CW01496992

A GREATER BRITAIN

RETHINKING THE UK'S GLOBAL STRATEGY

DR AZEEM IBRAHIM

FOREWORD BY
PROFESSOR SIR HEW STRACHAN

Biteback Publishing

First published in Great Britain in 2026 by
Biteback Publishing Ltd, London
Copyright © Azeem Ibrahim 2026

ISBN 978-1-78590-982-5

10 9 8 7 6 5 4 3 2 1

A CIP catalogue record for this book is available from the British Library.

Set in Adobe Caslon Pro

Printed and bound in Great Britain by
CPI Group (UK) Ltd, Croydon CR0 4YY

FSC
www.fsc.org
MIX
Paper | Supporting
responsible forestry
FSC® C013604

CONTENTS

FOREWORD
BY PROFESSOR SIR HEW STRACHAN

This is a challenging book – in the best possible sense. You won't agree with everything that Azeem Ibrahim says, and he would be disappointed if you did. He proposes a coherent programme of changes across areas of policy which, in most cases, government treats as though they are separate and independent. He seeks to create unity in the pursuit of the national interest. That objective does not mean that his is an argument for the resurrection of some imperial past. Although he can be 'anti-woke', he is not illiberal.

Azeem Ibrahim's prescriptions are designed to shore up Britain's place as a democracy and make it robust enough to be a leader in global multilateralism. Given that credential, *A Greater Britain* relies on debate and political difference, but it assumes that the final result of democracy in its best sense is consensus and a shared sense of direction. For Ibrahim, the lesson of populism is not that Britain is on a route to authoritarianism and certainly not to what he calls 'managed democracy' of the sort practised in Russia or Iran. Instead, it is that policies need to connect with the electorate, not with elite preoccupations forged according to the templates of academic theories or by the scaremongering of far-right nationalists.

This is an argument from the centre, even if it can at times borrow from ideas which have been brandished by those on the extremes of British politics.

Ibrahim, a Briton originally from Scotland and now working in the US, sees both democracy and the UK as in decline. The latter was dealt a hammer-blow by the 2008 crash; the mechanism for its recovery saved the banks at the expense of their private ac-count-holders. These taxpayers have still not recouped what they lost in real terms. As a result, falling productivity has required suc-cessive governments to increase taxes to generate sufficient funds to maintain expenditure, leading to a counter-productive spiral, worsened by the impact of the Covid pandemic. The result is that the status quo is not in fact static but, in Ibrahim's term, 'declinist'. His 'grand strategy' depends on 'going for growth'. Britain cannot deliver on its 'self-conception' as a 'moral, democratic nation' unless it has the economic resilience to sustain that ambition. This is not some absurd request 'to make Britain great again' but a design to make it better at what it would like to do – and, crucially, at what it should be capable of doing. His vision for Britain, set out in the introduction, is for it to be 'a lean, specialised, intermediary power'.

As the US pivots to Asia and as Britain confronts the costs of its withdrawal from the European Union, the UK should maximise the potential gains from its position between the two. The opportu-nities in the first instance are not so much those of geography but of political circumstance. The US is increasingly disinclined to sus-tain the multilateral international order which it set up after 1945; Europe is too bureaucratically and legally hamstrung to be fleet of foot. Britain, as a relatively small state, should build its relations with both but recognise its own dependence on the multilateral structures – the United Nations, the World Trade Organization and the principles of free trade – on which the post-Second World War system was built. China is manoeuvring itself into those structures but is not doing so as a liberal democracy. Although Britain cannot match China's Belt and Road Initiative, it can provide access to financial markets that are transparent and uncorrupted.

'Grand strategy' is the label which gives these ideas coherence. When the UK last debated the need for 'grand strategy' in 2010, after the return of the coalition government led by David Cameron, both the Prime Minister himself and those close to him were inclined to pooh-pooh the term as redolent of empire. They were echoed by pundits in the US, who were wont to argue that only great powers can have grand strategies. That is nonsense. Expanding powers that have yet to face the competition which their growth generates don't yet need grand strategies; contracting powers, facing relative decline, do. Britain did not need – or have – a grand strategy in the middle of the nineteenth century, when it was the first industrialised power in the world and when its goods commanded world markets. It *does* need one a century later when it does not have that primacy. One of the roles of grand strategy is prioritisation – the ability to accept the opportunity costs of hard choices without fudging the consequences (or not much).

Ibrahim puts national interest at the heart of a British grand strategy for the future. He addresses the unpalatable consequences which that objective creates for many: over climate change; refugees, asylum and migration; and human rights and international legal norms. Not for a moment does he dismiss those concerns. Rather, he suggests our preoccupation with them – and the need to find sensible ways through them – are part of Britain's brand as a multilateralist power committed to global order. His crucial point is that their resolutions are not ends in themselves but means to an end.

Although this is a book about grand strategy, it has little to say about hard power. (A chapter is dedicated to soft power, but it rightly argues that soft power is not an end in itself but a means to exercise influence – not least if it ultimately becomes necessary to wield hard power.) Ibrahim praises the 2025 Strategic Defence Review (SDR) for recognising Britain's economic weakness, but takes it to task for not addressing the issues of energy, climate, diplomacy, statecraft and finance. His criticism takes us to the heart of the problem. None of these policy areas lay within the scope of the SDR: its remit was confined specifically to defence and its scope, however broad, was limited to what the Treasury deemed affordable. His target should have been not the SDR but the National Security Strategy (NSS): its task in the past has been to cover the breadth of Ibrahim's demands. Perversely published after the SDR, the 2025 NSS was a much less substantial document. It failed to address wider policies left hanging by the SDR – and that is now the challenge.

The grand strategy which Ibrahim proposes is a task for the whole of government, not just the Ministry of Defence. Other departments, including the Foreign, Commonwealth and Development Office, the Home Office, the Ministry of Justice, the Department of Culture, Media and Sport, and, above all, the Treasury (to name only the most obvious) need to buy in to its conclusions. They won't do so of their own volition; for that to happen, all those agencies would have to subordinate the shibboleths of their own organisations to the demands of the national interest. Such change cannot be driven from the bottom up. For process to be replaced by results, its implementation must come from the top down – and, even if there is a will, there will be immense difficulties in finding a way.

The problems are both intellectual and institutional. The SDR reached most directly into others' domains with its attention to national resilience, in terms of home defence, of deterrence, of societal engagement and of public responsibility. The response to the Covid pandemic at community and local level across the UK showed that society is more responsive and resilient than its government thought – or than the then government was itself. Although the Conservatives' Integrated Review Refresh promised a National Resilience Strategy in 2023, it produced only a loose National Resilience Framework. Similarly, the Labour government's 2025 NSS left its response to a Resilience Action Plan, which passed by largely unrecognised when it was published in July 2025.

Ideas governing and shaping the national interest will also only gain traction if they have an institutional home. The one department of state in the UK with the requisite breadth is the Cabinet Office and the person and the body which it serves: the Prime Minister and the Cabinet. In 2010, the coalition government created a National Security Council (NSC) to formulate shared solutions and appointed a National Security Adviser (NSA) to support the Prime Minister and to chair the committee of officials whose ministries were represented on the NSC. No Prime Minister since then has followed a common pattern in how he or she handles the NSC. Under Boris Johnson, the council scarcely met, and he and Liz Truss effectively dismantled what they had inherited. The NSC has regained some ground since then, but in 2024 its precise authority and remit were clouded by the Prime Minister's appointment of Jonathan Powell as the NSA. Powell is undoubtedly a multilateralist and an experienced negotiator with a formidable reputation.

However, as a political appointee, he has no authority over civil servants; he is the first NSA not to have been a career civil servant. The government has refused to permit him, unlike his predecessors, to appear before the Joint Parliamentary Committee for the National Security Strategy. He is also operating out of No. 10, not the Cabinet Office. Such conditions are hardly conducive to creating either proper accountability, the committee's *raison d'être*, or to promoting public understanding of national strategy.

If the ideas advanced by Azeem Ibrahim's *A Greater Britain* are to get oxygen, they need to be heard, discussed and debated. That process won't start in government, or at least not at first. It will begin with you, the reader. The exchange of ideas can confront received wisdom and could ultimately shape policies. It is our best chance. According to the book's author, there is not much time. 'Britain is heading for economic and demographic decline so severe', Azeem Ibrahim concludes, 'that none of us may live long enough to see it recover.'

BRITAIN IN A FRACTURING WORLD ORDER

In 1945, as the Second World War came to an end, a bankrupt but victorious Britain helped lay the cornerstone of a new international order. The post-war Bretton Woods agreement – which set up a new system of international monetary rules under the aegis of the United Nations, establishing institutions like the International Monetary Fund (IMF) and the World Bank – promised stability, open markets and collective security under American leadership. When Winston Churchill returned to power in 1951, Britain still clung to all the trappings and accoutrements of a superpower. In fact, against every financial strain, Britain's armed forces grew to 872,000 men in service in 1952, given oxygen by US and Canadian loans despite harsh austerity and rationing at home. The Suez Crisis of 1956 proved that Britain could not withstand US economic and diplomatic pressure and marked the symbolic end of its ability to act without coalition, but Britain's direction of travel was clear: it was already dependent on the US and already anxious about its isolation from post-war Europe. Ambition and financial reality collided, but over the following three decades leaders failed to co-alesce around a new foreign policy to replace the 'three majestic circles' doctrine advocated by Churchill: Commonwealth, Europe and the English-speaking world, particularly the US.

The drift and decline of the late 1960s and 1970s can partly be explained by Britain's failure to choose a coherent path. Commentators of all political stripes often wrongly fall into a kind of teleological fatalism when discussing this period of British history: that we were fated to enter Europe or, equally, that we were destined to leave it. In fact, much came down to circumstance. The contextual reality of competing anxieties about the value of pound sterling, the US, our nuclear deterrent, the end of empire and a fear of missing out on Europe left many aspects of the British state in that paralysed dimension we now call 'managed decline'. We clung to our old industries at great cost – just as we had once clung to our foreign protectorates. The great irony, of course, was that Britain was in one sense refusing to adapt to the very economic and geostrategic order it was pivotal in bringing about in the first place.

Britain's position, post-Brexit and post-Covid, has so far been a frustrated repeat of those wasted decades. We are once again clinging to old habits and old assumptions and once more refusing to recognise our new reality. The new authoritarian threat coming from Russia and China, the dynamics of mass migration, the weakening of international institutions and the decline and impotence of Europe have together changed the way Britain must posture strategically. Yet no real change has been mustered. Revolutions in the digital economy, energy, AI and financial technology have given Britain considerable opportunities, yet our leadership has stifled them with tax, regulation and a naive and short-sighted energy policy. Just as in the late '60s, in our refusal to adapt we have once more turned to high tax and high spend, and by clinging to the old we have crowded out the new.

A Greater Britain is an attempt, built fundamentally from strategic analysis, to describe the new world Britain finds itself in and to design the foreign and domestic policy that will best allow it to deliver prosperity at home and secure its interests abroad. The book argues that Britain must become a lean, specialised intermediary power – pivoted towards the US in terms of security, while leading in key future industries through aggressive economic reform, permissive trade policy based on mutual recognition and strategic diplomacy rooted in realism, not nostalgia or naive appeasement.

* * *

For decades, the liberal international order underpinned unprecedented global economic growth and relative peace among the great powers. Having seen off its final rival after the Cold War, many believed that Western liberal democracy had triumphed for good – the 'end of history' in Francis Fukuyama's famous phrase. Particularly after Margaret Thatcher's reforms in the 1980s, Britain became a prime beneficiary of this international legal order – a highly globalised, high-wage, service-led economy deeply integrated in highly profitable value chains.

Britain and its allies assumed that open markets and democratic governance would spread inexorably. Our militaries are now therefore designed for counterterrorism, irregular warfare and peacekeeping operations rather than conventional war. Yet that democratising progress has gone into reverse, as conventional warfare returns to Europe and an alliance of authoritarian powers cooperates to undermine the democratic West, while offering an alternative power bloc for third countries to align with. The norms and institutions that once seemed unshakeable have been weakened by financial crises, geopolitical rivalries and a wave of anti-establishment sentiment. They are being replaced by new norms of non-interference and national sovereignty, which are more appealing to (and provide cover for) growing autocratic nations like Turkey, South Africa and even India to adopt a non-aligned stance, which gives yet more breathing room for autocracy. In my 2022 book *Authoritarian Century*, I argued that Western leaders after 1991 learned the wrong lesson from their ideological victory, embracing a complacent 'total liberalism' that ignores discontents and abandons dynamism in favour of a new orthodoxy. A global orthodoxy is less compelling and drives third nations away.

This hubris has had important consequences for Europe in particular, with the post-Maastricht Treaty (1992) European Union perhaps the purest institutional embodiment of 'total liberalism'. Following the 2008 financial crisis, the suffocating lack of economic dynamism (in part a structural product of the single currency and the consequent protectionism) has meant that Europe has failed to return to the same significant economic growth that the US has gone on to achieve. Indeed, stagnation in Europe actually spurred leaders to lean further into their orthodoxy. From 1 January 2010, when the Lisbon Treaty came into effect, to 1 January 2024, the volume of EU regulation increased by 101 per cent. It is no coincidence that Britain shares with Europe the same disappointing trends on investment, innovation, productivity and energy policy.

The political demoralisation caused by the Iraq War and 2008 financial crisis in the West was being acutely felt by the second half of the 2010s. A new strain of anti-establishment academic discourse arose, which sympathised strongly with enemies of the West, and which quite wrongly saw Western interventionism as the root cause of most of the world's poverty and violence. While headed by politicians including Jeremy Corbyn and Jean-Luc Mélenchon, the view permeated wider society and did considerable damage to the moral confidence of the West.

Russia and China began taking a more openly confrontational stance against Western democracies, while Britain and Europe in particular failed to take notice, in the naive hope that the world was, after all, still bound to democratise. Russia annexed Crimea in 2014, just as China began constructing artificial islands in the South China Sea. While Europe and the US *did* pursue sanctions against Russia, the sanctions were not coordinated with a coherent attempt to build strategic independence from, and capabilities against, Vladimir Putin's Russia. High-profile espionage cases were ignored, as Europe continued to increase its dependence on Russian gas while relying on both the Chinese manufacturing base and Chinese rare earth metals. Let us not forget the UK announced a 'golden era' of relations with China in 2015.

Russia in particular specialises in hybrid warfare and disruption below the threshold of open war. China has capabilities exceeded only by the US in cyberwarfare and cyberespionage, while it also has the economic heft to create an array of parallel international institutions – such as the Asian Infrastructure Investment Bank and the BRICS development bank – and projects like the Belt and Road Initiative (discussed in Chapter 1), to directly challenge Western soft power. Warnings about both Russia and China were consistently made at the highest levels of government. Yet much like our forebears in the 1950s, unreconciled with the realities of the end of empire, we were unwilling to recognise the risks and dynamics of the end of our unipolar world order.

The tumult in foreign policy circles following the return of Donald Trump to the White House in 2024 was therefore not an entirely unexpected jolt. Indeed, Trump's United States has finally done what the country has threatened to do for at least the last two decades: definitively shift its geostrategic focus from Europe to the Pacific. While this shift is well reasoned and perhaps necessary, it has severed an important anchor of the Western alliance at the same time as Western leadership is becoming increasingly temperamental and inward-focused. It comes, of course, as the EU struggles to project unified diplomatic or military power, while most of its constituent nations, similarly to Britain, lack any significant, deployable, conventional military strength, and have no credible plan to change that.

* * *

The pivot of the US away from Europe heralds the ceremonial retirement of the Atlantic Charter. Signed in 1941, several months before the US joined the war, the Atlantic Charter was the seminal document upon which the rules-based international order was to be established. Decolonisation, the United Nations, NATO and the principles of self-determination saw their most coherent and forceful defence therein. The Charter also provided the foundation for the General Agreement on Tariffs and Trade, the precursor to the World Trade Organization (WTO). It bears repeating once more that Britain has benefited enormously from these organisations, even if they have faced two decades of decline.

Instead of deepening integration under shared rules, nations are increasingly invoking national security and fabricating findings of anti-competitive market distortions to justify protectionist tariffs and export controls. The WTO, once the guarantor of a rules-based trading system, has effectively been paralysed – its highest appeals court has sat defunct for years after the United States blocked new judges. The admission of China into the WTO at the turn of the century turned out to be a Trojan Horse – high-profile backers concede that China has been largely responsible for the destruction of the WTO. Former Republican Representative Kevin Brady, who was one such backer, concluded, 'It's now clear China had no intention of living within a rules-based trading system.'

The IMF and World Bank, the twin pillars of Bretton Woods, are not yet beyond repair. While their governance has failed to adjust to the rise of emerging economies, the economic need to manage unpayable debts and geopolitical need to compete with more predatory Chinese finance mean their role remains secure, even if significant reform is required. The UN Security Council is often paralysed in the face of atrocities and wars, as great power vetoes by the five permanent members (the US, the UK, France, Russia and China) stymie collective action. International courts like the International Court of Justice (ICJ) exist but are increasingly weaponised by warring parties rather than universally respected, while the voting patterns of judges suggest, to put it mildly, that rulings are frequently political in nature.

While we are witnessing a partial return to the great-power politics of the early twentieth century, international institutions will continue to play a role. Even as we enter a more coldly realist world, these frameworks remain legally enshrined and are the most convenient forum for certain kinds of dispute settlement. Analysts are correct that the following decades will see a decline in multilateralism as the global order fragments, but this does not mean that soft power or institutional influence will hold no sway, nor that many challenges of the twenty-first century will not play out through an international institutional framework. Practically, however, these institutions will have to learn to coexist with rival claimants to international legitimacy.

At a national level, Freedom House reports that 2023 marked the eighteenth consecutive year of worldwide democratic decline. Many of the world's most established democracies have seen their norms eroded and institutions politicised, while outright autocracy has resurged in nations that once seemed on a path to liberalisation. Economically, decades of inequality and dislocation – aggravated by the 2008 financial crisis and rapid globalisation – left many citizens feeling betrayed by elites. Politically, mainstream parties often failed to address these grievances, creating fertile ground for firebrand outsiders. To a large extent, the economic and foreign policy failures associated with neoliberalism, or rather 'total liberalism', fatally undermined public faith in liberal democracy, yielding disaffected masses and opportunistic populists ready to capitalise on that anger.

In Brazil, and then in the United States itself, populists gained power and began to chip away at the very checks and balances that define liberal governance – attacking independent judiciaries and blurring ethical and procedural boundaries in pursuit of unchecked authority. In the case of Trump, perhaps the most totemic action was the suspension of access to federal buildings for firms such as Paul, Weiss 'pending a review of whether such clearances are consistent with the national interest'. Given that functioning as a law firm all but requires access to federal buildings – which includes the courts – this amounts to an embargo on any firm. Their crime was their politicised involvement in pro bono work against the government during Trump's first term. Within a week, Paul, Weiss LLP had publicly renounced its DEI initiatives and promised pro bono legal services to 'support the administration's initiatives'.[1] While, granted, firms like these had made themselves political while Trump was in opposition and could not command the trust of government, the fact remains that this would not have been possible only a decade ago. Both the law and the executive would have behaved better. We will explore the reasons for this, but it is important to note early on that there is intentionality in foreign interference to weaken these institutions.

Alliances founded on shared values have been strained by the rise of illiberal actors in member states. For example, the European Union has grappled with member governments in Hungary and Poland that challenge, if not the rule of law itself, then the principles of European and international law. Yet on the flip side, they have also intervened in Romanian elections, revealing that their opposition is consequentialist rather than strictly principled. Indeed, to a considerable extent, populists have succeeded precisely because liberal leaders, typified by those in European institutions, have felt empowered to ignore the votes and concerns of low-status voters. Liberalism must look inwards and recognise that elite control over the judiciary and bureaucracy has caused elite interests to come first, structurally. Concerns like the Chagos Islands, the transgender issue and net zero have been elevated to the very top of the British agenda, despite the fact that for the majority of Britons, these issues are moralising abstractions, while concerns about immigration, housing and price levels have only recently started to scratch through into concrete policy change.

Britain would rather remain engaged than give up on the institutions that have helped bring prosperity to the world, but loyalty must be to the rules-based order itself and not to the particular organisations and not at all costs. The reality Britain faces – and with which we must contend in this book – is that many international institutions are compromised by Russia and China and that we engage with these institutions ultimately to serve British interests. It is not for Britain to sacrifice its fundamental interests in order to serve international institutions but quite the other way around.

* * *

The key issue to unpick – in institutions as in foreign policy and defence – is the retreat of American leadership as the linchpin of the international order. The United States provided security guarantees, underwrote global institutions and acted as the ultimate backstop in most crises, at least those of significance for regional balances of power and global supply chains. The US's new, unpredictable global posture, which is partially a response to costly entanglements in Iraq and Afghanistan, demands that Britain acts with intentionality and strategy.

It is worth noting the shifting sands in geopolitics on top of the slower and more profound tectonic changes beneath. Recent US involvement against Iran may seem at first glance to indicate a renewed commitment to its former role as global policeman. Yet the details do not support that view. US involvement has for years been limited to strikes against key Iranian Revolutionary Guards Corps (IRGC) generals. The US bombing of Iranian nuclear targets came only after the significant destruction of Iran's proxies by Israel and in the context of a hot war between the two powers, in which the US's role, bargained by Trump, was ultimately de-escalatory. At every moment in said involvement, the key US anxiety was not to get drawn into the Middle East and to preserve as much capability as possible in the Pacific Theatre. The underlying trends, beyond the flux and noise, are of a less interventionist US focused increasingly on China.

Trump withdrew the US from international agreements (most notably the Paris Climate Accords and the Iran nuclear deal), slapped tariffs on allies as readily as on rivals and even reportedly mused about quitting NATO. He strongly prefers transactional bargaining and leverage over the integrative bargaining intrinsic to diplomatic 'repeat business'. Earlier missteps – particularly President Obama's hesitation to enforce his 'red line' in Syria in 2013 – had already signalled to some that Washington's resolve to enforce its rules was conditional. As Washington's focus has also shifted towards the Indo-Pacific and competition with China, and European leaders contend with a possible vacuum in their region, Britain must make another choice. While economically the question of 'Europe or America?' need not be binary, in terms of military posture Britain must pick a theatre of focus for the coming decades. That requires a clear-minded assessment of revisionist and revanchist powers, terrorism and economic interest; an understanding of Britain's strengths and specialised capabilities: technology, finance, cyber; and an operational analysis of where and with which allies Britain can best coordinate to further our interests.

Britain is no longer individually capable of projecting conventional power against near-peer rivals. Any operation it performs will have to be executed under the umbrella of the US Armed Forces. Compared to the UK pre-Suez, or indeed compared to the Britain during the Iraq War, our conventional hard power is wielded from Washington DC or alongside European allies. Yet, with Trump back in the White House, Britain now must deal with the reality that the rules-based international order is potentially losing its principal (and some might argue, sole) defender. While the indomitable US economy can survive outside the web of international treaties and agreements that it has constructed, the British economy cannot. A US in the process of disengaging from the world – with an increasingly isolationist stance from both political parties – combined with a growing anti-Western coalition of China and Russia, makes a tilt away from the United States less painful today than it has been at any other time in living memory.

Engagement from third nations in international institutions is key to Britain's strategy to retain global influence through these diplomatic channels. The value of our permanent seat at the UN Security Council and our newly acquired independent seat at the WTO relies on the ongoing relevance of these institutions and their robustness in the face of authoritarian challenge. Bolstering these institutions and maintaining third nations' engagement is contingent upon the West's continued ability to offer valuable economic partnerships. Much of the West hopes that its climate technology will reinforce our key value proposition: that our finance, our technology and our security expertise make partnerships with the West more valuable than with anyone else.

Yet, again, this is becoming less true each year. Chinese investment across Asia, Latin America and Africa is granting them still better access to key raw materials and rare earth metals. These investments buy influence to sway more votes at the UN, thereby sapping away Western diplomatic leadership one vote at a time; China uses this influence to install loyalists within global institutions. China's spending on research and development, the surest indicator of future tech dominance, now outstrips that of the United States.[2] They are also promoting the use of the renminbi

(RMB) with a $51 billion investment tied through their own financial system. As *Foreign Policy* has noted, the United States has long lagged behind China in overseas development finance. The International Development Finance Corporation (DFC), created under Trump, was intended to close that gap, but the shortfall existed well before his presidency. Moreover, with ageing populations and increasing demands for more and improved public services, a lack of growth is prompting politicians down a negative feedback loop of higher taxes to chase higher spending.

*   *   *

Many in the Global South view the US-led order as hypocritical or unfair, a perception that Chinese and Russian diplomats eagerly exploit. Moscow, for example, frames its clash with the West as a fight against neo-imperialism, claiming the US is a power in decline and that a moment of civilisational change is at hand. This has already had consequences around the world, not all of them bad. China's role in brokering de-escalation talks between Saudi Arabia and Iran would simply not have been possible for the US to pull off. In a way that would have been simply unthinkable at the turn of the century, there is a new reality where the US's diplomatic reputation and moral authority have diminished enough that it is possible to resolve conflict without them and without their pesky and demanding 'principles' getting in the way.

There is now a need to engage the wider world on terms that counter the appeal of the authoritarian model. But we must also recognise that the private interest of global leaders prefers non-interference and unconstrained power over the difficult politics and power-sharing inherent in liberal democracy. Once we have accepted this, we can start to compete with clarity of mind. We can – and must – start to strategise, post-Fukuyama, about how to leverage the strengths of liberalism and freedom to compete in the authoritarian century. The successful model, illustrated thematically throughout this book, will involve hard investment that plays to our strengths.

* * *

A central theme of Britain's future will be the viability of achieving a subtle balance. How can the UK champion multilateralism and a rules-based order while also advancing its national interests? What balance can be struck between idealism and realism – between values and pragmatism – in Britain's external engagements? A second theme is the power of incentives – and whether the government is aware of such power. Whether we're designing climate policy, an immigration system or a tax regime, we must be willing to recognise how current policy creates perverse incentives that undermine our goals and push Britain down a path neither policymakers nor the public would have chosen. We need to be willing to hold our noses and make quite radical changes to ensure our foreign and domestic policies are incentive-compatible.

Fundamentally, this analysis rests upon the cultivation of economic growth and capability here on this island. Where can Britain exert genuine leadership or add value on the global stage? Which niches – be it climate action, conflict mediation, technology governance or development finance – offer the UK a chance to be a convener and problem-solver respected by others? What domestic changes are required?

No introduction to Britain's position would be complete without a description of our dire economic situation. There is no point denying, therefore, that this book is political. The author's prognosis regarding Britain is that our prospects are deteriorating faster now than at any point in any of our lifetimes. To be frank, Britain is heading for economic and demographic decline so severe that none of us may live long enough to see it recover. Indeed, Britain's deterioration – political, moral, institutional – is accelerating. Our situation is far from unsalvageable; in fact, Britain has abundant opportunities and advantages that it continues, at present, to squander.

In recent years, both of Britain's main parties have shown themselves incapable of constraining the bureaucracy or the judiciary. The government of Prime Minister Keir Starmer and Chancellor Rachel Reeves began with an unprecedented run of calamitous and unnecessary fiscal decisions characterised by a failure to understand incentives: a non-dom regime change that pushed 16,500 millionaires to leave within a year; a private school VAT imposition that massively underestimated the number who would queue up for state schools; a national insurance hike that beat recruitment back to its lowest level since the pandemic; and a public sector pay 'settlement' that simply elevated pay expectations elsewhere. It bodes very ill for any attempt to curb record levels of government spending, when the government could not cut winter fuel, disability nor welfare payments due to enormous backbench revolt. The country lacks serious economic governance, and it will pay not only through higher tax and inflation but through a collapse in the very 'investment' the government invited us to judge it by. Foreign direct investment therefore fell in the space of a year to the lowest level since 2007. Britain must find a way out of this broken consensus – and it has no time to lose.

The need for a balance between idealism and realism, between regional theatres, between multilateralism and independence, does not mean that Britain's domestic policy must itself be 'moderate', 'balanced' or 'subtle' – at least not in the sense that these words are often meant in politics. When Britain's status quo is so fundamentally declinist, proposals for incrementalism or rhetorical claims that the 'adults are back in the room' fail to notice the self-reinforcing tailspin the country has entered into. More of the same, or trimming around the edges, simply will not do.

Since the turn of the century, Britain has embarked upon three simultaneous experiments in economics and statecraft. The first saw an engorgement of the state and of those bodies and individuals which depend directly and indirectly upon it. This includes quangos, civil servants and human rights lawyers as much as it does the record-breaking constituency of thirty-six million who live in households receiving more in direct benefits than they pay in taxes.[3] We may think only of the BBC and other state-owned companies, but large portions of the British private sector – from McKinsey & Company to the social care sector – have come to expect and rely upon extraordinarily 'generous' contracts from the taxpayer. The civil service outsources basic administrative tasks to such consultancies, while councils and departments have created such demanding and anti-competitive requirements that they have left themselves at the mercy of care monopolies of their own creation. As state-sector pay rises continue, the benefit bill proves impossible to cut; not only is a millionaire leaving every forty-five minutes but our young entrepreneurs and doctors are quitting Britain.

The second experiment is that of mass migration. With successive years of net immigration in the high hundreds of thousands, the places of these millionaires and young workers are replaced two or three times over by predominantly unskilled migrants. The jury verdict is in when it comes to low-skilled migration: it is simultaneously a fiscal, social and political drain, impoverishing Europe while dividing it socially and politically deeper and more hopelessly than at any time since the Thirty Years' War.

The third experiment was the shifting of the legal foundation of the state from Parliament, the Bill of Rights and the law lords to the Human Rights Act (HRA), the European Convention of Human Rights (ECHR) and the Supreme Court. The supplementary legislation and the quangos they spawned – including the Fixed Term Parliaments Act, Equality Act, Climate Change Act and the spectrum of organisations from Natural England and the Environment Agency to the Forestry Commission – have together worked to fundamentally disconnect the activity of the state from the mandate and will of Parliament. It is no coincidence that these produced the largest amount of lawfare, growth-blocking and cost-raising. These three experiments, linked in so far as they reinforce and overlap one another, have sent Britain perilously close to the point of no return.

The net effect is institutional damage, economic stagnation, social and political division and the demoralisation of Britain and her diplomats on the world stage. A generation of lawyers, politicians and professionals have been raised both to rely on the state and to sustain themselves through perpetuating the status quo of generous contracts. This has seen the gradual expansion of the HRA and the application of the ECHR to cover circumstances it was never envisioned to apply to, as well as the proliferation of political platitudes – such as that 'diversity is our strength' – to downplay, deflect and in many cases conspire to cover up the damage that these experiments have caused and continue to cause. No vision for a Britain that projects power and influence, mediates conflict and leads on technology, climate and finance, nor even one capable of defending itself against threats from without or within, can succeed without rebuilding these foundations.

Just as with an addict, the first step is to admit we have a problem and recognise the full extent of it before we start making grand promises about how we're going to fix it. We will start by substantiating our two key premises. First, that the breakdown of the old international order is more profound than just Trump; it threatens fundamental British interests and will require us to abandon old assumptions and practices, or else the global balance of power will tip against us. Second, that British statecraft and domestic institutions are in terminal decline and are causing irreversible damage to the UK.

From this foundation, the body of this book is a treatise analysing and then proposing a way forward – a blueprint for each key decision: climate, foreign policy and soft power, refugee policy, international legal norms, trade, counterterrorism, domestic economic policy and international finance. In each area, Britain must break its historic habit and adapt fast; it must be ruthlessly pragmatic, cooperative but clear-eyed. Britain has key advantages that we must not squander. Having set about a programme of domestic reform – from cutting wasteful spending to instituting a more dynamic, lower-regulation economy with globally competitive taxation that will set it up for the coming century – Britain must invest in new sources of hard and soft power, including a tactical nuclear deterrent independent from the US. It must learn when to reinforce the international legal order, and when to start competing in the new paradigm. Britain cannot rely on dispersed sources of soft power to advance our interests on their own; we must actively and cohesively leverage our many sources of soft power. We must make these work in the same direction with a new strategic doctrine – the Knowledge Power Doctrine – through which we can convert soft power into strategic policy and agenda-setting influence. The stakes are high: our ability to navigate this authoritarian century will not only determine our national fortunes but also influence the future of the international order that emerges from today's period of global convulsion and dissension. The task is daunting, but it is not beyond Britain to reinvent itself as a dynamic, solution-oriented power for the twenty-first century.

CHAPTER 1

THE CHALLENGES OF AN AUTHORITARIAN CENTURY

In the West's triumphalist moment, which reached its zenith in the years following the collapse of the USSR, it seemed the ideals of open society, human rights and market liberalisation had no serious rival. In this seductive vision of a world in which Western liberalism had 'won', the US-led order overplayed its hand, expecting that it could bring Russia and China into the fold while hitting down on incalcitrant regimes like those of Iraq and Libya. This belief that the US could democratise the world instead helped foment a coalition against it. Today, those very democratic ideals are in retreat across much of the globe. In both long-standing democracies and countries that only recently embraced pluralism, liberal norms are under attack. An authoritarian and populist backlash has gathered momentum – not driven by a new global ideology as in the twentieth century, but by an atavistic return to nativist, nationalist and xenophobic politics. Democratic institutions and practices that were once thought to be consolidating have begun to erode. From large emerging powers to smaller states, many regimes have slid backwards into authoritarianism, often degenerating from previously functional democracies into hybrid forms of autocracy. At the same time, international cooperation has weakened as countries turn inward, proclaiming the primacy of national sovereignty over the once prevailing spirit of multilateralism.

This global 'democratic recession' is illustrated by examples which themselves range from concerning to critical. India, the world's largest democracy, has edged towards ethnic majoritarian rule under Prime Minister Narendra Modi, rewriting citizenship laws and electoral practices in ways designed to subtly disenfranchise its Muslim minority. Brazil, under the presidency of Jair Bolsonaro, witnessed constant assaults on democratic norms and environmental protections, propelled by a reactionary agenda. Under his successor, Lula, the country briefly tended towards outspoken support of Venezuelan socialist dictator Nicolás Maduro, ostensibly because of affinity between their ideological positions.

The first watershed moment that suggested this might happen in the Anglosphere was upon Trump's defeat at the 2020 election – culminating in major disturbances to the peaceful transfer of power. Since his re-election in 2024, Trump has blurred the lines of the US Department of Justice's autonomy, using it to disrupt his enemies and turn a blind eye to his allies, arguably in exactly the same way as it had been leveraged against him by his Democrat rivals. In eastern Europe, Hungary and, to a lesser extent, Poland have backtracked on liberal principles: Hungary's self-declared 'illiberal' government openly defies European Union standards on the rule of law, while Poland's ruling party has made independent courts and media vassals of the presidential office. In Turkey, a NATO member, democratic institutions have been hollowed out by President Erdoğan's increasingly authoritarian grip; he is also promoting Islamic Turkish nationalism and turning away from the secular Turkish state built by Atatürk. Russia has transformed from the fragile democracy of the 1990s into a personalised irredentist autocracy with a proven track record of interference in foreign elections. China, which never liberalised politically even as it opened its economy, now champions a confident authoritarian model on the world stage, bolstered by a terrifying technological panopticon. With the help of its terrorist paramilitary IRGC, Iran has built a narco-trafficking, gun-running terror cell network that spans four continents and an array of terrorist armies in the form of Hamas, Hezbollah, Palestinian Islamic Jihad, Kataib Sayyid al Shuhada and the Badr Organization, alongside myriad smaller forces scattered across the Levant and Bahrain. In every region, examples abound of elected leaders abusing mandates to entrench their own power, stoke ethnic or religious nationalism and undermine opposition. Liberal democracy's promise of openness and pluralism is being rejected by leaders and movements who claim that only a strong hand – their own – can defend 'the people' against threats and decadence.

Underlying this trend is a fragility within the liberal project itself. Liberal democracy, since its Enlightenment origins, rests on the principle of equal and inherent human worth. Its grand historical task has been to build societies in which all individuals are treated with dignity, enjoy fundamental rights and are free to pursue their own wellbeing. By its nature, a liberal society is always a work in progress – never perfect, but legitimised by steady movement guided by reasoned public debate. This Rawlsian concept of 'public reasons' – that matters of basic justice must use reasons accessible and acceptable to all members of a pluralistic society, rather than appeals to any particular comprehensive doctrine like religion or identity – put Western societies among the most open, tolerant, reflective and innovative societies in human history. This very openness, however, makes liberal societies vulnerable to reactionary forces that resist change and to disillusionment when progress seems to stall. The illiberal critique of liberalism, made by Carl Schmitt, an avowed German Nazi, is still perhaps the most visceral one, with his almost Hobbesian conception of politics as fundamentally about friend and enemy.[1] Liberal democracy, Schmitt argues, has a tendency to exclude issues important to the fringes, and in many cases prohibit them, which provokes these elements either to break up democratic institutions or resort to violence.

Part of the backlash we are witnessing (at least in those formerly democratic states) is rooted in liberal democracy's unkept promises: corrupt elites, stark inequalities, cultural dislocation, mass migration and economic stagnation have led many to lose faith in democratic institutions. Britain must guard against these at home and, where possible, abroad. Opportunistic demagogues exploit this loss of faith, offering simplistic answers and scapegoats in place of the liberal vision of gradual progress. As Schmitt warns, we embolden them if we become too squeamish to include their worries (at least those that stop short of calls to violate fundamental rights) in mainstream political debate. In short, the ideals of liberalism – tolerance, rule of law, universal rights – are under siege both from without and within. The world may be entering an authoritarian century regardless of what Britain does. Unless our fellow democracies can understand what went wrong and muster a strategic response, the rules of diplomacy, trade and warfare may revert to a struggle phase reminiscent of the interwar period where democratic and authoritarian nations club together to rival one another.

At its core, liberalism is a political philosophy of human equality and individual rights. It holds that all people are entitled to the same fundamental freedoms and protections, and that government exists to secure these rights, not to privilege one group over another. Upon this 'egalitarian plateau', as Ronald Dworkin puts it, a range of liberal political philosophies, from Rawlsian social democracy to libertarianism, are built.[2] Out of these principles naturally emerges democracy – a system of government accountable to the people and conducive to human wellbeing. While, in concept at least, not all liberalism requires democracy, liberal democracy, in essence, marries this egalitarian ethos with representative institutions: regular free elections, the rule of law, constitutional limits on power and respect for dissent and minority views. Crucially, liberal democracy is an evolving experiment. It is relatively new in historical terms and remains imperfect even in the nations that have longest practised it.

Thinkers including (perhaps most prominently, in Britain's case) Michael Oakeshott have argued that no such perfect institutions exist, and that they serve a particular people tending to the business of government and responding to events.[3] Attempts to permanently enshrine certain views, or institute immutable organs of the state to guard certain interests, are the projects of pure rationalists who fail to recognise what they do not know – not least the future. The British constitution – unwritten though robust through practice – is precious precisely because it refuses to be beholden to the conceit of those who think they can design a perfect state to deal with our very imperfect world.

No democracy fully lives up to its ideals at all times; the project of expanding rights and improving governance is always ongoing. Yet again, such expansion of positive rights (rights *to* something as opposed to a right *against* something being done to you) may have the effect of shaking the very foundational democratic principle or precipitating a democratic end-state. Free speech, to name one example, has come under threat in the West through precisely this mechanism – a well-meaning expansionist conception of political rights that ends up criminalising speech. Liberalism therefore thrives on confidence – the willingness to debate and take on rivals – and the more expansive the scope of that democracy, the more resilient it will be to the threats Carl Schmitt described. Confidence to debate also ensures humility is built into liberalism – its strength is the capacity for self-correction and inclusion of genuinely diverse voices. However, when that self-correction falters, or when large sections of society feel excluded and aggrieved, the legitimacy of the entire system comes into question.

Opposing the liberal democratic model is an increasingly prevalent alternative we might call 'managed democracy'.⁴ Managed democracies adopt the *form* of democratic governance – constitutions, elections, parliaments, courts – but gut them of substance. Power in such regimes is tightly controlled by a dominant individual or party, and explicitly illiberal values guide the state. Dissent is curtailed, the playing field is heavily skewed through media control and harassment of the opposition, and the ruling elite claims to govern in the 'true' interest of the people but without genuine accountability. In the world today, this model has become the most prevalent challenger to liberal democracy. After the end of the Cold War, many assumed the primary threats to democracy (fascism, Soviet communism, militant theocracy) had been defeated or marginalised. But in their wake, the managed democracy model has risen to fill the void.

It is observable in a diverse array of states: Vladimir Putin's Russia is a paradigmatic example, maintaining the façade of elections and parties while in reality a small circle around Putin makes all crucial decisions and suppresses any real opposition. Viktor Orbán's Hungary similarly keeps the mechanics of democracy (elections, a legislature) but tilts them so heavily – through gerrymandering, media domination and the muzzling of civil society – that the ruling party faces no real check on its power. In Iran, an unelected theocratic Guardian Council holds ultimate authority over which candidates may run and what laws may pass, ensuring that the electoral system can never alter the Islamic Republic's core ideological character. Even formally democratic India shows signs of this pattern: the ruling party has worked to limit the electorate and redefine who counts as a 'true' Indian, for instance via citizenship laws that exclude Muslims and other measures that edge the country towards ethno-religious majoritarian rule.

These regimes share common features. All project a veneer of mass participation: they hold votes, allow some opposition on paper and maintain institutions that resemble those of democracies; but in practice they consolidate authority in one faction or leader. Elections may be held, but they are often rigged or tightly managed; opposition parties exist, but many are fake or systematically undermined; a press operates, but it is bullied or bought into propaganda service. Such systems have deep historical antecedents. In the late nineteenth-century German and Austro-Hungarian Empires, for example, voting rights were expanded without granting legislatures real governing power – an early form of managed democracy. What is startling is the return of this model in the twenty-first century after a period in which liberal democracy seemed ascendant. Over the past two decades, more and more countries have slid into this hybrid form. Most authoritarian-leaning states today are no longer outright totalitarian dictatorships; instead, they maintain enough democratic window dressing to mollify citizens or international observers, even as they entrench autocratic rule behind the scenes.

Crucially, I stress that managed democracies are not simply

halfway houses en route to full democracy. Rather, they tend to become stable and entrenched systems in their own right, explicitly hostile to liberal ideals and capable of enduring over time. Such regimes are the de facto ideological and geopolitical rivals to liberal democracy in our era. They cooperate with and learn from each other, share tactics of repression and propaganda, supply one another with munitions and present themselves to the world as a viable alternative. This recognition leads to a sobering conclusion: if liberal democracy is to survive and prevail, it must treat these regimes as formidable competitors in a contest over the future of the international order. Naivety and hubris in foreign policy is not an option. Likewise, naivety in thinking that we can avoid this fate by legalising politics is a recipe for disaster.

The 1990s began with the Soviet collapse and China still relatively weak and inward-facing. At that time, it appeared that Western-style liberal democracy, coupled with market capitalism, had no serious adversary left. One model – often labelled the Washington Consensus – was held up as the template for all nations: open markets, deregulation, privatisation and liberal democratic politics, grounded in the belief that this combination would yield peace and prosperity everywhere. For a while, this confidence seemed justified. Many countries in eastern Europe, Latin America and Asia embraced democratic reforms and joined the global capitalist economy. The world saw more integrated markets, the spread of the internet and information flows and an apparent convergence towards liberal norms. By the late 1990s, liberal democracy appeared to be on an irreversible forward march.

Yet even at its zenith, this post-Cold War order contained the seeds of its present troubles. In hindsight, we can observe that Western triumphalists overlooked significant frailties in their own system. Industrial jobs declined in the face of automation and off-shoring and whole communities were left behind in the rush of hyper-globalisation. Generally speaking, nations more than made up for the loss of less advanced manufacturing with a pivot to more complex manufacturing and high-skill service sector employment. But on a localised and individual basis, entire regions were left behind, from northern England to Rust Belt Pennsylvania. Traditional party systems have struggled to adapt to rapid economic shifts. Still, for a time, overall growth masked these stresses: the booming 1990s delivered higher living standards for many, and the memory of the stagnation and turmoil of the 1970s made the new consensus look comparatively successful.

Success dulled the urgency to address the model's flaws with confidence, humility and reasoned debate. Financial markets were liberalised further, assuming that market actors would responsibly manage risk. Democratic oversight of economic processes waned; politics became increasingly technocratic and aligned with the interests of global finance. Meanwhile, outside the West, countries that adopted market reforms but not liberal politics (like China) were not pressured to democratise, under the assumption that economic progress would eventually bring political openness on its own. In hindsight, these were grave errors. We should have scored while we were ahead.

The unaddressed weaknesses of the new order burst into the open with the arrogance of the Iraq War followed by the global financial crisis of 2008. The crisis was a dramatic validation of the sceptics: it revealed how recklessly the financial elite had been behaving and how vulnerable the system was to collapse. While, in most cases, we want markets to respond to news and rumours, we emphatically do not want those 'animal spirits' bearing down around high street banks, where a mere suspicion of insolvency can bring about the feared run on the bank. Trillions of dollars in speculative investments (like the notorious subprime mortgage securities) evaporated, triggering bank failures and a severe recession across the Western world.

Our collective response to the crisis further weakened the Midas-touched cachet of liberal democracy. Governments moved swiftly to bail out banks and stabilise the financial system – a step seen as necessary to prevent complete economic meltdown. But ordinary citizens paid the price: the ensuing recession cost millions of people their jobs and homes, and most governments imposed austerity measures to manage the debts incurred by the bailouts. Banks deemed 'too big to fail' were rescued with public funds; bankers often kept their bonuses, even as unemployment and foreclosures ravaged middle- and working-class communities. Over the next years, even as economies recovered on paper, wages stagnated and job security declined for much of the population. Some of this was necessary, some of it was not. The best practice, clearly, is that solvent institutions buy those that are struggling for a nominal sum. HSBC bought Silicon Valley Bank UK for £1 in 2023, securing people's deposits of £6.7 billion from the line of creditors without bailing out shareholders.

The decision was made to bail out the banks. The crisis and its aftermath shattered the public's trust that incumbent governments were accountable to the people's needs. Instead, governments unfortunate enough to be in power (on both the centre-left and centre-right) appeared beholden to financial interests and unresponsive to the pain of ordinary citizens. It is a familiar argument, perhaps first made by Joseph Stiglitz in his *Globalization and Its Discontents*, that it was into this breach the populists stepped, keenly followed by the growing number of 'left-behind' voters.[5] But we are not a closed system – part of the damage done was to stall and then reverse the democratisation process in developing countries. Authoritarian states were also left with primed and angry populations throughout the West that irregular and informational warfare, particularly conducted by Russia, could target and help mobilise.

In Britain as across Europe, the 2015 refugee crisis provided a lightning rod for populist parties. Images of hundreds of thousands of asylum seekers – many from Syria, Iraq and North Africa – entering Europe were seized upon by far-right leaders to stoke fear of an 'invasion'. Ambitious politicians amplified prejudices and fears about foreigners to argue for sealing borders and restoring an idealised national homogeneity. The weaponisation of the refugee issue helped populists rally support in countries like Germany (the Alternative für Deutschland), France (Marine Le Pen's National Rally), Italy (Matteo Salvini's Lega) and smaller states in Scandinavia and Central Europe.

In the US, populism's rise culminated in the election of Donald Trump as President in 2016 – a development almost unthinkable even a single year prior. Trump, a political outsider, ran a proudly anti-establishment, anti-globalist campaign. He tapped into deep wells of resentment in American society: anger at trade deals which were shipping jobs overseas, anger at Washington politicians (both Republicans and Democrats) perceived as elitist and ineffectual, and a cultural backlash against the country's growing diversity and progressive social norms. Trump's slogans, and his branding of the press as the 'enemy of the people', broke many of the unwritten rules of American politics. Yet they resonated with millions who felt betrayed by the course of the country, and who saw in Trump, at last, someone willing to give voice to their concerns.

Trump demonstrated how this total liberalism, in all its hypocrisy, could be destroyed not through a coup but through the ballot box. The party system which had conspired to exclude had been turned against itself, and nobody should mourn its loss. However, American democracy has now traded elitism, incumbency and stasis for a politics with systemically weaker institutions. With Trump's return, the rate of institutional damage has eclipsed that seen in his first term. Populism also made strong inroads on the left in some countries (for example, the rise of Syriza in Greece amid public fury at EU-imposed austerity, or the popularity of politicians like Bernie Sanders in the US and Jeremy Corbyn in the UK, who challenged the centrist consensus). I note, however, that these left-populist currents, while significant, generally did not cross the same red lines of liberal democracy that the ethno-nationalist right did. In Britain, for instance, the Labour Party under Corbyn espoused anti-elite rhetoric and radical economic changes but ultimately failed to win power and was succeeded by a more moderate leadership. By contrast, right-wing populism often directly challenges liberal pluralism by seeking to redefine the nation in exclusionary terms (Hungary's Orbán, for example, openly declares he is building an 'illiberal state' to defend Christian Hungarian identity).

At any rate, by the close of the 2010s, it became clear that populism was not a transient phenomenon but a durable force reshaping policy and discourse. A striking aspect of that revival is how it had been abetted by the information revolution. Conspiracy theories, propaganda and misinformation are not new to politics; the advent of social media and digital communication has radically amplified their spread and impact.

In previous eras, gatekeepers like reputable news organisations had a monopoly on mass communication, which filtered out the most egregious falsehoods in so far as they harmed the affluent classes. Today, however, billions of people receive information via online feeds that prioritise engagement over accuracy. Extremist and conspiratorial content often spreads faster and wider than factual reporting, because it is more emotionally charged and algorithmically boosted by user interactions. This has created an environment in which alternative realities can flourish. Populist and authoritarian groups exploit this by crafting simplistic, emotionally resonant stories that blame society's problems on nefarious plots, and then disseminating those stories with unprecedented reach.

One emblematic phenomenon was the rise of the QAnon conspiracy theory, perhaps the purest case study in modern misinformation. QAnon originated on anonymous internet forums and posited that a secret cabal of satanic, paedophilic elites (often alleged to include top Democrats and global figures) was controlling world events, and that Donald Trump was heroically working to expose and destroy them. Absurd as this narrative sounds, it masterfully wove together many existing conspiracy tropes, from old antisemitic myths to anti-vaccine paranoia and 'deep state' fears, into a single grand unified theory. By 2020, QAnon adherents had entered Republican electoral politics, with some winning local or even Congressional offices. Here was a vivid example of modern disinformation destabilising a major political party: ambitious politicians felt pressure not to ridicule the conspiratorial views of their base. The result was a Republican Party increasingly 'inoculated' against reality, willing to deny verified facts (like the results of elections or the safety of vaccines) for expediency's sake. The incentives to unravel the narrative were simply not there.

This digital ecosystem of disinformation has directly undermined liberal democratic discourse and left it exposed to foreign influence.

It becomes exceedingly difficult to have reasoned debate or to reach consensus on basic facts if large segments of the public are living in alternate informational realities. Policy responses to genuine problems (a pandemic, for example, or a security threat) are hampered when misinformation spreads faster than truth. Russia, in particular, has deployed online disinformation as a cheap and effective geopolitical weapon: troll farms and fake accounts push divisive content into foreign societies. Western intelligence agencies have uncovered extensive Russian interference operations along these lines, and similar tactics are used by other authoritarian governments and non-state extremists. The challenge is immense: how to preserve an open internet that enriches public debate, builds democratic confidence and humility, while preventing malicious actors (foreign or domestic) from poisoning that openness to destabilise democracy?

* * *

The challenge is certainly less complex for authoritarian states and managed democracies. Russia's post-Cold War trajectory embodies many of the themes of democratic backsliding and authoritarian adaptation. In the 1990s, Russia experimented chaotically with democracy and market reform, suffering economic collapse and no small measure of national humiliation in the process. By the end of that decade, average Russians associated 'democracy' with poverty, corruption and disorder. This set the stage for Vladimir Putin, a former KGB officer, to rise to power in 2000 as a stabilising strongman. Over the next two decades, Putin systematically reversed Russia's democratic gains, constructing a regime that is the paradigmatic managed democracy.

Putin and his ruling circle (centred on the United Russia party and security services) control the media narrative, harass or jail serious opponents and rig electoral procedures to ensure their continued dominance. Independent television and newspapers were either taken over by pro-Kremlin oligarchs or shut down; journalists and activists who probed too deeply into state abuses faced intimidation or worse (many high-profile critics, from investigative reporters to opposition politician Boris Nemtsov, were assassinated under murky circumstances). Over time, checks and balances were neutered: Parliament became a rubber stamp, regional governors were brought to heel and the judiciary lost any autonomy. By amending the constitution and shuffling offices between President and Prime Minister, Putin has effectively made himself leader for life. Under this veneer of democracy – with a constitution, courts, elections – Russia transitioned from managed democracy to authoritarian state centred on one man's personalised rule and a clique of loyalists enriched by their proximity to power.

The Putin regime buttresses its legitimacy with a nationalist and traditionalist ideology with a distinctly irredentist character. It champions a vision of Russia as a distinct Eurasian civilisation, committed to conservative social values and orthodox religion, standing against a decadent, hypocritical West. State propaganda incessantly pushes this narrative, portraying Putin as the saviour of the nation's stability and pride. This same propaganda, repackaged in *Russia Today* for Western leftists and the far right, has spread the idea that Ukraine is to blame for Russia's invasion of it. The regime also invokes external threats to rally domestic support: NATO expansion, Western sanctions and criticism of Russia's human rights are all cast as proof that the West is encircling Russia and trying to keep it down. Again, this narrative is exported to a West that is already weakened by the legitimacy loss from the financial crisis and refugee crisis, and under active attack by Russian propagandists. Many Russians, having endured the chaos of the 1990s, have been willing to trade some freedoms for the relative order and economic recovery (buoyed by oil revenues) that Putin delivered in his first decade. However, this 'social contract' – less freedom in exchange for stability and modest prosperity – began to fray as the economy stagnated in the 2010s and corruption remained rife. Putin responded not by liberalising but by doubling down on authoritarian control and stoking nationalist fervour to distract from domestic woes.

A defining feature of Putin's rule has been its assertive challenge to the liberal international order. Putin did not accept the post-Cold War settlement in which Russia lost superpower status and NATO and the EU expanded eastward. Instead, he set out to revise the balance of power in Russia's favour. Militarily, this meant interventions and aggression in Russia's neighbourhood: the invasion of Georgia in 2008, the seizure of Crimea from Ukraine in 2014 and the full-scale war launched against Ukraine in 2022 all reflect Putin's determination to reclaim influence over former Soviet lands and thwart their drift towards Western alliances. These actions flouted international law and norms, demonstrating Putin's rejection of the rules-based order championed by liberal democracies. Diplomatically, Russia has forged a functional alliance with other authoritarian states (like Iran and China, and formerly Syria), often coordinating positions to counter Western initiatives at the United Nations and other forums.

*　*　*

Russia's most insidious impact on the global democratic recession has been through its adept use of hybrid warfare and the spread of disinformation. Lacking the economic might of China or the soft-power appeal of Western culture, Putin's Russia turned to asymmetric tactics to weaken its rivals. The Kremlin harnessed the openness of democratic societies to meddle in their politics, employing cyber hacks, leaked information and armies of online trolls to influence public opinion abroad. During the 2016 US Presidential election, Russian hackers stole emails from political organisations and individuals and released them strategically to damage Hillary Clinton's campaign, while a Russian 'troll farm' in St Petersburg pumped out divisive social media content masquerading as the work of US activists.[6] Russia has funded large parts of the green and anti-fracking elements in the UK and European Union. Similar interference was documented in elections and referendums across Europe, including the Brexit campaign and the French presidential elections. The goals were twofold: to tilt outcomes in favour of those more aligned to Moscow's interests (often populists who admired Putin or took a softer line on Russia) and, more generally, to sow chaos and distrust, making it harder for democracies to pursue coherent, assertive policies abroad.

We will discuss in the coming chapter the role of political culture in the West, with growing leftist progressivism from its roots in postmodern academia. 'Woke' ideology has in some cases adopted Russian narratives, and in others has weakened the confidence of the West to stand up for its own interests. A confused and obscurantist trend in the West, characterised by accusations of racism, classism and sexism in the form of third-wave feminism (as well as transgender ideology), along with sympathy for enemies of the West and even terrorists – past and present – deepened a 'culture war', the flames of which have been fanned by Russia.

Putin's Russia has in many ways pioneered the authoritarian

playbook for the twenty-first century: crush domestic dissent, promote a unifying illiberal ideology at home and attack liberal democracy abroad via clandestine means rather than open confrontation. This model has inspired copycats and admirers. In the context of a leftist cultural moment, far-right leaders in Europe came to view Putin as a defender of nationalist sovereignty and 'traditional values', aligning with him ideologically. The Kremlin has provided support (either financial or through the media) to sympathetic parties – from the National Rally in France to the Freedom Party in Austria – as part of its effort to cultivate a network of pro-Russian voices within Western democracies. Such alliances show how authoritarianism can be transnational, with autocrats reinforcing each other's narratives and goals.

In short, Russia under Putin stands out as a case of democratic reversal that has had outsized international consequences. It went from a tentative liberalising path to a consolidated authoritarian regime that actively works to undermine liberal democracy elsewhere. If Russia wrote, and continues to write, the destabilising playbook, it is China that is the ascendant authoritarian power that will define the twenty-first century.

* * *

China represents an alternative path that largely bypassed liberal democracy altogether. The People's Republic of China, ruled by the Chinese Communist Party (CCP) since 1949, was never a democracy. But for the first decades of post-Mao reform (1980s–2000s), many in the West assumed that China's increasing integration with the global economy and exposure to outside ideas would lead, eventually, to political liberalisation.[7] That expectation has not been borne out. Instead, China has combined authoritarian one-party rule with market-driven growth to dramatic effect, lifting hundreds of millions out of poverty and emerging as the main geopolitical competitor to the United States – all while tightening internal control and projecting influence outward.

Under Xi Jinping, who became General Secretary of the CCP in 2012, China's trajectory has become explicitly more authoritarian. Xi swiftly consolidated power, eliminating the term limits and collective leadership norms that were meant to prevent a return to Mao-style dictatorship. He has amassed personal authority, being hailed as the 'core' leader and enshrining his ideological contributions in the Party constitution.[8] Domestically, Xi's tenure has seen a harsh crackdown on dissent and tightening of social control. Independent human rights lawyers, civil society organisations and grassroots activists (including those advocating for ethnic minority rights or #MeToo issues) have been arrested or silenced. The CCP under Xi has deployed cutting-edge surveillance technology to monitor its citizens on a massive scale: a panopticon of street cameras with facial recognition, AI systems that track online behaviour and communications and big-data analysis to flag 'abnormal' activities. This surveillance state is epitomised by conditions in Xinjiang, a western region home to the Muslim Uyghur population and the location of the ongoing Uyghur genocide. There, under the guise of anti-terrorism, authorities have built a high-tech police state, complete with checkpoints, ubiquitous cameras and involuntary data collection (including DNA and iris scans) from millions of Uyghurs. Up to 1 million Uyghurs and other Muslim minorities have been detained in what the government calls 're-education' camps – facilities that survivors describe as forced indoctrination centres aiming to strip them of their culture and faith. Reports of forced labour, sterilisation and other abuses in Xinjiang point to a campaign of cultural extermination.[9] This represents authoritarian repression at its most extreme, justified by Beijing as necessary for stability and development.

Another flashpoint has been Hong Kong, formerly a semi-autonomous city with a strong tradition of rule of law and free speech. Britain's interest and history here is tragic. Assurances given by the CCP at the moment of handover in 1997 have been comprehensively reneged upon. After large pro-democracy protests erupted in Hong Kong in 2019, Beijing imposed a sweeping National Security Law that effectively ended the 'One Country, Two Systems' arrangement years ahead of schedule. Activists, journalists and opposition politicians in Hong Kong were arrested or driven into exile, and the city's once vibrant democratic institutions were neutered. This demonstrated that the CCP would not tolerate even a small enclave of freedom under its sovereignty, let alone countenance democratisation on the mainland. It raises serious questions for the West about whether a tougher stance on China, earlier on, could have forced a bona fide democratisation.

Economically, China continues to embrace some market mechanisms but always under party supervision. The CCP has cracked down on private sector figures who challenge its authority (such as tech billionaire Jack Ma, who disappeared from public view for months after criticising regulators). The message is clear: prosperity is welcome, but political loyalty is non-negotiable. Through initiatives like the Social Credit System (which scores citizens and businesses on trustworthiness, punishing behaviour the state deems undesirable) and heavy censorship of the internet (the so-called 'Great Firewall'), China is pioneering an Orwellian fusion of data-driven efficiency with authoritarian oversight.

On the global stage, China has become the leading advocate and benefactor of a post-liberal order. Its signature foreign policy project, the Belt and Road Initiative (often called the BRI), has seen China invest in infrastructure across Asia, Africa and Latin America. While ostensibly apolitical, the initiative's deals often come with an implicit 'authoritarian bargain': Chinese loans and development assistance do not ask recipients to meet governance or human rights standards (unlike Western aid). Instead, China offers a model of rapid development without democratic constraints – they are effectively saying, 'We will help you build roads, railways and ports, and we won't ask what you do with your political system in return.' This appeals to many leaders in developing countries who are weary of Western conditionality about reforms or corruption.[10] However, the BRI has also drawn criticism for creating debt dependencies and for enabling local corruption, as well as giving China strategic footholds (e.g. control of ports or mineral resources) that can translate into political leverage.

At international institutions, China has grown more confident in asserting its preferences. It has pushed for language that emphasises state sovereignty and non-interference, to ward off any attempts at outside scrutiny of its own conduct. In bodies like the UN Human Rights Council, Chinese diplomats work alongside Russia and others to dilute human rights initiatives and to promote the idea that development (rather than individual rights) should be the primary metric of a government's legitimacy. China champions concepts like 'Internet sovereignty', arguing that each state should control its own cyberspace, a principle aimed at legitimising online censorship and surveillance. Beijing also established new institutions like the Asian Infrastructure Investment Bank as alternatives to Western-dominated ones, dragging countries into their economic sphere as Western loans dry up. Likewise, Chinese spending on cutting-edge research and development now outstrips the US – the surest indicator that a 500-year Western advantage in technology may soon evaporate.

Unlike Russia, China became more repressive even as it grew richer. For rulers in other countries, China offers an attractive template: you can have growth, national pride and technological advancement and still retain absolute political control and one-party rule. For people under authoritarian rule, China's rise may weaken their hope for democratisation, as their governments have a powerful patron and model to emulate. It is plausible, however frightening, that third countries become less like us, and more like China.

That said, China's model is not without its own contradictions and costs. The lack of political freedom and rule of law can lead to gross injustices, mass unrest (as seen in Hong Kong or in periodic protests around China over local grievances) and policy mistakes due to suppressed feedback (for example, the early mishandling and cover-up of the Covid outbreak in Wuhan was exacerbated by officials' fear of reporting bad news up the chain). Internationally, China's aggressive moves – military build-ups in the South China Sea, threats to Taiwan and 'wolf warrior' diplomacy that brooks no criticism – have begun to produce a backlash, spurring closer cooperation among other nations wary of Chinese domination, particularly in south-east Asia where Chinese maritime expansionism continues. Thus, the contest between liberal and authoritarian systems is far from settled; it is dynamic, with push and counter-push. This is evident not just in geopolitics but also in the realm of ideas, where China and Russia promote 'civilisational' governance models while the West (at least in principle) continues to advocate universal human rights and democratic values.

Iran shares characteristics of Russian-style authoritarianism much more than Chinese, yet the three are often grouped as part of an Authoritarian Axis.[11] They are a key supplier to Russia in their invasion of Ukraine and to China in feeding their insatiable demand for oil and gas. While China is able to cooperate (and even offer outright diplomatic assistance) with Iran, there is scant evidence that either Russia or China would seek to defend Iran against the United States.

* * *

The key upshot is this: these authoritarian powers are at their most dangerous when their strategic interests align. Opportunism is therefore a key variable that the West must learn to control. The US once held a 'two war construct' – similar to Britain's 1889 'two power standard' (which required that Britain's navy be as large as the next two largest navies combined) – which sought to preserve at all times its ability to fight two wars in two different theatres, simultaneously. For all the truth in the fact that Europe cannot adequately defend itself, the US has also seen a dramatic reduction in relative defence spending on its own. The brief US logistical shift to the Middle East during the Twelve-Day War between Israel and Iran in 2025 put Taiwan on high alert. Tipping points around the globe and the connectedness of one theatre to another binds their interests and increases their gains from cooperation.

We can directly reduce the extent to which Russia's and China's interests align by increasing our collective defence spending. In particular, Europe seeing to its own defence is crucial to give the US capacity to limit the possibility of a tipping point in the Middle East and the Pacific, and Trump was absolutely right to insist on it.

This principle also applies to the many smaller third nations with their own concerns about how the global international order works for them, in addition to their own negotiated conflicts with their own rivals. The grand strategy of the US – characterised by the principle of 'offshore balancing' – works as follows: the US must retain the *capacity* to maintain the balance of power in key parts of the world. It is not necessary to dominate any region (except its home region, the Americas) but rather stop any other power or combination of powers from taking over. The logic of the US pivot to the Far East is revealed in that there is no realistic potential hegemon in Europe or the Middle East. But there is one in China. Through increased defence spending, the West can minimise the extent to which aggression in eastern Europe or the Middle East diverts resources from East Asia, and therefore reduce the alignment of strategic interests between Russia and China.

How then can the West, and Britain in particular, fight back while stabilising our own democracies and delivering growth and prosperity for our citizens? A motivating goal of this book is to address that question by outlining strategies to reinforce democratic resilience against these threats, in particular ones that strengthen our hand by building capability and hard power, while facilitating adjustment to this new world of great power competition. We will analyse Britain's best response, our best available economic and diplomatic stance to counter threats of terror, global warming, weakening global institutions and legal norms, as well as to compete with authoritarians ideologically. One place to start is to recognise that Britain and Europe have massively declined in relative global influence, not just from their lack of military prowess and underinvestment in the industrial, energy, technological and strategic resources of the future, but from a more ideological failure, both in government and societally, to identify their own values and interests and to project them consistently in matters of foreign policy.

The Twelve-Day War again provides some illustrative examples. Neither Keir Starmer nor French President Emmanuel Macron played the role they could have played in the conflict. Both were equivocating, both were issuing platitudes about peace and 'expressions of concern' which failed to rise to the occasion or even take note of the reasons the two sides were at war. To be clear, supporting de-escalation over US or even British bombing of Iran is a defensible goal about which one may reasonably disagree. What is indefensible is the feeble way in which it was attempted. British naval assets in the region (including the aircraft carrier HMS *Queen Elizabeth*) were not diverted to gain bargaining power. Starmer, then Home Secretary David Lammy and his Defence Secretary John Healey were united in a campaign of faux ignorance, pretending that Trump had no intention of bombing Iran's nuclear sites – all this in order to create a less-than-compelling illusion that the UK and US were on the same page, only to then inevitably perform a volte-face by backing the strikes after the fact. It would be difficult to intentionally contrive so ineffectual an approach to a conflict Britain has been intimately involved in since 2002. It is no surprise Trump made an otherwise irrelevant G7 summit memorable by leaving it early.

The confidence and humility that makes democratic liberalism more resilient at home also makes it more effective on the global stage. A Britain without the moral authority to act must recognise the need for profound cultural change. For our current purposes, suffice it to say there is no silver bullet to magically restore liberalism's primacy. In *Authoritarian Century*, I sketched a kind of roadmap for how liberal democracies can regain their footing. It builds first from domestic reforms, international coordination and ideological rejuvenation. The overarching theme is that liberal democracy must fix its internal weaknesses and confidently stand up to external challengers at the same time. It's a monumental undertaking, but it is the only path forward if we are to avoid an authoritarian century. Elucidating this point, and spelling out what that means for Britain, is necessary.

Indeed, the UK's 2025 Strategic Defence Review shows that, to a considerable extent, Britain is aware of the weakness of its strategic outlook in the face of these threats. It recognises that hostile state actors, terrorism, cyber threats and disinformation are creating a more dangerous environment and asserts the need for Britain to modernise its defences while reinforcing key alliances, particularly NATO.[12] In that sense, Britain's strategists are starting from the same premises that we are. The review reinforces the enduring importance of Euro-Atlantic security, but also acknowledges the strategic weight of the Indo-Pacific and the global contest between democratic and authoritarian systems. The unstated premise is that realistically, as this book will show, where the US goes, the UK must follow. Central to the review is the belief that defending liberal democratic values is a national security imperative. It explicitly names Russia as the most acute threat to European security while underestimating China as merely posing a systemic challenge. This is perhaps explained by the Labour government's misguided attempt at rapprochement with Beijing. The UK is committing to a strategy of integrated deterrence, combining diplomatic, economic, technological and military tools to respond to adversaries. This includes investing in advanced capabilities such as artificial intelligence, cyber defence and space technologies, while maintaining the UK's nuclear deterrent and role as a reliable military partner.

Where the review fails to rise to the level of events is not in its conception but in its content. The economic, energy, climate, diplomatic and fiscal strategy of the UK is, to be blunt, catastrophically wrong. Advantages in cyber, AI and finance are being squandered due to economic mismanagement, failures of basic statecraft and a political and social culture that fails to identify British interests and to connect them to concrete policy decisions.

*   *   *

One of the most significant consequences of this diplomatic realignment has been in the realm of cybersecurity. China has used its cyber capabilities not only to steal valuable intellectual property and technological advances from British firms, but also to pose a direct operational threat to both UK military systems and civilian infrastructure. This has included attacks on Members of Parliament and the Electoral Commission. A previous UK government press release, which attributed these cyberattacks to Chinese state-linked organisations, now carries a disclaimer noting it was issued under the 2022–24 Rishi Sunak administration. Since taking office, Keir Starmer has notably avoided referring to China as a 'threat', instead characterising his approach as one of 'predictable and pragmatic partnership'.[13] This has since backfired politically as well as strategically, by reportedly causing the collapse of a high-stakes case against two agents accused of spying for China, causing significant embarrassment for the government.

The UK's failure to take earlier action – both in regard to Ukraine and China – between 1997 and 2016 has cost the country valuable time in achieving strategic independence from Russian energy and Chinese manufacturing dependencies. The long-term damage from

Britain's foreign policy has had economic consequences, particularly through the erosion and offshoring of key industries, most notably advanced manufacturing, shipbuilding and military-industrial production. This naivety was compounded by undeliverable and distracting promises about cheap and reliable green energy. While the decline of steel manufacturing receives much of the public's attention, this is less concerning given its global abundance and the willingness of allied nations to supply it. Our imports overwhelmingly come from European allies, as well as Canada and the US. A far greater vulnerability lies in Britain's dependence on China for rare earth elements – materials essential to both advanced technology and the green energy transition, a supply China has demonstrated it is willing to weaponise. China currently provides 46.3 per cent of Europe's rare earth supply; without securing access to these materials on open global markets, not only will Western climate goals become unattainable, but China will continue to dominate the production of solar panels and electric vehicles – consolidating its economic advantage.

A recent report by the Center for Strategic and International Studies (CSIS) warns that the US's defence industrial base is not adequately prepared for a possible confrontation with China.[14] With munitions stockpiles already depleted by ongoing conflicts in Ukraine and the Middle East, CSIS simulations suggest the US could exhaust its supply of long-range precision-guided missiles within a week, making sustained military engagement extremely difficult. China is well aware of these production shortfalls, and this knowledge increases the likelihood of risk-taking in areas such as Taiwan and the South China Sea. The fragility of critical supply chains – particularly for strategic metals – limits Western options both militarily and diplomatically.

Gallium stands out as a particularly strategic metal, with China producing 98 per cent of the global supply. It is vital for the manufacture of cutting-edge military hardware and high-performance semiconductors that underpin systems like GPS. Gallium-based components are crucial for 5G networks, solar power technology and electric vehicles. They are also key to modern missile defence platforms such as the Lower-Tier Air and Missile Defense Sensor (LTAMDS), used in Patriot missile systems. Raytheon, one of the system's designers, has described LTAMDS as 'transformational', capable of detecting threats at far greater distances than current technologies – a capability essential to protecting US assets in any conflict with China, Russia or other major powers. As demand for higher-performance chips surpasses what silicon can deliver, both commercial and military industries are expected to increase their reliance on gallium. According to CSIS, a US Geological Survey study found that even a 30 per cent disruption in gallium supply could result in a $602 billion loss to US GDP – equivalent to 2.1 per cent of national output.

This broader underestimation of authoritarian threats has also contributed to a deeper failure: the erosion of commitment to the rules-based international order, a system from which the UK has historically benefited. That order is now under sustained pressure – in part because of the lack of political will to defend it.

CHAPTER 2

THE DECLINE OF BRITISH STATECRAFT

Once upon a time, Britain had a fierce reputation as an efficient and effective machine of diplomacy and statecraft. Through a judicious use of diplomatic mission, commercial influence and naval power – essentially, both carrot and stick – Britain brought about the balance of power and economic conditions it needed for growth, trade and empire. Despite that pedigree, Britain has suffered a string of failed deployments, decisions and negotiations. Some are so calamitous as to call into question the competence of the Foreign Office itself. Other core parts of British statecraft – what we call the practice of conducting state affairs for the betterment of the country – seem to operate, quite astonishingly, without a coherent idea of what the 'betterment of the country' actually consists of.

At first pass that may seem a rather brave opening gambit. Our leaders are, almost to a man, well-educated and well-meaning. Yet one source of our decline has its roots in academia – in bad students as much as in bad professors. The theory behind constructive and 'credible' foreign policy is a sound one. In international relations, we talk about integrative versus distributive bargaining. Trump is the archetypal distributive bargainer, meaning he sees agreements as all-or-nothing one-time events with winners and losers, and ignores that countries have options other than to trade with the US. Integrative bargaining understands that there will be another agreement next year, and that a zero-sum approach this year will jeopardise the next negotiation. Trump forgets that the 'game' is repeated forever, *integrated* across different negotiations and that countries, like companies, make their money on repeat business. Striking extractive deals and parroting the language of a protection racket, only to then change one's mind and reverse tariffs, is the opposite of an integrative approach. One significant recent example of the failure of this strategy is how Norway was anxious to ditch its US F-35s as they no longer saw the US as an honest broker against Russia that will keep them supplied with spare parts, and worry that there may be a 'kill switch' to stop US military hardware being used in ways Trump won't approve of. They got over their concerns, yet the episode reminded commentators how integrative foreign policy is more sustainable and maximises outcomes over the longer term.[1]

Our leaders, both civil servants and cabinet ministers, are familiar with the conclusion. Indeed, in Britain, diplomatic statecraft has been markedly bipartisan and consensus-based since the late 1990s. Axioms of British statecraft have been these core ideas of 'credibility', 'reputation' and so forth. Both are incredibly rich concepts when describing an effective approach to getting our way as a nation, sustainably and over the long term. Increasingly, however, these axioms have become divorced from their intended goal: the promotion of British interests. No nation should seek to be credible or have a good reputation at the expense of its own interests. They are desirable goals instrumentally, not intrinsically. They should never have been elevated in the minds of politicians to be goals in their own right. Secondly, they have become much thinner concepts, increasingly used to justify any compromise even when there's no direct and foreseeable way that it could improve outcomes for Britain in future.

The decline in British statecraft in the dimension of 'bad ideas' is best separated into two explanatory categories. The first is the top-down failure among strategists and leaders to conceive of British interests and to privilege them over the interests of others. The second is the bottom-up effect of social, legal and political progressivism that obscures and undermines good statecraft from within.

It is not necessary to detail in full how the Chagos Archipelago handover, to take just one example, manifestly harms British interests and the interests of our allies. Diego Garcia is a strategically vital hub in the Indian Ocean, serving as a linchpin for US and UK power projection, logistics and surveillance across the Middle East, Africa and Asia. Its location enables rapid military response, airstrike capability, sustained naval operations and intelligence gathering critical to regional and global security. The Diego Garcia island base was not under a legal threat severe enough to threaten its operation. The legal judgment that went against the UK (with Chinese and Russian judges on the bench) was non-binding.[2] It was owned and operated with complete sovereignty and autonomy and was able to project aerial power across the Indian Ocean as far as Afghanistan and Iran. As this new era of great power competition dawns, the position of Diego Garcia, already perhaps the most geostrategically important base operated by any NATO power, will only grow in importance. The handover sees instead Mauritius – an avowed ally of China – given sovereignty and now sharing several key aspects of jurisdiction over the base itself. They are to have joint jurisdiction even in terms of secure radio transmissions and must now be warned whenever an operation is launched from the base. The lease is to last ninety-nine years. There are no provisions strong enough to stop the other islands being turned into military bases – even Chinese ones.

The claims from leadership and the bureaucracy that such a deal was vital for the 'safety and security of the British people' are simply wrong. Memorandums and parliamentary documentation argue, without any substantive evidence to support it, that there was an ongoing risk of a future *binding* agreement ruling that the base could no longer operate. There is no mechanism by which an advisory opinion can become a binding judgment. There is no facility whatsoever by which a case of this kind could produce one. As Lord West of Spithead, former First Sea Lord, argues in his report on the matter, the flawed legal reasoning 'undermines the Government's claim' that the long-term future of Diego Garcia 'is more secure under this agreement than without it'.[3]

The consequences of the deal for the base will be felt over the course of the next century. As Lord West writes, these bases are 'an invaluable currency' – and this one has been kneecapped. True legal uncertainty is assured by the terms of the new treaty. A lack of integrity for secure military communications is unforgiveable. The risks of a lease compared to sovereignty are severe. The operational frictions imposed are also intolerable. Contracts on the base must either be given to Mauritian businesses or a written explanation must be sent to Port Louis as to why not. Contractors are to be Mauritians wherever possible – it is compromising that Britain and the US are to cede absolute control over those allowed onto the base. In annexes to the agreement, the UK commits to notifying

Mauritius of the location of all equipment on Diego Garica that it is upgrading or repairing.

In theory, the UK–US base and Mauritius 'shall jointly decide' about whether the other islands can be used by other nations' (read: China's) militaries. Realistically, however, the UK would be left protesting under the terms of the lease to a joint commission. If Mauritius wanted to lease out another island to the Chinese, no legal action could practically prevent them. Likewise, if Mauritius were to break the terms of this new lease, there would be realistically very little the UK could seek to do about it (note here that Mauritius was paid £3 million to drop their claims to it back in 1965 and have reneged on that agreement, which *was* binding under international law). We would obviously not be willing to vacate the base – and would quickly learn what *actual* legal uncertainty looks like.

China sees Mauritius as a key economic partner, ratifying the Mauritius–China Free Trade Agreement in 2021 as their first such deep trade relationship with any African country. They see Mauritius's so-called 'Ocean Economy' – their marine and offshore resources, now including those surrounding Chagos – as key fuel for growing Chinese demand. Chinese investment and influence on the island is burgeoning; a raft of Chinese-built infrastructure projects, from airports to the highways and data infrastructure, have been built using Chinese loans. Defenders of the deal (including Keir Starmer's special envoy in the negotiations, Jonathan Powell) blithely protest that Mauritius is not a member of China's $1 trillion Belt and Road Initiative, which is true. And yet with the amount of Chinese capital onshore, they may as well be. China have been vying for an Indian Ocean base for more than a decade, so it is no wonder that China celebrated the UK–Mauritius deal as a 'massive achievement'. The fact that a nominal £30 billion will be sent over the next ninety-nine years (which is to come out of our defence spending) to their ally is just the icing on the cake.

It is vital that we learn lessons from this calamitous deal and draw conclusions about how it happened. That it is a bad deal should be self-evident. What is more valuable to Britain, going forward, is an understanding of how on earth such a poor agreement came to pass. As above, it is most instructive to split the societal causes from the governmental ones, and to see where they relate. These apply beyond Chagos and have been undermining British statecraft in dozens of similar negotiations in the last two decades.

The governmental reasons must begin with the way leaders understand and interpret legal advice. The civil service is not allowed to propose policies or courses of action which contravene 'international law'; however, as Lord Sumption points out, their internal interpretation of the law is highly politicised, particularly in international law and human rights law. Despite this, the utterance 'international law' has a sincerity and gravity to it even when the substance is a non-binding agreement. But the issue of legality has a much longer history in the Chagos case. The ICJ ruling itself contravenes the principle that no state should be compelled to have its bilateral disputes submitted for judicial settlement without its consent. With regards to the ICJ, 'the purpose of the advisory function is not to settle – at least directly – disputes between States, but to offer legal advice to the organs and institutions requesting the opinion'. It appears as if elected and non-elected officials were aware of this fact to varying degrees. Helen Goodman, upon hearing the advice, declared that the 'International Court of Justice found that the UK's control of the Chagos Islands is illegal and wrong'.

There is a significant factor in this failure of statecraft that sees the lawyers themselves as agents active against British interests. Lord Hermer, for instance, currently serving as Attorney General (and who met Keir Starmer as a colleague at Doughty Street Chambers where together they practiced human rights law), is responsible for the legal advice provided to the UK government. He himself went on to practice at Matrix Chambers, alongside Phillipe Sands KC, who has for a decade and a half served as Mauritius's chief legal counsel. When the ICJ gave its advice, Sands commented that '[the UK's] arguments that Chagos is about security and a bilateral matter between it and Mauritius were given short shrift'. Leaving aside the question of whether this intentionally misleads, it is clear from this deal that Chagos is very much about security.

* * *

Both Conservative and Labour leadership has been under pressure from a dimension the UK is particularly vulnerable to: shyness over empire and demands for decolonisation. Britain's leaders embarrass very easily over this issue. But good statecraft demands that our case is made robustly and that, if necessary, we bite the bullet. It is worth noting that being prone to embarrassment of this sort becomes a top-down pressure on good governance, as ministers, just like business leaders, create obligations on those below them in order to protect themselves from uncomfortable conversations, which is the ultimate purpose of all Diversity, Equity and Inclusion initiatives. Indeed, talks with Mauritius were reopened because of what can only be described as the mild colonial embarrassment of appearing not to negotiate with Mauritius while describing the issue as a bilateral dispute. Those ministers from the Conservative government originally involved had no intention of bringing about a deal of this kind. Yet they sent their departments out to negotiate, not with a clear vision of what they hoped to achieve, or a risk assessment of where such talks might lead, but rather with the goal of playing nice and kicking the can down the road. Unfortunately, to mix metaphors, that 'can' was reopened when it came across the desk of Sir Keir Starmer (the best-case scenario for Mauritian negotiators).

To avoid ambiguity: the rising pressure and obscurantism of progressive high-status opinions complicating statecraft is a separate phenomenon to the rising authoritarian threat worldwide. The particular ethical and political values that are being challenged by that rising authoritarian threat (a threat which, unsurprisingly, progressivism tends to ignore), and the particular domestic and international institutions that are being undermined, paint a very serious picture indeed. Globally, we are not simply in one of those periods where political ascendency shifts from the centre-left to the centre-right (or vice versa); it is a much more profound rejection of an entire model for the organisation of society. The role of new relativist postmodern ideologies in the West has unfortunately been to desensitise us to the rising authoritarian threat by complicating our self-conception as moral, democratic nations and to instil a false belief that our liberal values are universally held.

It is worth noting that embarrassment of this sort is, of course, also a bottom-up consequence of legal, social and political progressivism. Not Chagos, nor the Elgin Marbles, nor any other purported question of decolonisation would see consequential numbers of votes won if Britain were to abandon its 'colonial' claim. There is no political payoff to these issues; these are issues which politicians choose to bring to the public attention. Andrew Breitbart's most enduring observation about American politics was that 'politics is downstream of culture'. In particular, this type of politics is downstream of a culture prevalent among affluent classes. There are certain high-status beliefs common throughout Western nations (including outside the Anglosphere); these are recognisable as left-wing but have replaced older issues of class with new issues of race, cosmopolitanism and climate change. We would identify this new alignment as new or 'woke' left, as compared to the old left, but with luxury and high-status beliefs that come to include some on the centre-right as well as the centre-left.

These new left beliefs are, roundly, the kind which would go down well at a dinner party. What unites them is the elevation of morality and moral purity, and the desire as the holder of the belief to distinguish oneself from lower-status belief systems. Supporting 'decolonisation' is a high-status opinion, lauded and funded at universities, in the arts and in workplaces as much as in government departments. It is high status particularly in the sense that it allows the holder of the belief to separate themselves from low-status opinions that include nationalism, pride in one's history and racism. Critics of 'woke' politics often focus on 'luxury beliefs', a subcategory of high-status beliefs which are also expensive to hold. Supporting high levels of migration, for instance, is a luxury belief, since you have to be wealthy enough to live away from the negative consequences, and may benefit from asset appreciation and cheaper labour. Criticism of immigration is low status.

A final insight to introduce is that made by Bryan Caplan in his book *The Myth of the Rational Voter*.[4] Among many other piercing observations on politics made from the perspective of economics, Caplan notes that holding opinions according to your private interests, or even in the national interest, won't often maximise your wellbeing (for instance, you might stand to benefit enormously if the top rate of income tax were cut). You may convince a small number and have an infinitesimally small chance of changing the election result in a single constituency. However, the costs of your opinion are real and immediate. You may lose friends, risk upset, forgo opportunities or feel psychological guilt. If you acquiesce to the high-status opinion, you are likely to gain social status. Caplan's concept of 'rational irrationality' is one part of a picture which explains why it can be advantageous socially and economically to vote for things that are against your own interests or against the coherent interests of a nation state. This happens at the large group – i.e. the cultural – level.

This speaks to the inability of our leaders to properly conceptualise British interests separately to their own. The cultural milieu in which we expect our government departments and leaders to execute effective statecraft rewards high-status opinion over fundamental interests (most net zero policy comes under this category). In turn, the organs of the state, particularly the judiciary, sculpts the Overton window – the range of action deemed acceptable for the state to take – according to the precepts of high-status opinion. The theme of judicial overreach, or more accurately, the crowding out of politics by law, is most eloquently treated by Lord Sumption in his *Trials of the State: Law and the Decline of Politics*.[5] The tendency of the courts to inject themselves into what are political issues, and to make declaratory announcements about values and rights, is another mechanism by which high-status opinion drives a failure of statecraft. The result is baffling decisions, such as the one taken to enshrine net zero by 2050 into UK law by statute.

In this brave new world of law – of which human rights law is the most egregious offender – many foundational principles of common law have been diminished in order to allow for fresh law to be creat-ed from the bench. Parliamentary legislation, or indeed the ECHR, serves as what Sumption calls a 'clarion call': an inspiration for ac-tivist legal practitioners to take it further than the legislation could ever have conceivably been intended to go.[6] Sumption, a veteran of the Supreme Court and a giant of the commercial bar, provides an extensive account of where this has developed from, and where the profession is heading; one cause is the fact that private practitioners (the likes of Starmer, Hermer and Sands) are much more able law-yers than those drafting government legislation. Aside from barris-ters such as these, politicised judges made tendentious use of other international accords including the UN Refugee Convention, the Paris Agreement, the Convention on the Rights of the Child and even the Aarhus Convention, which provides for public access to information, involvement in decision-making and 'access to justice' in environmental matters. The Climate Change Act, Equality Act and Human Rights Act are particularly problematic in how they constrain reasonable private and state action and place a burden on government so high that all manner of necessary decisions – from airport expansions and house-building to border security and the deportation of foreign criminals – have become incredibly difficult.

The issue of an overreaching judiciary will receive a more thor-ough treatment later in this book. For now, suffice it to note how Lord Sumption's analysis was received: Jessica Simor KC, a bar-rister at Matrix Chambers alongside Hermer and Sands, criticised Sumption, writing, 'The former Supreme Court justice is fanning the flames of nationalism,' and that 'those who care about the future will read and despair'.[7] The moralism and political sensationalism in these words betrays the claim Simor and others make that even very mundane rights are so fundamental that they must be put beyond the reach of politics. Their desire to put them there is itself political. The gradual expansion of the scope of human rights and equalities law, once limited to the most fundamental rights, now gives courts the power to review sentencing, immigration, employment law, environmental and even planning law on the grounds of human rights. Courts frequently produce obscene judgments on this basis. One immigration court allowed Ghanaian visa overstayer Joyce Baidoo – who had been convicted and jailed for fraud – to remain in the UK on human rights grounds since she would encounter 'significant obstacles' in reintegrating in Ghana due to her long absence, and that leaving the UK would have a 'detrimental impact on her mental health'. Another case, involving Next warehouse and store workers, saw courts effectively legislate from the bench that two dissimilar jobs must pay the same because men are more likely to do one, and women the other.[8] However, to protest this incursion of the judiciary into the political or the economic is deemed low status indeed, since it involves either trusting the grubby, uncouth and suspicious realm of politics and its majoritarian rule, or the market.

Some concrete examples may be necessary to convince the reader that some of our courts are as radical as we have claimed. Hermer rightly receives criticism for the extent to which he has constrained democratic politics in service to his own radical opinion. In the new guidance he gave government lawyers in 2025, Hermer instructed that all lawyers must inform him personally if any minister may be about to break the law; he also inserted twenty-three new references to international law and removed instructions left by his predecessors that prevented lawyers becoming a 'block' on government policy. But Hermer is just the most visible of a large constituency of barristers and judges who occupy themselves with finding novel methods to bend legislation to their own political preference. One particularly productive loophole has been Article 8 of the European Convention on Human Rights, which has given us such legal howlers as the criminal allowed to stay since his stepson didn't like Albanian chicken nuggets.

Rebecca Chapman is one of the most prolific abusers of this loophole, and also of Article 3, which concerns claims based on medical conditions – a subject upon which she published a practical guidebook in 2021.[9] Yet not only does she represent clients (including a lesbian couple allowed to stay since, although homosexuality is legal in Albania, homophobia is 'rampant in rural areas'), she also sits as a judge on the same upper-tier immigration tribunal where she practices as a barrister. Fellow barristers from Chapman's chambers, Garden Court, go further; for instance, Greg Ó Ceallaigh KC has said the Tories should be 'dealt with as you would deal with the Nazis', while Nick Bano has written that 'landlords and house price speculators [should be driven] from the face of the Earth'. Another of their colleagues, barrister Michael Goold, won a case for Extinction Rebellion activists who had committed criminal damage against the Treasury building, claiming 'anyone who knew the full scale of the climate crisis would have consented to the damage'.[10]

The problems this presents for the law are grave; the problems it presents for politics and statecraft even graver. Starmer (or indeed any British leader), as well as the civil service, are both produced and constrained by the functioning of these institutions and the culture that produced them. An absolutist culture on international law could make one forget that these are, at their core, treaties written and signed by states many decades ago to deal with the problems they faced and foresaw in good faith. Britain's position on international law is radical, of course, but it is not within the gift even of Parliament to reform it. The Conservative governments issued many more remedial orders from Parliament to 'provide a speedy response to adverse human rights judgements' when courts declared time and again 'incompatibilities' between legislation and the HRA. Yet when the government often fails to appeal, when its own lawyers are produced and sustained by the same law that they seek to change and when courts still consider primary legislation over the remedial orders, there's very little that can be done.

What is perhaps remarkable about Chagos is that despite being presented with the perfect opportunity to back out of the arrangement when Mauritius sought to renegotiate the deal, no part of the British state was able to reverse course on such a critical issue of diplomacy and statecraft. It cut through several lines of vulnerability: on the law, on nationalism and on empire. Our leadership and civil service was unable to deal with cultural and personal pressure from below and institutional and legal pressure from above. Our institutions and culture have created an environment where bad ideas reap political and personal rewards.

Some final comparative points are needed to fully scope out this problem of bad ideas. When comparing the UK to other countries, commentators often look first to the origin of the ideas: the United States. Perhaps France, however, is the most developed in terms of limiting the impact of these ideas on institutions, particularly schools, universities and government departments. To be clear, France did not get off to a strong start. Just as Britain's sensibilities are vulnerable to talk of empire, so France's are vulnerable to rhetoric about French linguistic and cultural exceptionalism. The growth of woke ideas in France masqueraded as anti-American influence and the assertion of a distinctly French academic sphere;

French thought and postmodern thought were deemed one and the same. Second-hand dealers in these ideas, as theorist Friedrich Hayek would call them, found success in attracting state funding for their activism. Alliance Citoyenne, a French organisation that promotes unionisation and direct action, receives 15 per cent of its budget from the French state, which it uses in large part to train activists to lobby the state itself. This builds upon the observation that woke ideas are very saleable and incredibly profitable. This is as true for NGOs and activist movements as much as it is for large management consultancies.

French progressive influence of this kind shares with its Anglosphere equivalent the elevation of 'communities' over any prior conception of a national community. Its prescription for how multiculturalism must work is therefore not that existing institutional values are expanded and reinforced, but rather that multicultural success requires asserting and affirming the separateness and equality of 'communities'. The French, however, have a more robust secular, republican and philosophical conception of citizenship compared to the liberal individualist conception prevalent in the Anglosphere. (This is not to say that Anglo-Saxon conceptions of liberty are not robust compared to progressivism's ideas. Rather, the secular and republican conception of citizenship legitimises a wider range of countermeasures against communitarianism for France. France, in brief, is comfortable in some degree of enforcement of a universalised 'Frenchness' to take precedence over ethnic, regional and religious identities.) French academia has been clearer and more resolute in the identification and condemnation of these ideas which threaten *la laïcité* – particularly the threat from communitarian thought. French academia has therefore produced reactions that would be unimaginable in the UK, including 'Le manifest des 100' – an open letter in *Le Monde* signed by one hundred French academics to oppose '*l'islamogauchisme*' (Islamo-leftism) at universities.

Similarly, Ilana Cicurel, an MEP and member of Macron's centrist party, remarked, 'We see a drift, the temptation to reduce people to their identities in the name of the fight against discrimination.' Jean-Michel Blanquer, perhaps the political leader of the French anti-woke movement, urged his countrymen to 'look at how the Chinese use TikTok or the way Qatar uses Al Jazeera, and how they exploit woke themes'. We might think that these claims are typical from those on the right of politics – that France is not unique. Yet what has separated France from the trajectory of the UK, the US, Ireland and many others, is the republican tradition of the left itself. The ever-irreverent French left has proved itself less amenable to woke politics than most centre-right parties in Europe. While France's institutions are by no means unscathed, their political culture means their leaders face stronger incentives not to acquiesce. In May 2025, Macron was presented with a report, drafted by two senior civil servants, detailing and evidencing the 'entryism' of Muslim Brotherhood partisans into French institutions. The report was accepted and 'new proposals' were immediately sought after. It is unlikely that such a report would ever be commissioned in the UK, unlikelier still that it would be penned by civil servants and perhaps unimaginable that it would not be buried before making it to the Prime Minister.

The second comparative point is historical. This is not the first time that militant influence has been exerted on universities. Marxism in the 1950s and 1960s and critical sociology into the 1980s rocked campuses. Each of these bears a similarity to the current progressive cultural moment in that both found formal academic support for political motives. 'Studies', including gender studies, postcolonial studies and so forth, were established with academic credentials with the goal of expounding a particular set of political ideas. We might call this academic capture. What differentiates these periods from ours, however, is that there was much less success exporting these ideas into government and the practice of statecraft since they, by comparison, did not break enough ground into the culture of the affluent political classes.

Again, a key element of their proliferation was that the payoff for holding these ideas was much higher than in any previous wave of militant progressivism. Nicolai J. Foss and Peter G. Klein's paper 'Why Do Companies Go Woke?' attempted to explain why so many companies were eagerly adopting woke business practices despite there being no evidence of their improving company performance.[11] Insights from agency theory and institutional theory, many of which we have discussed throughout this chapter, show how internal advocacy of woke goals at the middle management level can increase job security, career opportunities and decision-making influence. The very same processes exist inside government departments and within non-economic social hierarchies. Even in social settings, status can be asserted by criticising the language of others against progressive value systems. Neither campaigns for nuclear disarmament, Marxism in the 1950s nor later waves of campus upheavals provided the same incentives for self-regarding agents in an organisation.[12] This time, academic capture has ultimately led to the historic capture of the broader institutions of the state.

The moral failure of this progressivism stems from its suspicion of British interests as racist and inherently coming at the expense of minorities, both at home and abroad. It is a political position developed across disciplines which seeks to blame Western and particularly British and American colonialism for the immiseration of the world's poor. While productive discussions can and should be had about the impact of Western interventionism across the globe, progressivism's moral and intellectual weakness sees it sympathising with authoritarians of every stripe. Even in the best-case scenario, those who subscribe to this belief system tend to support the case of foreigners against the interests of Britain and her allies as a reflexive rule of thumb. The power struggle between exploiters and exploited is the fundamental lens through which any dispute must be settled. It is only in the case of Ukraine that the left has endorsed the actions of Western powers, leaving only the most radical on the European far left and far right to have sided with Putin, on the grounds that, after all, the West must always be the imperialist provocateur.[13] On the subject of Chagos, reparations, Syria, Iranian proxies and more – the anti-Western optics, skilfully leveraged by our enemies, come first, and British interests themselves are an irrelevant and illegitimate concern.

It is not the moral concern that dooms ideologues to misidentify British interests, but rather the anti-British element of that moral framework. Chagos again provides the perfect example. It matters not to the activist barristers that the Chagossians did not wish to see their homeland transferred to Mauritius. It does not matter that Mauritius has *criminalised* on threat of imprisonment for up to ten years the failure to describe Chagos as Mauritian – a law passed in November 2021 specifically to target and threaten Chagossians who did not recognise Mauritius's tenuous claim to their homeland. Both governments refused a plebiscite among the displaced Chagossians to discover which nation, or neither, they assent to governing them. Chagossians have been poorly treated by the UK – that much is clear. Yet arguably they have been treated worse still by the Mauritians, who many (or indeed *most*) Chagossians see as having co-opted their claim to the island and presented it as their own. Aside from any discussion over whether Britain's leaders should have entertained advice from the ICJ over one of its key bases in the first place, two wrongs don't make a right. The simplistic and moralising wokeism has handed the issue of Chagossian resettlement of the islands to the Mauritians, who are under no obligation whatsoever to see that land is returned to those who actually have claim to it.

In May 2025, upon the announcement of the deal, Briton Phillipe Sands, Mauritius's legal counsel and co-founder of Matrix Chambers, affected to worry about 'undermining the right of self-determination under international law' since the rights carved out for the Diego Garcia base could interfere with Mauritius's 'infrastructure and other land developments to facilitate Chagossian resettlement'. While this is a plainly performative 'worry' – considering no allowance whatsoever has been made to seek the consent of the Chagossians at any point in this process – it seems unlikely, given how badly the Chagossians have been treated, that development of the islands will be 'to facilitate Chagossian resettlement' at all. No provisions of the treaty signed by the UK give assurances that the Chagossians will be guaranteed the right to resettle. No provisions assure us that the benefits from the development of the island and its Exclusive Economic Zone's maritime resources, currently a protected biosphere, will accrue principally to the Chagossians and not to the Mauritians themselves. Given how central the conception of *victimhood* is in the theory and practice of this new progressivism, it is a terrible irony that they have forgotten the truly wronged party: the Chagossians.

Indeed, Jean Francois-Nellan, of campaign group Chagossian

Voices, was 'appalled but not surprised' to hear that only three weeks after the deal's ink had dried, Mauritius was set to use the British funds from the Diego Garcia lease to pay off its own debt and not to serve the interests of the Chagossians in whose name they had claimed the islands. He wrote at that time that '[the budget] completely omits the Chagossians, the very people whose displacement gave rise to the international legal fight Mauritius continues to wage'.

This damage to Britain's interests – leaving aside the damage to its finances and the budget for deployable strength elsewhere – may indeed have involved handing the Chagossians to the wolves. The reason is simply that this new orthodoxy among our affluent classes admits no possibility that Britain, seen by some as the perpetrator of original sin on a global scale, could be a better custodian of minority rights than an African pretender state claiming to represent them. Sands surmises that the agreement was 'crucial for both countries but especially Britain, as it seeks to enhance its global role and reputation, bringing down the flag on its last colony in Africa'. His evidence was perhaps the most instructive part of his piece, with Sands writing, 'Britain's legal claim was hopeless, and it undermined efforts to garner international support in other matters, such as Russia's illegal occupation of Ukraine.'

The argument that the legal status of Chagos was harming Britain's global reputation is not compelling. Sands cannot point to a single example of 'whataboutery' levied against British diplomacy over Chagos by any nation except Mauritius, the People's Republic of China and Sands himself in his book *The Last Colony*.[14] Not even Starmer himself was willing to repeat the claim. At any rate, the idea that the reputational damage could be so stark that the international community would see equivalence between Britain's claim of over 200 years of continuous sovereignty over Chagos, and Russia's apparent appeal to sham referendums and the right of conquest, is demonstrably false. The charge that our leaders have no idea what the 'betterment of the country' consists of is therefore laid out.

*   *   *

Taken together, our leaders and institutions face perverse incentives to promote value systems over national and institutional interest. They routinely receive low-quality legal advice which is itself compromised by high-status interests, while British judges are increasingly comfortable affecting significant changes to the law from the bench. From above and below, 'national interest' (economic, cultural and military) as a concept has become deeply unfashionable, even seen as racist and imperialist, and has been diluted in much of public discourse to a universalised conception of interest which elevates the interests of others to being a component of our own interest. This obscurantist role of woke ideology, combined with technological and informational warfare, has compromised our cultural resilience to the influence and hostile actions of authoritarian states overseas. Global warming, refugee movements and, yes, key military assets have their status as interests challenged by this nexus of embarrassment, obscurantism and status-seeking. The combined effect on our leadership and civil service is that of split motives and unclear thinking. We began this chapter discussing the concepts of 'credibility' – a strong and valuable idea in international relations diluted in this cultural environment to justify the weakening of Britain's hard power and negotiating power.

While Chagos has guided this exploration, two further case

studies are illuminating: the EU and China. The first regards the negotiations with the EU from 2017 and the subsequent 'reset' in 2025. The Conservative government at the time took very seriously the idea that a series of generous commitments and promises early on would later pay dividends in the form of a more favourable and friendly accord. Theresa May – not pro-Brexit in so far as the 2016 referendum was concerned – understood that the principal motive of Britain's voters was to see a reduction in immigration, not to leave the economic institutions of the bloc. To that end, she offered in 2017 to bind the UK to the EU regulatory regime, but was rebuffed. In hindsight, it seems rather odd that that offer was rejected on the grounds that Britain must be treated as a 'third country' and that there could be no 'cherry picking' over free movement. It was only by 2018 that the EU negotiators, led by Michel Barnier, had realised that it was Northern Ireland that held the key to tie up the British negotiators, and that an opportunity had emerged in the form of a minority government with a majority opposed to Brexit.

It mattered not that Britain had committed not to erect a hard border in Ireland, and that it was the EU which had suddenly started threatening to do so. Britain could not identify the vexatiousness of this framing and was unwilling to denounce it thoroughly. A timetable for negotiations had been expertly produced by Brussels such that 'nothing was agreed until everything was agreed', and that no compromise on the 'four freedoms' (movement of people, goods, capital and services) was possible. Both pieces of framing should have been rejected. The former was a strategy to end-load the negotiations such that the EU could extract maximum concessions from Britain on its various key asks (budgetary contributions, access to UK fishing waters and regulatory capture of the UK to retain its share of the British market) on the back of its historical and cultural vulnerability over the Troubles. The latter was straightforwardly a negotiating gambit to draw out British counterproposals. It is self-evident that the 'four freedoms' can be divorced from each other because, in the end, the withdrawal agreement and Trade and Cooperation Agreement (TCA) did exactly that. Yet given the way the issue was discussed in the British media and the way Conservative politicians spoke about it at the time, one would be forgiven for thinking that the 'four freedoms' were a species of transcendental moral truth.

The *Financial Times* gushed that 'Europe's four freedoms are its very essence.'[15] Clearly not. Yet the dogma had significant purchase in the UK: Prime Minister Theresa May repeated the logic that 'European leaders have said many times that membership means accepting the four freedoms', and that therefore, in leaving, the four were indivisible. That May's claim is a non sequitur is not the principal point here. Rather, the point is that to accept the EU's framing was a strategic error and an error of statecraft. There was, in the end, no limit to the damage this would permanently do by laying the blame for the effects of apparently immutable EU rules at the feet of the UK Prime Minister. Even after 2019, with the ascendency of a fresh pro-Brexit mandate and a large majority in Parliament, this early agreement to the EU timetable and the premises upon which it began led to the Northern Ireland Protocol, about which May had said two years earlier, 'No UK Prime Minister could ever agree to it.'[16]

The UK should have learned from this experience. The EU made masterful use of timetabling. They were able to signal credibly that their red lines were non-negotiable – despite their eventual agreement showing that the 'four freedoms' were rhetorical – and therefore that compromise must come from the UK. Allan Drazen and

Paul R. Masson have explained the issue of policy rules very well: claiming to have rules and sticking to them, except if the damage in specific circumstances would not be compensated by the increased credibility of the rule itself, proved to be a good strategy for the EU negotiators.[17] By the time the negotiations were entering their final stages, and fisheries were being introduced as a new red line for the EU, Parliament passed a law making an exit from the EU illegal except with an agreement signed off by Brussels. With the time to our scheduled departure ticking down, Britain's red lines, no matter how reasonable and undemanding, were irrelevant. This is, of course, such a spectacular negotiating victory for the EU that not even they could see it coming. Even six years on, it is not clear whether pro-European members of the House of Commons fully understood the extent to which they were compromising the British negotiating position, or whether they intended to strengthen the EU position to make the Prime Minister's position untenable. At any rate, they succeeded in both.

The EU also got their 'hooks' in early. Gaining hooks doesn't in essence mean bullying, threats or subversion. It means communicating effectively and identifying weaknesses in your opposite numbers. What is crucial to understand, from a negotiating and diplomatic standpoint, is that the hook over the Northern Ireland border, with a part played very well by Irish Taoiseach Leo Varadkar, was by no means inevitable. There was no particular reason why the EU should have been able to hold the border over our heads rather than us holding it over theirs. With no precedent for a country leaving the EU, we ought not to have so readily accepted EU timetabling and framing for the discussions. We lacked the diplomatic skill and, indeed, a clear vision of what we wanted from the negotiations. Those who theorised Brexit and who convinced the public of that vision were not then in government, with the Prime Minister and the majority of cabinet having opposed this enormous constitutional change in the first place.

The advice to not rush into negotiations before you have decided what you want, why you want it, how you will try to get it, as well as what your partners want, why they want it and how they may try to get it, is sound but hardly revolutionary. Yet in these EU negotiations, just as in Chagos, Britain began discussions without its house in order. In the case of Chagos, it is remarkable that Britain was engaging in discussions *at all* while pronouncing that the UK did not recognise a Mauritian claim to the archipelago. Of course, we have discussed already that low-quality British legal advice and postcolonial sensibilities compromised Chagos from the start. Time will reveal exactly what forces, internal or external to the British state, pushed Chagos back onto the agenda when it had been summarily shut down only a few years prior. As of 2025, it appears that it was placed back on the agenda by Starmer and Hermer.

There is a lack of coherent strategic thinking before opening discussions – and a lack of tactical nous once discussions begin. But not every element of statecraft and diplomacy is a negotiation. Much of the day-to-day business of government is about managing relationships and postures in the various theatres of geopolitics. We might start with the observation that isolation rarely shifts behaviour. Grandstanding may enhance your public reputation at home, but will often mean giving up your chance to advance national interests. The question of appeasement and isolation concerning Vladimir Putin will concern scholars for many years to come. So too will the Starmer government's decision to commence a rapprochement with the People's Republic of China, following his consistent attempts to forge a 'strong' relationship with the emerging great power. Regardless of the merit of a closer relationship with and greater dependence on China – a central component of myriad aspects of Britain's strategy for this century – the approach of the British Embassy in China is praiseworthy. Given the goals passed to them from Westminster, the best way to engage with an authoritarian state is without grandstanding but equally without grovelling and compromising on integrity. The balance between private discussions and public statements must be achieved tactfully.

Diplomats must first understand what motivates their counterparts. Authoritarian states are not all the same – neither are they all incapable of rational discussion and dealmaking. British diplomats in China have done an admirable job in learning the structure, culture, influences and survival instincts of Chinese diplomatic personalities. They have learned, even if their new ministers in Westminster have not, that not all contact, in any scenario, is progress for a UK–China relationship. Just as Britain experienced at the hands of EU negotiators, if the rules of engagement are set by a rival power, we are likely to find ourselves set up for failure. Another area where Starmer's pro-China pivot (emulating David Cameron's pivot in the first half of the 2010s) is complicating matters is that in many cases amateur diplomacy confuses *relationships* with *friendships*. When China seeks to compromise British strategic interests across a dozen strategic lines (including, no less, a covert and then flagrant undermining of the British position in Diego Garcia) and Britain is concerned principally with 'credibility' and the optics of friendship, we have a diplomatic mismatch – and our leadership fails to recognise the nature of the unfolding bargaining. It is hard to see how Starmer's rapprochement can continue given the unrelenting hostile overtures coming from Beijing. New infrastructure, including the new Chinese 'super embassy' in London, will surely be blocked. To be clear, engagement is critical – even with authoritarians – but that does not extend to compromising our trustworthiness with our allies where our relationships are crucial.

The dramatic lengths to which the US and Five Eyes (an intelligence alliance formed by Australia, Canada, New Zealand, the UK and the US) partners had to go to reverse the UK's position on the Huawei 5G rollout had already raised eyebrows. Washington mounted an unusually intense lobbying campaign that included high-level intelligence briefings, diplomatic interventions and even threats to restrict intelligence sharing if London refused to reconsider. With academic, industrial and technological espionage increasing – along with *true* violations of international law in the form of man-made island claims in the South China Sea and the genocide of the Uighurs – it is important to ask again: what is the sustainable objective Britain (read: Starmer) wants from this rapprochement? For a leadership that claims to be concerned with Britain's diplomatic reputation, it is remarkable that we have shown ourselves willing to tarnish it with respect to our Five Eyes partners, all in an attempt to ingratiate ourselves with nations without a clear idea of what we seek to achieve. More recently, there was scandal over the government's refusal to label China an 'enemy' which thereby undermined the legal case against two likely Chinese spies. The answer at this point appears to be framed in terms of climate change cooperation. Our green strategy is the subject of a later chapter of this book. Suffice it to say here that compromising security interests is a high price to pay for any kind of cooperation when viable alternatives exist.

Britain remains unwilling to improve when it comes to posture, relationships and negotiation. In the 2025 'reset' of relations with the EU, Britain again had an entirely incoherent idea of what it intended to get out of the renegotiations. In yet another example of amateurishly confusing *relationships* with *friendships*, Starmer saw his 'reset' as an opportunity for a totally unreciprocated gesture of goodwill by which he would sign away leverage over matters of significant EU interest without demanding anything in exchange. The naive attempt was yet again an exercise in incoherently building 'reputation'. It bears repeating that reputation and credibility are tools and strategies developed to *serve* British interests. It is not coherent therefore to *sacrifice* British interests in order to develop reputation and credibility, nor is it likely that reputation or credibility could be generated by failing to robustly defend one's national interest on the global stage.

There was a string of key EU demands as part of the renegotiation: renewed fishing access to UK waters, UK contribution to an EU common defence pact and fund, closer UK alignment with EU policy on sanitary and phytosanitary standards (SPS) and youth mobility of EU citizens into the UK. Each of these (except alignment on SPS) the UK ought to have been willing to oblige, but good statecraft demands, as we have said, that one knows what one intends to get out of a negotiation, while recognising the interests of one's counterpart. That means that the UK should have been sober about what it sought in return. Some ideas include the robust interception and return of those who have made illegal Channel crossings, moves to achieve mutual recognition of standards for professional qualifications, reductions in the number of border checks and the softening of the border in the Irish Sea. Starmer and his team asked for *none* of this. They granted fishing rights to EU vessels for twelve more years in exchange for precisely nothing. To have recognised the power of this bargaining chip for the French and to have done nothing with it, while record Channel crossings continued, speaks volumes. Starmer didn't even seek to achieve reciprocal access to the overfished EU fishing grounds – any UK vessels and those of the Channel Islands must negotiate separately with the individual EU member state, and they are guaranteed nothing.

The defence pact was another key EU demand. There is, to be clear, good reason for Britain to cooperate with European partners to defend their eastern border. Security guarantees could have been offered, for instance, in exchange for the equal treatment of British firms in EU defence contracts and for guaranteed proportional contributions of military aid to Ukraine. But neither of these were asked for or achieved. Starmer instead negotiated that Britain pay into the procurement fund, controlled by the EU, in the hope that we get our money's worth of equipment and our fair share of the contracts. If the long history of our membership of the bloc is anything to go by, British firms will be overlooked for the vast majority of the contracts. This is not a satisfactory outcome for obliging an EU demand. Many commentators have alleged that Starmer did not recognise the strength of the British negotiating position; on the balance of evidence, he probably was aware, but was thrown off by naive expectations that international agreements are built from blank cheques and blind faith.

Britain now finds itself paying into mobility schemes it had no professed interest in joining. It has also made an open-ended commitment to permanently align British SPS standards with those of the EU. For such a massive compromise on the regulatory autonomy of the UK (which, as we will discuss in a separate chapter, is a crucial element of a trade policy for the next century), you would expect nothing less than the dissolution of the customs border along the Irish Sea. After all, agricultural produce had long been the principal concern upon which the apparent need for a hard border was tenuously justified. Yet in the event, the EU will not be removing any infrastructure.

There is one key piece of this puzzle missing: the lobbying by groups including Best for Britain to align Britain with the EU market. The reasoning of these groups was reflected almost verbatim by former Secretary of State for Business and Trade Jonathan Reynolds and Keir Starmer. As the argument goes, since the EU is, taken together, our largest trade partner, it makes sense to compromise our trading relationship with every other nation on earth in other to improve our EU relationship. Two implicit assumptions here are false. Firstly, it takes for granted that the EU relationship can be significantly improved. Even Best for Britain's own modelling showed that the effect on GDP growth of SPS alignment on agrifood is not statistically significant.[18] This assumption becomes graver still when one realises that the reason the EU is such a large trade partner is precisely because we have a comprehensive TCA with them already. Secondly, our largest single trade partner, the US, is larger than our second (Germany), third (Ireland) and fourth (the Netherlands) largest markets combined, despite the fact that until recently no full trade agreement had been in place since the post-war Marshall Plan. It is likely that analysis similar to that undertaken by Best for Britain, despite its flaws, led Starmer to believe that an SPS agreement with Europe would lead to growth. This will strike most economists as profoundly wishful thinking. In any event, it would not excuse the negotiating practice of acquiescing to an EU SPS demand without securing any British interest in return.

*   *   *

The foundation of any revival of British influence will have to be a return to form on negotiation and statecraft. This will require cultural as well as philosophical change, in order for British institutions to correctly reorientate themselves with Britain's fundamental interests. It is not enough to simply name and shame leadership, the civil service, the courts or pervasive ideology; it is necessary that Britain comes to understand how these failures play off each other and that a genuine cultural upheaval is precipitated. Britain must collectively move on from its squeamishness over empire if we are to hold our own country in high esteem and avoid being held to moral ransom by former colonies. That includes celebrating Britain's contribution to its former colonies, and the wider world, as well as the colonies' contribution to Britain.

Many who journeyed to Britain in the decades immediately after the First World War did so with a profound sense of British identity. Millions, from every background, chose to fight for it because of the values it espoused. That included the opportunity of replacing status with contract, free trade, the early abolition of the slave trade (and the decades-long mission to stamp out the practice across the Gulf of Guinea and the Caribbean), entrepreneurship, industrial innovation, sportsmanship and individual freedom. Indeed, the fact that, as a culture, we are so ready to pass judgement on the British Empire, and not on any of its contemporaries – the Mughals, the Qing dynasty, African slave states, Arab slave pirates or even more recent perpetrators from the Turkish genocides against Armenians, Greeks and Georgians – lets slip one simple fact: many consider the British Empire (and the early United States) uniquely ripe for judgement by today's standards and international norms. That speaks both to how comparatively morally responsive the empire was and also how instrumental it was in bringing about the international legal norms under which the greatest period of peace, expansion of democracy and alleviation of poverty in human history has flourished.

There is no need to glorify it or proselytise this case on its behalf. To do so would likely be counterproductive, at any rate. It is only necessary to overturn those aspects of self-deprecation which are causing problems for statecraft. To be robust when, for instance, Caribbean states make vexatious claims for massive financial payments. To have the confidence to retort when disingenuous claims are made about Britain's past in an attempt to signal status and self-aggrandise. The goal is not to bury discussion of empire, nor to force those at school and university to hear a fair case made for it, but simply to challenge in open debate allegations that seek to harm our reputation as and when they are made. We certainly should not be collaborating with or coddling those who seek to undermine our soft power. On the contrary, the British state must be in the business of making the strongest possible case for itself, except where it has manifestly done wrong.

Firstly, projecting a positive and confident national story is good for our standing among nations. This is widely understood by our enemies and their national press. It is why Russia Today, Qatar's Al Jazeera and China Central Television have each echoed and amplified British self-flagellation and produced media making the least sympathetic case possible against Britain.[19] That our own state-owned media, the BBC, produces content indistinguishable from that of Al Jazeera, says plenty about our public broadcaster. The result is that no matter the good Britain does, it never seems to seize the initiative in its own global image. It does not matter that the UK has sought to create, over the last twenty years, the world's first true, developed multicultural state, and that to that end it has spent hundreds of billions of pounds to support migrants. It does not matter that, for many years, Britain was the most welcoming place on earth to new arrivals. Britain rarely makes any fuss at all over the billions it spends in overseas aid. If aid really is to be critical to our influence, it seems remarkable that your average journalist couldn't tell you a single overseas project funded by Britain.

The African Continental Free Trade Area (AfCFTA) is the largest trade bloc on earth by trade area. It currently faces troubles over implementation which are likely to continue for many years yet, but it marks for many African nations their first bona fide exposure to global markets since independence. Britain built and paid for their Accra headquarters and helped get the organisation off the ground. Britain supported 6 million girls into education. British taxpayers bankroll the British International Investment Programme providing over £7 billion to the developing world, and continues to contribute to the almost £6 billion European Development Fund (further obscuring the fact that Britain might deserve credit). The reader is forgiven for having likely never heard of any of this. A predictable consequence of focusing on ancient history and optics is that our £14 billion-a-year foreign aid budget is of little consequence. With nobody making the case for Britain's positive global role, and many foreign and domestic opportunists willing to make the case against, our aid budget ends up looking like an apology rather than something deserving of genuine praise and thanks. Cultural change and courageous leadership are needed to get British statecraft back on track.

More recently, the BBC became engulfed in a scandal as it was revealed to have doctored a speech Trump gave on 6 January 2021, the day he was accused of inciting insurrection, to bolster the claim that Trump had directly encouraged violence. The documentary which contained the misleading edit aired before the 2024 election. Trump decried that the BBC are 'from a Foreign Country [*sic*], one that many consider our Number One Ally [*sic*]'. In the same scandal, a catalogue of other failures emerged, including the printing of falsehoods about the war in Gaza from the BBC Arabic service (which took them from Al Jazeera), and the 'effective censorship' of reporting on transgender issues. As well as being bad news for relations with the White House, this evidence suggests that cultural issues within the media mean high-status opinions take priority over journalistic duties, let alone over Britain's reputational or geopolitical interests.

Taken together, a change in communicative style is also crucial if we are to leave behind our extended period as a geopolitical non-entity. During the Twelve-Day War between Israel and Iran in 2025, Britain manoeuvred itself into a position where it got no credit for half-hearted attempts at de-escalation and no credit for the support we might have offered our allies. Equivocation, dithering and platitudinous non-statements meant there was no reason whatsoever for either side to listen to a word Starmer or the British Parliament had to say on the matter. If Britain knew what it wanted and why it wanted it, we would have the courage to stand on that platform and influence global events.

* * *

The final dimension of the fundamental vulnerability of the British state concerns negotiations with both unions and the private sector. Within the first weeks of Starmer's Labour government, we saw a 'settlement' over public sector pay, particularly for junior doctors. Yet no real negotiations took place. There were no concessions on productivity or on the implementation of technology to save on administrative costs. The government argued, post hoc, that now they had 'solved' the dispute, the NHS could 'get back to work'. At a stroke, they had deepened the deficit to the tune of tens of billions.

Predictably, this gave succour to a host of other industrial disputes; demands over pay and conditions – including working from home and shorter working hours – were raised (and these disputes continue to this day). All that they had increased was the incentive to be disagreeable. Labour believed that it was Tory selfishness – a hardball politics of obstructionism – which was holding the NHS back. Yet they had only managed to reduce output per worker and output per pound to a new record low. The kicker is that such metrics were not their concern in the first place. They conceive of junior doctors and public sector workers as the 'good guys', and so see capitulating in negotiations as the moral thing to do. If you don't sincerely care about getting a good deal for Britain and its beleaguered taxpayer, even when you lose, you win.

The wins for the unions pale in comparison to the negotiation masterclass conducted by the private sector. Britain's almost entirely foreign-owned steel industry has perfected the art of rent-seeking. They recognised their strong hook: politicians who remember the 1980s do not have the stomach to lay off steel workers, no matter the cost. While piling environmental and energy costs onto producers, Jingye (British Steel – now nationalised), Tata and Liberty Steel each enjoy a revolving door of bailouts and state funding, trading on the fact they know no British government will ever allow them to shut up shop. The big consultancy firms, at the same time, receive £3.4 billion in government contracts (up 57 per cent on pre-Covid), while the civil service itself has ballooned to a peacetime record of 515,085 personnel with a record budget. The Department for Health and Social Care (DHSC) is perhaps the least competent of them all. They notoriously lost 75 per cent of the £12 billion of personal protective equipment (PPE) they panic-bought. The method of outsourcing used by the social care system becomes progressively worse each year, since local authorities have effectively regulated local social care providers into becoming monopolies and have built closed-door systems for allocating care work to contractors. Without any opportunity to meet their legal obligations except through them, the DHSC and local authorities have handed care providers near total price-setting power.

The skilful management of state affairs requires that we should be able to identify and rectify these flagrant abuses of taxpayer funds. On top of this is the 'sprawling empire' of quangos (quasi-autonomous non-governmental organisations) which cost the taxpayer an eyewatering £124 billion a year. By way of comparison, savings from the government's now-reversed Winter Fuel Allowance cut was to be £1.4 billion a year, and its now-reversed welfare cuts were to save less than £4.8 billion *by the end of the decade*. These quangos are funded by the government and exert considerable influence over the way taxpayers' money is spent. In April 2025, Starmer's government declared that every quango across government will be reviewed and each department will have to justify its quangos, or else the organisations will face closure. This is positive, but no clear criteria were given about what constitutes a justification. In political reality, quangos exist in order to insulate ministers from unpopular decisions and allow them to dodge responsibility for mistakes. They tend to be staffed by civil servants (and so suffer from the same high-status cultural incentive issues discussed above) and due to their single-issue nature, have become increasingly radical, in what psychologists call a 'purity spiral'.[20] Quangos like Natural England have deviated so far from their mandate and have, unfortunately, become increasingly puritanical and myopic, since there is little need or requirement to consider unintended consequences, and they are unplugged from the real decision-making taking place in the department and elsewhere in government.

The revolving door between most quangos and departments is one reason why they are so difficult to cut. Everyone involved has a private interest as the gravy train chugs on. Another reason is that seats on quangos pay handsomely, and can be given as rewards to politicians, donors and even rivals to buy their favour. It is not enough that quangos should justify their existence in terms of their objective: they must justify it in terms of the outcomes they have achieved. Those reasons, to borrow a Rawlsian term, should be public reasons – not just reasons that are to the private benefit of the minister.[21]

*   *   *

British statecraft – the skilful management of state affairs both domestically and internationally – is harmed by bad culture, bad incentives, bad ideas and bad law. It is necessary for the UK to turn a new corner. Strong leadership, a shrinking of the size of the state and a limitation on the scope of law will help produce this cultural change and limit the more dangerous consequences for Britain. Implementing good law, defending good ideas and projecting vision and confidence will help tear down the incentives to holding high-status, obscurantist opinions. Reforming law while simultaneously taking concrete steps to root out ideologies that leave us vulnerable to authoritarian states is the only way to build Britain in a way that preserves those values which have served us, and the world, so well.

CHAPTER 3

CLIMATE EMERGENCY

As Britain prepares for a new century with authoritarian states growing in strength and confidence, the issue of climate change will form an ever-increasing part of international diplomacy. Climate change is a fact.[1] It will occur. But it must be thought of not as a unique threat over which all countries can join hands, but instead as an arena for geopolitical contest and competition, like any other. It will be like the threats posed by war and the rumours of war, like the competition for resources each country engages in, like the race to dominate international institutions.

The UK's international climate policy hinges on two core strengths: developing specialised expertise (particularly in financial innovation and select technologies) and building diplomatic coalitions to spread knowledge and enforce cooperation. While Britain is unlikely to lead in manufacturing or in setting most global regulations, it is well placed to shape climate finance and support green innovation, especially in the developing world. By focusing on these areas, the UK can convert climate leadership into broader influence across defence, energy and diplomacy. Strategic independence also gives the UK flexibility, allowing it to accept beneficial partnerships (such as the market for low-cost Chinese electric vehicles) while confidently rejecting high-risk ones, like Chinese-built 5G networks.

The challenge from totalitarian states is very stark. They will not only be reluctant to cooperate on climate change when they want to, they will also form strategic opposition to those institutions which draw other countries into closer ties with open and democratic societies. This is a domain, a debate, a competition, like any other. It must be thought of as such. The reset of the US in the traditional foreign policy theatres of free trade and interventionism heightens the need for a recalculation on climate policy.

Climate change policy also affects great power dynamics with respect to Russia and China. Both are heavy producers and consumers of fossil fuel energy. Russia is a net exporter of hydrocarbons and China is a manufacturing powerhouse that still relies on cheap and dirty energy, especially coal and oil. Russia additionally stands to benefit not only from a destabilised rules-based order – as recent years have shown – but also from global warming itself. As weak and poor countries are destabilised, Russia can benefit. Even the melting of the ice caps helps Russia: polar melting opens a navigable route along Russia's Arctic coast. But these dynamics play in the background, as a divided West competes strategically for support and climate cooperation from unaligned nations.

Climate change policy is one area which attracts a disproportionate amount of discussion over 'credibility' and 'soft power'. That is for good reason. It is the purest case of an issue where coordination is not just preferable but required. There is no prize for decarbonising first, but there are significant costs if no nation decarbonises. This problem of collective action is the natural stomping ground for theorists of soft power and influence, as well as of international agreements and frameworks, while international aid is at the core of most nation's strategies. It is therefore an ideal place to begin. Soft power, then, is a form of non-coercive influence – it involves shaping other actors' preferences, so they voluntarily adopt one's own goals, and building reputational authority. The orthodox view is that soft power emanates from three main resources: culture, political values and foreign policy legitimacy. While hard power relies on coercion or incentives, soft power operates by shaping hearts and minds. The orthodoxy continues to hold that soft power is more durable in international relations. Its relevance endures today: democracies, in particular, rely on it to build trust, reinforce alliances and ultimately sustain global influence without over-reliance on force.

As the century progresses, states will move into networks of co-operation in all manner of ways, in response to common threats and incentives. Climate change poses real threats to the stability of the world; it warrants its own cooperation, in its own right. Yet the issue interacts directly with increasing energy scarcity, the in-dustrial price of electricity (which affects production and prices), as well as with nuclear and security concerns. A changing climate also means unprecedented migration, and it threatens the stability of water-scarce states. Even as Britain and the West decline as a pro-portion of both global GDP and world population, and the balance of military strength shifts eastwards, the UK has the capacity to use its power to influence the architecture of global political insti-tutions. While Britain's soft power remains strong, the UK should exert its influence on climate change not just to secure climate goals but to ensure global institutions protect Britain's vital global inter-ests. This chapter considers how this can be achieved.

*   *   *

Ever since the Paris Agreement, agreed at the COP21 summit, all global powers are formally committed to the related goals of mitigation, adaptation and maintaining the financial arrangements to ensure both.[2] The Paris Agreement spawned a commitment to hold 'the increase in the global average temperature to well below 2°C above pre-industrial levels' and to try 'to limit the temperature increase to 1.5°C above pre-industrial levels'. How legally binding such a commitment is depends upon domestic law and the state of mind of officials in charge of implementing its strictures. In the case of the UK, the Paris Agreement was ratified during the early months of the Prime Ministership of Theresa May, and it has proven to be robust. Not one of May's successors seriously challenged Britain's commitment to net zero, despite growing public disquiet. For example, a legal challenge against a third runway at Heathrow Airport was launched, which based many of its arguments on the Paris Agreement and Britain's legal commitments. That case went all the way to the Supreme Court before the runway was, in theory, deemed lawful. It is a shame that planning law has now replaced environmental law as the next blocker.

Governments in Europe and overseas with a more flexible approach to the rule of law, and indeed those countries with less specific nationally determined contributions (NDCs) – the individual climate actions each state agrees to – have been able to flout the spirit of the agreement more flagrantly. Britain is thus bound by chains of its own making. If it can convince other countries to keep to their own agreements, so much the better. But otherwise, Britain has a great challenge ahead. Its own prosperity may be affected by following rules no one else cares to adopt. This is something Britain's politicians must think seriously about.

The 1.5°C threshold and 2°C threshold are both held by some to be 'tipping points' at which the various strands of climate break-down will become worse and lead to 'exponential' problems. Both targets have become totemic for climate ambition. They have their origins in the 1970s, when perhaps the most influential environ-mental economist, William Nordhaus, showed that a two-degree rise would place global temperatures in a range not seen for several thousand years.[3] Nordhaus thought it prudent to keep temperatures within these recent limits. Well-intentioned academics have per-haps ascribed more significance to these particular targets than any of their original authors would have bargained for, and academic findings have been widely misinterpreted to fuel alarmism.

For the last two decades, climate economists have studied the mathematics of 'long-tailed risks': those potential outcomes with a very small chance of happening, but a cataclysmic cost should they occur. If we think about how likely something is to happen, we can better use our resources to prevent the things that have the greatest chance of happening and with the gravest consequences. Harvard University climate economist Martin Weitzman's notorious 'dismal theorem' showed how very unlikely but impossible-to-rule-out risks of catastrophic loss can justify effectively unlimited insurance. This means that when analysis is produced advising that global temperature rises are limited to 2°C due to the potential for cata-strophic damage, that is emphatically *not* the same as claiming that more than a 2°C rise would *inevitably* lead to catastrophic damage (though it certainly hasn't prevented activists and politicians from giving that impression). They benefit from saying that the world will either end or be severely affected if global temperature rises are not halted in their tracks.

Of course, this does not mean that 'tipping points' do not exist. Malcolm Gladwell's 2000 book *The Tipping Point* – which discussed the moments at which things became inevitable or highly likely at relatively low thresholds – convincingly showed that compounded environmental stresses can add up to much more than the sum of their parts.[4] The argument for keeping temperatures within their recent historical range is strong, even if we sensibly realise that going past 2°C warming will not necessarily doom the planet into a climate tailspin.

In Paris it was agreed that to limit global warming to 1.5°C, greenhouse gas emissions must peak before 2025 at the latest and decline 43 per cent by 2030. The US initially signed up to the Paris Agreement, but it left in 2020 under the first Presidency of Donald Trump before rejoining in 2021 under Joe Biden. Of the major producers of greenhouse gases, only Iran is outside the Paris Agreement. Libya has yet to agree but it currently has relatively limited hydrocarbon production due to the country's ongoing civil war. Since 2019, Russia signed up to the Paris Accord – and is notionally committed to its shared international targets.

Despite its ambition, there are significant problems both with the structure of the Paris Agreement and its ability to encourage states to meet the global targets. The NDCs are set by each state in relative isolation and a given state can choose to focus purely on mitigation if it so chooses, largely leaving the cutting of emissions to others. The intention is that each successive COP conference would evaluate the impact of these national goals to see if they were being achieved and if, cumulatively, they led to meeting the 1.5 per cent target. The nature of cooperation here lacks enforcement. Britain under Ed Miliband has perhaps gone further than any other nation on earth in terms of pulling the trigger on economic damage in order to meet climate targets. In a collective action problem, this isn't where we should seek to be.

All the recent evidence suggests that the 1.5°C target will be significantly breached.[5] In the very best-case scenario, we can hope for no increase in annual emissions from 2030, rather than the downward trend which the Paris Agreement maintains is needed. Linked to this, there are already commercial plans to extract more than double the volume of fossil fuels in the year 2030 than are consistent with meeting the 1.5°C target; and the amount spent on adaptation to a net zero world is falling even as the impacts of climate change become more real. The latest report from the World Meteorological Organization as part of its annual survey showed that 2023 was the warmest year on record, with new records set for the levels of greenhouse gases, sea temperature rise and the loss of glacial ice. More recent surveys indicate that 2025 will be warmer still.

The framework for action set out in the Paris Agreements built on the earlier Kyoto Accords. The core building block of these treaties is the nationally (but also collaboratively in the case of the EU) set NDCs to bring about the reduction of greenhouse gases. As such, there are no targets at the state level, but the expectation was that each round of these would set more rigorous targets. Linked to this are the long-term low greenhouse gas emission strategies (or LT-LEDS) setting out the longer-term goal to which the NDCs must work (however, these are not mandatory, as such). One of the tasks for each party to the COP conferences is to assess whether the NDCs are adequate in combination, given that there is considerable leeway as they are meant to take into account 'different national circumstances'.

While this strand is essentially state-centred, the Paris Agreement contains three ways for cross-state support to occur. Developed countries are expected to provide financial assistance to more vulnerable, less developed states. This funding can be both for mitigation – to reduce emissions – and for adaptation: as they struggle to cope with the inevitable shocks and disruption, there will be more assistance required for poorer countries with weak or inefficient central governments. These agreements are supported by other accords and rules around technology transfer from the poor world to the rich, intended to achieve the twin goals of mitigation and adaptation and to encourage developed countries to assist in capacity building in more vulnerable regions. The latter element has long been seen as having an important role in global security. It is vital for national and international security that poor states are not destabilised by climate change or the efforts to address it. Without support, these governments may struggle and fall, opening the door to all manner of problems.[6]

The issue with this framework lies in the implementation. The NDC approach allows key states to fail to meet the degree of change needed (in the language of the accords, this is what is meant by the slippery term 'different national circumstances'). And while in theory the direction should be towards stricter targets, the reality is that states such as the US are planning to expand their production of oil and gas, not curtail it. Equally, there have been reports that critical systems such as carbon offsets – by which emitters and polluters can undertake measures which are meant to absorb additional carbon, like the planting of trees – simply do not work and are leading to unintended consequences.[7] Not only do they fail to bring about the claimed reductions in greenhouse gases, the projects used may well be doing additional damage. In particular, white papers looking into carbon offset markets found that only 10 per cent of such schemes meet reasonable sustainability criteria, despite their being backed by a consortium of more than fifty of the world's largest companies. Former Bank of England Governor and Prime Minister of Canada Mark Carney's taskforce came to similar conclusions. Perhaps the most damning truth about carbon offset schemes is that they frequently misrepresent what would have happened had the carbon credit not been issued. In order for the carbon credit to have in fact reduced carbon emissions, there must be a CO_2-sequestering activity that would not have happened were it not for the credit, or a CO_2-producing activity that was prevented using carbon credits as an incentive. However, in many cases carbon credits are issued to 'protect' forest that was at no credible risk of being deforested, or granted for solar farms which were being built anyway without the credit's incentive. In both cases, the credits would not produce any actual climate benefit but are sold as if they would.

Perhaps more damaging to countries like Britain is that the Paris Agreement model of cooperation suffers from profoundly weak incentives. Paris effectively functions on a 'name and shame' design.[8] Those states which fail to meet their goals are exposed to criticism, but not much else. This might work for Britain, a country whose leadership respects international law and does not willingly embrace courses which bring it into conflict with international institutions. Yet so many states are not like this; their leaders do not care, having a more direct sense of their own national interest. There is no mechanism for limiting the appeal of free-riding. Since the state of the climate is an external cost imposed on the whole world, those who do not keep their word or honour agreements can benefit from other countries' expensive efforts while making no such effort themselves.

Successful climate agreements like the Montreal Protocol, which eliminated the use of ozone-damaging chlorofluorocarbons (CFCs) in aerosols, by contrast, made heavy use of powerful incentives.[9]

Countries which failed to sign up were not allowed to trade their CFC products with those that had. There was a treaty through which developed nations would help developing ones finance the new capital investment to move on from CFCs. India, a country which had sought to expand the production of CFC products, found itself without a market and so was all but forced to cooperate and eliminate CFCs. There was, of course, more going on behind the scenes than that alone. Patents for CFC products were expiring, and their makers stood to make money with new green alternatives. The lessons for the Paris Agreement could not be clearer: diplomats and governments need a more sophisticated, incentive-driven arsenal of carrots and sticks, including trade access, technology transfers and finance, to coerce and entice countries to keep to their word. And there also needs to be profitable and sustainable green technology replacements ready and raring to go, so that the transition can happen fast and without hardship.

But Paris has one great function: public relations. It is still worth Britain both looking good and seeming ready to *do* good in the eyes of the world. Britain faces a clear incentive to design a more incentive-compatible and effective alternative to Paris. It must make a better future come to pass, in its own interests and the world's.

* * *

When it comes to climate change, the UK's domestic position matters, particularly in terms of its ability to make demands on the wider international community. At the time of the 2021 COP26 conference in Glasgow, it could be reasonably claimed that the UK was acting in a manner deserving of wider credit within the framework of Paris. The stances of both the UK government and the devolved administrations (especially Scotland) set out serious commitment. In addition, the UK COP President, Alok Sharma, was widely seen as effective and engaging in leading the negotiations. He has since lobbied successive UK governments to take the security implications of climate change seriously.[10]

However, the rapid turnover of UK Prime Ministers since then has weakened the Conservative Party's commitments on climate change to the point where they have little credibility. Meanwhile, the SNP's unsupported aspirations have had to be reduced due to their lack of feasibility. Finally, the Labour Party has stepped back considerably from its earlier ambitious commitments in this area and replaced them with an incoherent and in some cases radical approach that is proving neither effective nor financially sustainable. By 2025, Secretary of State for Energy Security and Net Zero Ed Miliband's changes had pushed £4.2 billion of unforeseen costs onto energy bills, while savings that were supposed to cut energy bills by £300 (according to Labour's manifesto) backfired and added further costs. Miliband's critics, and it is hard not to join them, say he will consign Britain to expensive electricity and power cuts. He says he will make the country as green as it has ever been. So far, nothing definitive has been done, while there are suggestions that his ill-conceived ban on oil exploration will not last for long.[11] Labour have instead focused on the creation of their GB Energy project, an attempt to pick winners while also somehow making the very investments the private sector deems unprofitable.

The Conservative Party is torn between the environmentalism of Alok Sharma and the Conservative Environmental Network and those who followed former Prime Minister Rishi Sunak in trading off environmental goals for economic ones. Labour have become more radical since entering office and yet simultaneously less interested in making their example desirable for other nations to follow. This is the risk of climate policy which is not incentive-compatible: you run the risk of broadcasting the high upfront costs and enduringly high prices. It remains likely, at the point of writing, that the money allocated to GB Energy is largely spent on green investment, though it may also be spent on the grid and on battery and energy infrastructure, which will increase the viability of future green investments.

This matters for several reasons. First, if the UK is to have a credible voice internationally, it must have matching credible domestic policies. Within the framework of Paris, 'doing your bit' gives you licence to both praise and shame others. Larger domestic investment in green technology also drives up our utility as a partner for the energy transition, as it strengthens our position in the development of the most profitable technologies. In geostrategic terms, strong and consistent action on climate throughout the West will command disproportionately more respect from third nations. If there are outliers not doing their bit, even in the developed world, it makes shirking much easier for developing nations.

The UK's role in international climate policy has two key facets: developing several specific areas of expertise and diplomatically assembling broader coalitions. Specifically, the UK must remain at the forefront of technological innovation as well as the innovation of new bonds, loans and equity schemes to raise capital globally for green investment. It is only in combination with tactful diplomacy that the UK can be a global leader in spreading knowhow and developing the institutional architecture to encourage and enforce cooperation. Attaining such leadership is a goal in itself, but is also an opportunity to influence on defence, energy and other more traditional areas of international diplomacy.

Britain need not pretend that it can do everything. Our advantages – particularly our financial sector and diplomatic links with the Commonwealth – stand us in good stead to incubate both new technologies and new models and frameworks for financing climate transition in the developing world. We are highly unlikely to become a competitive manufacturing hub for most of these new technologies. We are also unlikely to have any real prospect of sculpting the regulatory frameworks that govern them, except in particular areas (including nuclear fusion, where we stand among the global leaders). In this competition for soft power (and in terms of energy – an input for all military-industrial and economic production – for hard power) we must play to our strengths. We must lend our weight to our allies to take the lead and pool our resources into those industries where we can really lead.

Sometimes we can both support *and* lead. The US and the EU are the two most capable economies in the world and represent the entire liberal West except CANZUK (Canada, Australia, New Zealand and the UK). They have both blundered by exacting large tariffs on Chinese electric vehicles, in many cases doubling the price of their own energy transition. They've done this, ostensibly, to 'protect' an EV industry that is already protected by unprecedented subsidies in both the US and the EU. The UK, happily, has ignored calls to do the same. One advantage of strategic independence is that when an economy like China offers to subsidise our energy transition, we can say yes. When China offers to build our 5G networks however – with all the risks this poses for spying and sabotage – we can flatly and confidently decline.

* * *

The security issues related to the climate emergency can be broken down into three areas: the security of the UK itself; the security of countries affected by the worst impacts; and the consequences for the wider global system. In all these framings, there is a need for an approach to security that goes beyond the identification of risks and understands how climate change will become, and in some cases already is, a major driver of conflict both between and within states.

The level of domestic security is outside the scope of this book but will become increasingly important. We are already seeing reduced crop yields due to weather changes, for example. Elements of the UK's infrastructure are struggling with higher peak temperatures and with less frequent but more intense rainfall. Heatstroke and productivity losses from high temperatures occur when most homes and some businesses are not equipped with air conditioning. Invasive species – both plant and animal – are finding it easier to survive and spread, with risks both to human health and agricultural productivity. Even in isolation, these issues each have the ability to reduce the social wealth of the UK and weaken the internal political settlement. To state the obvious, there is no fundamental difference in effect if a major production chain collapses for domestic or international reasons.

As towns are hit with repeated incidents of major flooding, those living there are finding it impossible to insure their properties and the damage from one storm is not being cleared before another storm occurs. Equally, climate-related disruption elsewhere has direct consequences for the UK domestically. Loss of key agricultural products can follow on from climatic disruption and the interruption of key supply chains such as the Panama Canal being jeopardised by drought.[12] Indeed, it comes at a time when armed conflict has reduced the viability of the Suez Canal, again affecting both the price and availability of goods. For an economy built on the assumptions of globalisation, any such event has the ability to threaten the UK's wider security and, as these events compound, they start to become a serious drag on economic performance.

Not only is climate change destabilising many states, it is also fuelling the global refugee and migrant crises. Desperate people – and there may be some 216 million of them – will need to go somewhere.[13] Native populations who feel ignored become very easy to radicalise, especially given ethno-religious and cultural differences between migrant populations and Europeans. The current consensus, from the Labour Party to the populist right, is that this is a problem to be minimised by both legal and logistical actions to prevent borders being crossed illegally. Addressing climate change, while far from the only cause of mass migration, would help diffuse future conflict at source and minimise the numbers without leaving desperate people without help.

This in turn starkly affects the security of the countries for whom climate change-induced hardship will be most severe. Notably, the COP28 in Dubai, held in 2023, marked a growing interest in security-related discussions. In effect, climate change is now seen as a 'threat multiplier', something that may make latent crises more volatile and trigger fresh rounds of international instability. The UK is already taking this seriously, in particular by trying to focus attention on the need for analysis and data about emerging problems. However, this is a highly specialist task. The focus needs to fall in part on how climate change will amplify existing problems (especially of regime collapse) but also how the UK's allies, and adversaries, may adapt to climate change.

Disputes over resources and land may change from the pattern we have grown used to since the 1950s and even more from the relatively benign post-1990 era. The quicker these issues are identified, the quicker the UK can both determine its own response and help others. The flip side is the economic and strategic risk that comes with having unaffordable, uncompetitive energy, and the additional risk of having insufficient energy or other inputs as a result of having pursued net zero. Any honest assessment of the balance of these two risks would transparently show that the risk of energy poverty and of lacking the strategic goods to defend our interests are more severe than the risks of climate change in so far as our national security is concerned. Moreover, Britain will bear the security costs of other nations' climate emissions even as it bears the costs of abating our own emissions. A straightforward question must guide policymakers in this trade-off: are the emissions generated and any subsequent emissions caused by other nations' following our example worth sacrificing the strategic or economic good in question? In the case of North Sea oil and gas or an expanded Heathrow, it is obvious that the benefits outweigh the costs. Britain's failure to develop these strategic goods is government failure on a generational scale.

Indeed, policies such as 'Clean Power 2030' – the laughable idea that Britain can generate 95 per cent of its power from clean sources by 2030 – and the need to spend £800 billion in today's prices to reach net zero by 2050, look unlikely to meet our test. The economic fact is that £800 billion of spending will have an even greater opportunity cost. If an investment in a heat pump raises costs, then billions spent on them will cost billions more in ongoing costs. If net zero costs growth or causes companies to collapse, it will cost billions in forgone tax receipts. If it costs primary steel – as it seems to have done – the cost will have to be quantified in terms of sovereign power sacrificed. By 2036 the lost tax receipts from the lost output caused by net zero policies will overtake the investment itself as the largest associated cost to the Exchequer.[14] The upshot is clear: climate change may well be a policy objective about which we should not be short-sighted, but equally, we must not be short-sighted about the risks or costs of overzealously pursuing net zero. Even on our own terms and with our primary aim – to inspire other nations to follow our example – we are failing. More than anything, we are demonstrating that the promise of cheap, renewable and reliable power is an empty one.[15]

* * *

The UK, and liberal nations in general, has a key asset that can be used to further our interests and the cause of climate change abatement: they are inherently safer and more attractive destinations for capital, even capital which originates in totalitarian states. Their attractiveness is not just due to sound property rights or access to the widest possible array of projects to finance – it is backed up by the stability and diversification of the economies which support them. As well as having large economies, they have an outsized capacity to borrow and lend competitively.

The role of climate finance is not just to address climate change but to provide an alternative source of funding to authoritarian alternatives such as the Chinese Belt and Road Initiative – now widely seen as a trap into which foolhardy countries can fall and not just a source of free money to finance megaprojects. Becoming a debtor to an authoritarian regime carries risks both for the debtor country but also for the West in general: countries can be pulled out of our sphere of influence, weakening the resolve of collective action and emboldening those who would profit from the destabilisation of democratic states to go further still. China, for instance, doesn't attach the same strict conditions that the West does. It is through this process that 'climate aid' and 'climate investment' have become euphemisms for general investment in a developing country for manifold reasons – something quite appropriate once seen in the light of the alternatives.

One proposal to leverage our larger and more efficient capital markets advocates the creation of tax-exempt bonds and loans for green investment.[16] These bonds could also be made internationally tax-exempt through reciprocal agreement. Countries would be incentivised to agree to bring Western capital (much of which originates in the Global East but seeks stability in the dollar, pound and euro) in large quantities. Investors would enjoy tax-free returns both at home and abroad. Green investments would benefit from a significantly higher rate of return without tax.[17] Whatever form it takes, it will be Western banks that finance the green transition at the lowest cost, and this offers an exceptional opportunity for Britain in particular to innovate new financial products with enhanced climate incentives.

* * *

The UK's departure from the European Union necessitates a pivot if it is not to also mean a weakening of influence over our international interests and those of our allies. The Commonwealth is a leading candidate of mostly English-speaking, common law and democratic states across six continents. In this context, the Commonwealth offers considerable scope. The total membership is fifty-five nations ranging in size from India to small nations in the Pacific such as Nauru (with a population of around 12,000). Of the richer states, Australia is vulnerable due to its already arid climate and also valuable as it has remained a large-scale producer of fossil fuels. It also has large regions which offer potential for cheap solar energy creation, as well as uranium, gold and other rare earth metals which promise to power the energy transition. Canada faces challenges (and some limited opportunities) from the major shifts of weather patterns in the Arctic and, again, is a major fossil fuel producer in the form of the highly polluting tar sands in the west. In effect, both of these face different direct problems as well as needing to address the practical consequences of weaning their economies away from industries heavily implicated in climate change.

At the other end of the scale, African states run the range from those who have seen recent economic development and increases in relative wealth to those which have at times risked becoming failed states. In the case of the latter, the lack of state capacity makes them vulnerable to its effects, but also less potent at preventing such failures in the first place. If they intend to try, they may find that their development partners are from totalitarian states. The small island states face particular vulnerabilities, including the loss of land to the oceans and a potential link between climate change and the incidence of natural disasters, including hurricanes, death of fish populations from heating and acidification and the death of coral reefs that attract crucial tourist revenue.

In 2018, the UK committed the Commonwealth to 'mitigate climate change, reduce vulnerability and increase resilience'. This notional commitment was re-affirmed by the UK government in 2023 with a plan to 'strengthen the resilience of the most vulnerable members to climate change, nature loss and environmental degradation'. It should be noted that these goals have been set against a background of diminishing UK non-climate aid, with this dropping by almost £4 billion between 2018 and 2021 and continuing to fall since.[18] This can be seen as the UK becoming more selective in its choice of aid recipients (and attaching more and more climate-related criteria to the receipt of aid).

Useful building blocks, then, are already in place. The Commonwealth Climate Change Programme is focused on improving the resilience of more vulnerable members, and the related finance hub helps countries access funds and support, bringing together geographically disparate countries.[19] Related to this are shared programmes designed to ease the process of responding to, and recovering from, natural disasters. There are also wider programmes addressing problems such as desertification and loss of biodiversity. While an ideal UK policy would select climate development partners more strategically in response to limitations in fiscal capacity and in response to moves to court third nations made by totalitarian states, the UK could certainly do much worse than to partner with broadly like-minded Anglophone nations.

Political oscillations and multiple pressures on fiscal power (including the near £1 trillion borrowed and spent since Covid; the 2022 bonds crisis; and household and business cost-push inflation following Russia's invasion of Ukraine) have together pushed British international climate development much further down the list of priorities, for both parties and the electorate. While it will always be necessary to trade off climate goals for fiscal ones, a stronger argument can be made by linking diplomatic, aid and climate goals together, which is something the Commonwealth does very well, with cross-party appeal.

CANZUK, a muted variant of the AUKUS and Five Eyes military partnership between the Western Anglophone nations, has potential for a deep trade agreement (DTA, of which, more on page 177) and also a wider system of friendly investment, capital and labour movement and regulatory accords. With CANZUK as the centre of gravity, influence could develop and grow to include the wider Commonwealth. It is worth highlighting that, while Commonwealth member states would enjoy the benefits of closer economic, regulatory and trading ties with one another, the UK itself would be seated as the leader of a large coalition of nations and at the same time promote free trade and offer an alternative market to China. The Commonwealth contains the world's largest supply of most rare earth metals and elemental resources that can feed the energy transition and bolster security infrastructure. Australia alone has the largest reserve of lithium and the second-largest supply of cobalt; Canada, Indonesia and South Africa together can secure mutual supplies for the next century.

In addition, the UK remains an important member of other key international bodies. At one hand is the UN and its related agencies but, given the security aspect, membership of the informal Five Eyes intelligence network and of NATO are also important. When considering the UK's role as a leader of a climate, financial and trading partnership, and as a leading author and architect of international institutions, our membership of the Comprehensive and Progressive Trans-Pacific Partnership (CPTPP) and permanent membership of the UN Security Council are key assets for consolidating European power in the next century and ensuring we're ahead of European competitors for influence in the Global South.

The UK is well placed to act as a global leader in responding to climate change, certainly far beyond simply meeting its commitments to net zero at a domestic level. It remains a major hub in the global finance system with the ability to shape new financial products to finance the green transition and exert influence on it.[20] The Commonwealth, for many reasons, gives the UK a natural leadership role, including as it does rich countries that face common economic, political and security threats, as well as poor countries that need help to both cope and adapt to particular strands of the climate emergency. In effect, models of cooperation, sharing, funding and joint approaches that can work across such a diverse body can also be offered as models more widely. The best practices that Britian can incubate within the Commonwealth can set the standard for wider international cooperation.

A powerful proposal would include a Commonwealth Accord, similar in aim to Paris except that it is bound together and functions on the basis of strong incentives (trade and financial access) rather than the naming-and-shaming model of the Paris Accords. The latter suffers gravely from periodic disengagement from the US under Trump and from other Western nations dialling back climate targets. Driving open global markets to Western trade and finance is also, happily, a key geostrategic buffer against Chinese economic warfare.

To ensure such a role, the UK must get its own house in order. In general, the political right must recognise that the leadership role the UK must play, and the fiscal cost that this will inevitably involve, is a long-term strategy to secure British interests into the next century. The left must realise that a tax-and-spend and regulatory approach to climate change is unsustainable and eliminates market incentives to transition. Our current approach, which involves the world's highest energy costs (four times higher than the

US) and the fastest rising taxes in the G7, places enormous burdens on living standards while simultaneously reducing the payoffs to investment and innovation.[21]

There is a policy trilemma between energy transition, living standards and relative equality, but successive British governments have failed to recognise that. They have crowded out private investment in nuclear, gas and renewables with high taxes and burdensome regulations, especially in planning. Recognising this, they have attempted to replace private investment with public projects, and to fix prices by offering subsidised prices to renewable suppliers, also at taxpayers' expense. The result is less investment at much higher cost, necessitating higher taxes and lower living standards, which reinforces low rates of return and further spurns the investment Britain needs for its transition. The geopolitical independence of Brexit is certainly a double-edged sword. Our successes are more impactful, but our failures more painful than if we were made to follow the crowd. With the US pulling back from the world, if we specialise we have an opportunity to identify the key green industry where we can lead, and to do so through international forums to support international legal norms and build influence and security for the UK.

However, as we will continue to explore in this book, the UK as a globally integrated island economy cannot afford an undermined global order in the way that the US can. Stepping up to reinforce the global order has high concentrated costs but even higher dispersed benefits. Getting the balance right – leading where appropriate and being an importer and rule-taker from the legal order where we are uncompetitive – is the key to Britain's success. If we are to move on from a period of managed decline, it will mean specialisation.

The challenge of climate change offers up this book's central argument in miniature. Raising our gaze to international forums with an ambition to shape the global rules in the areas where we have a comparative advantage: this is the essence of global, inter-governmental, institutional leadership. As crisis approaches, the UK has an opportunity to seize outsized influence in a new axis of power – that of the international organisation. As we proceed, we must develop a strategy to achieve exactly this, developing a key offering and power base with which to buy currency in these international forums.

CHAPTER 4

GLOBAL DEMOGRAPHICS AND REFUGEES

The global refugee crisis is not going to go away. In fact, forced migration has been a growing feature of the world, particularly since the 1990s – and it is increasing every year. Illegal immigration and refugee movements are growing in tandem, and migrants are increasingly overwhelming refugee systems designed for a very different post-war world. The direct impact of climate change may force many millions of people to move, and without free and open markets for scarce inputs, conflict over resources may again trigger migration. Unfortunately, the world is trending towards a more permissive environment for international aggression and for corruption. Both have the capacity to drive refugee movements into the West.

Larger still than forced migration is voluntary migration. In the European Union in 2023, some 43 million residents were born outside the EU. As a proportion of the total population of non-EU citizens, 21 per cent lived in Europe for work, 34 per cent came to join their families, 15 per cent to claim asylum, 4 per cent for education and 26 per cent for 'other' reasons. In the UK, 42 per cent of all immigrants who have ever arrived in the country arrived between 2011 and 2021. Adjusting to 2024, that number surpasses 50 per cent. The scale of sustained movement in global populations is unprecedented at any point in human history. According to Migration Watch, following the 2021 census, more than four-fifths of the UK's increase in population is due to immigration. Britain's natural population fell from 2023 to 2024; more people died than were born. Yet the total population is still estimated to have grown, and this growth is wholly down to migration.

The effects of migration cut across Britain's various strategic dimensions. Far right and Islamist extremism feed off each other – and large-scale migration is the fuel. Britain is seeing the emigration of particularly young, educated workers, the effects of which interact with migration by putting upward pressure on housing prices and causing the transformation of formerly affordable neighbourhoods in cities (where previous generations of young people once bought their first homes) into increasingly unappealing ethnic enclaves. Emigration to Europe, the US and Dubai in particular presents long-term economic challenges: those emigrating are typically high-skilled Britons while those arriving are overwhelmingly low-skilled migrants from Africa, the Middle East and the Indian subcontinent. Migration also cuts through British strategy on the Commonwealth – where it presents opportunities to benefit from familial links to boost business ties with Commonwealth states. Finally, it hits at the very heart of the strategic necessity to bolster British democratic culture, returning it to confidence and humility. With every election (and referendum) for the last twenty years won by parties promising lower migration – only for the opposite to have happened in the event – migration is perhaps the single most unifying unaddressed concern of the British people, skilfully exploited by populists like Nigel Farage.

At the end of 2023, there were nearly 120 million people worldwide displaced as refugees.[1] This is an underestimate since many forcibly displaced people are not being recorded formally, as they never enter the formal UNHCR (the UN refugee agency) systems. Forty-seven million refugees are children and 2 million of these were born as refugees. Seventy million are still in their original country (internally displaced) and are being supported under one or other of the UNHCR's mandates (so again this understates the global problem). Of the global refugee population, 73 per cent come from five countries (Afghanistan, Syria, Venezuela, Ukraine and South Sudan). Of note, only one of these countries – Venezuela – is not experiencing sustained conflict but does suffer under the autocratic rule of dictator Nicolás Maduro.

Most refugees have historically stayed as close to their home country as possible and in some cases, such as Yemen and Gaza, find it near-impossible to leave their home country, despite the ongoing conflicts. Overall, this concentrates the refugees in low- to middle-income countries, while migrants concentrate in high-income countries. There are now over a million Rohingya in formal or informal camps in southern Bangladesh, and dealing with this influx is a serious problem for a country that has very limited resources. Around 39 per cent of refugees are confined to five countries (Iran, Turkey, Colombia, Germany and Pakistan) and of these only Germany could be described as even moderately wealthy.

In the UK, 85,000 people sought asylum in 2023, and the Home Office already had a backlog of 215,000 cases.[2] In 2022, 21,000 people had their claim processed and were granted refugee status on any grounds.[3] The obvious consequence is a rapid increase in the backlog of unprocessed claims, with individuals trapped in a limbo where they have very few rights until their claim is processed. For example, in Britain, asylum seekers cannot legally work but many do anyway, illegally, because life without work can be grim. This is just one example of how migration of all kinds distorts the economy. It is vital that Britain's leaders learn the nature of these distortions, and do not close their eyes to them. Only if they know how migration really affects Britain can our leaders govern the country well.

In total, asylum seekers and refugees make up around 11 per cent of all immigrants to the UK. The cost of housing asylum seekers, including those who have had their claims rejected but for one of a number of reasons are not being returned to their country of origin, is in many cases extremely high. The UK as a whole spent £4.3 billion on costs associated with asylum seekers in 2023, compared to £3.7 billion in 2022. Very high costs are also imposed upon local authorities, which are in many cases responsible for providing accommodation and services. The costs for accommodating one child can reach £15,000 a week – with many councils warning of possible bankruptcy as a result.

Beyond fiscal issues, immigration, especially at the scale currently being seen, has a significant impact on economic outcomes. The broad consensus is that immigration has increased or decreased British GDP by around 1 per cent, although most economists cannot agree on what assumptions should be carried forward, particularly assumptions about how economic activity might change dynamically over time.[4] However, on a per capita level, this means the population is growing faster than output, meaning a reduction in GDP per capita. There are winners and losers from immigration, but constraints on housing in recent years, as well as inelasticity in the supply of other key infrastructure and public services, has meant that average living standards have certainly fallen as a result.

This crisis is a global one. It has largely been produced by the lower cost and accessibility of long-distance travel, as well as by the increased access to information and awareness among migrants of applicable rules. It is also one with significant direct and indirect security implications. From the Paris attacks of 2015 onwards, Europe's principal terror threat has come from immigrant communities. While there are examples of first-generation immigrants involved in terror attacks, including in the Paris attacks, the vast majority are committed instead by the descendants of migrants. This suggests that Europe and the UK must, in the first instance, develop more robust immigration systems. This, of course, is something much easier said than done.

There are also security risks with refugee populations. One attacker, referred to as Ahmad al-Mohammad, used fake ID to pose as a Syrian to gain access to France via the Greek island of Leros.[5] In the second instance, we must do a better job of integrating those who arrive to avoid both security and criminality risks. While the UK does not collect such information, government reports from Denmark suggest immigrants from the MENAPT countries (the Middle East, North Africa, Pakistan and Turkey) have three-and-a-half times the rate of criminality compared to ethnic Danes. This increases to five-and-a-half times for their descendants.

This is an immense social problem, and it creates other social problems in its wake. Other ethnic groups notice these disproportions. If they feel that some are given free passes by the state, they become restive and unhappy. In discussions of migration, the feelings of those already in the country are easily forgotten, but if those people remain a majority, their opinions and their interests are vital and must be taken into account by governments.

One important element is the insecurity experienced by refugees both individually and collectively. Linked to this is the need to reduce reliance on illegal migration routes. Modern migration revolves around organised criminal gangs and the resulting link between these activities, drugs, corruption and in some cases funding for terrorism must not be ignored. In Libya, people smuggling is both a source of revenue for the country's armed factions and is perhaps the easiest way for them to make money, outweighing even trade in drugs and arms.

It is notable that the US has not, on the whole, suffered with elevated rates of terror incidents committed by immigrants or their descendants, nor is there any evidence that illegal immigrants crossing over the southern border from Latin America have elevated rates of criminality – and certainly not at the same rates seen in Europe – although this does not stop Trump from claiming otherwise. Quite often, comparative investigations are therefore most instructive in terms of policy, especially since immigration can be of such different character between destination countries, even when migrants have the same national origin. One example might be that of Lebanese migrants, who, when immigrating to Australia (and also Germany and Canada), have become notorious for narcotics, weapons trafficking, extortion and prostitution through the Lebanese mafia.

There is no such organised crime element in the UK or the US, nor in France. So much of the story of immigration is concealed by the data, only to be seen in case study. For instance, in the UK, there are some 1.6 million Britons of Pakistani descent. Some 60 to 70 per cent were estimated to have come from the Mirpur, Kotli and Bhimber districts of rural Azad Kashmir following flooding in the 1960s.[6] There are so many peculiarities which affect particular groups, known as cohort effects, which makes analysis of this type both difficult and beyond the scope of this book.

Migration and asylum differ legally in more than one important sense – in theory, we have control domestically over the former. In reality, closing down immigration routes including family reunion (which, as above, accounts for 34 per cent of Europe's foreign-born population), education and others, would likely be met in court with as much opposition as would changes to our asylum policy. They are both governed de facto, then, by international treaty, including the ECHR, though asylum policy even more so.

For our purposes, it is only necessary to understand that migration and asylum can build resilient and productive communities for the UK, and deepen commercial and cultural ties with the world, but can also bring criminality and significant security risks. Different political groups are tempted to oversimplify the question of immigration and asylum. The economic, sociological, criminological and security questions are complex in their own right. But, of course, the geopolitics of migration is even more so. Hostile actors including Russia (and, more recently, the Russian ally Belarus) have been using the mass displacement of persons as a tool to destabilise Europe. This was accomplished in the Syrian civil war, in which up to 20 million people were internally displaced, 5 or so million of whom fled abroad. One of the largest global smugglers of narcotics, weapons and people is the Iranian IRGC, which works with proxies in Latin America to attempt to destabilise the US and to profit through smuggling. Attempting to see this phenomenon purely through an economic or humanitarian lens, as politicians of all stripes often do, misses the geopolitical complexities entirely.

In short, the UK needs global influence if it is to change the rules that have been governing global population movements since the Second World War, to make them robust to hostile state action and exploitation.

Both of Britain's main parties, yet again, are promising significantly lower net migration. On 12 May 2025, Starmer's remarks at the launch of an immigration white paper drew widespread criticism for its argument that the UK risks becoming an 'island of strangers' without controls on immigration.[7] As David Miller pondered in the *New Statesman*:

> It's long been known that the societies that have gone furthest in pursuit of social democratic policies – the Scandinavian democracies especially – have also been societies that enjoy a high level of social trust. Trust between citizens is what encourages them to support policies from which they may not benefit directly, not only in the area of social justice but on long-term issues, such as combatting climate change.

Starmer, in using such language (regardless of whether it was intended more as a political veneer to stem the growth of Reform), draws upon a long political, philosophical and psychological history starting perhaps with Alexis de Tocqueville in his *Democracy in America*, which framed the entire foundation of American success as a matter of social mores and high social trust. There is a tendency, particularly given how high-status pro-immigration views are, to assume that concerns about migration must be racist or uneducated. This is a reflection Britain must lose, and fast. Backbench Labour MP Diane Abbott branded Starmer's remarks 'fundamentally racist'. They weren't. Disingenuous comparisons have been made to

Enoch Powell's 'rivers of blood' speech, but the closer match in fact is Theresa May's 'citizens of nowhere' comments from 2016.

In response to May's speech, the BBC published an anonymous opinion piece declaring that a 'philosopher' had determined that 'we are all citizens of the world'.[8] As in many other cases, reading the archives of news and commentary from a decade ago shows us just how far the debate has come. At any rate, platitudes such as these and attempts to characterise the entire category of concern as racist have not made the issue go away. The Tories, Reform and Labour all belatedly agree that migration is too high, and yet have no credible plan to stop it. This points to British governmental failure bolstered by bad political culture and the corrosive network effect of high-status opinions.

* * *

The UK runs several discrete schemes to help people from particular locations. By May 2024, this had brought in 207,000 people from Ukraine; a scheme to help people move from refugee camps in Syria helped 20,000 people move between 2014 and 2020; and a scheme set up in the aftermath of the Taliban taking power in Afghanistan helped 27,000 between 2021 and 2024. There is an ongoing scheme to help those looking to move from Hong Kong who hold British National (Overseas) status. Around 100,000 have moved to the UK under this scheme so far.[9]

Beyond this country-specific approach, the UK runs generic schemes in addition to the discrete ones; a resettlement scheme for people in refugee camps, either linked to local authorities or community groups, and a scheme for those with a family member who already has some degree of residency. In theory, this creates a framework where people can apply for asylum while in a refugee camp, especially if they can show family or other ties to the UK. In practice these schemes are of little value (as the Home Office acts as if it prefers would-be asylum seekers to arrive in the UK), but they could be repurposed into an effective tool for creating safe routes for asylum seekers. The family route has been affected by the approach set out in the 2022 Nationality and Borders Act, specifically by treating those who enter the UK by lawful means differently to illegal entrants. The goal, straightforwardly, was to ensure that these refugees should always opt to arrive by ferry or plane rather than by illegal small boat smugglers.

UK law is governed by the UN Refugee Convention, a 1967 Protocol added to the 1951 Refugee Convention, which states that a refugee is unable to return to their country of origin 'owing to a well-founded fear of being persecuted for reasons of race, religion, nationality, membership of a particular social group, or political opinion'. An asylum seeker is someone who has applied for refugee status in a particular country and whose status is yet to be determined. While waiting for this decision, asylum seekers are protected from being sent to a country where they could face persecution and have permission to remain in their current country.

The ECHR and the UNHCR Handbook, Chapter VI, provide further guidance that UK courts adhere to, supererogatory to the Refugee Convention. The UN Convention on the Rights of the Child also has significant influence on both government policy and the court decisions being reached. Immigration lawyers are aware of these conventions and are using them in ways that could not realistically have been anticipated in 1967. One particular way, discussed by Lord Sumption, sees the European Court of Human Rights treating the ECHR as a 'living document', with its actual text being ignored in favour of more expansive court judgments. It is a legal structure that is, Sumption argues, quite incompatible with common law, the proud tradition of British and English law.

Save for a few specific instances, someone must be physically in the UK to claim asylum. The only routes to the UK are a visa for some other purpose (such as tourism), use of false documents to enter, or reliance on smuggling gangs.[10] The Dublin Convention, which governs EU asylum affairs, requires that refugees should stay in the first safe European country they enter, though this was not effective at facilitating deportations, nor at dissuading migrants from journeying deeper into Europe. The UK is not a member of the Convention, having left the EU, but it was enshrined in UK law. According to the Convention, in some cases those who are deemed to have passed a safe country are given a lesser status if their application is accepted. Perhaps unadvisedly, Labour have revoked this clause, which no doubt contributed to boat crossings to July 2025 being 50 per cent higher than the year before (though the government blames the weather).[11] Almost by definition, the great majority of unlawful entrants to the UK come from the territory of a EU member state via the English Channel. The Conservative government has placed great emphasis on removing anyone who enters illegally but who is able to claim refugee status to a third country, an example of which was the short-lived Rwanda scheme. The scheme was introduced because mass migration was not being solved by any other lever at the disposal of the Home Office.

The Rwanda scheme, officially the UK and Rwanda Migration and Economic Development Partnership, was an attempt to solve the small boats crisis and the legal impediments to deportation in a single policy. The UK could meet its obligations under all of its treaties by deporting all those who attempt that illegal route to

Rwanda, to have their asylum claims processed there. If successful, they would be granted settlement status in Rwanda. The policy effectively aimed to remove any and all incentives to attempting an illegal journey across the Channel. Any would-be claimant with a valid claim would face overwhelming incentives to cross into the UK legally, for instance with a tourist visa. The plan was broadly unpopular, although in the months since its revocation, it has attracted many converts as the lack of alternatives focused minds.

Rwanda was cancelled by Starmer's Labour government upon taking office in July 2024. At the time of writing, it is still unclear if the government has the intention of finding an alternative policy which produces the same incentives for population movements to be regular and legal, although the European Commission and many European neighbours are exploring similar offshore processing, with Albania as well as with Rwanda itself. In July 2025, Starmer signed an agreement with France which promises a 'one in, one out' approach to Channel migrants. The plan has elements of a successful policy – being immediately deported back to France would be a deterrent to making the journey – although fails in that too small a proportion of migrants are deported to act as an effective deterrent. As we have already seen, there is nothing to stop a returned migrant from making the journey again, so long as France continues to fail in its obligations as a maritime nation and signatory of the Refugee Convention. It is also weaker than previous policy, given that the migrants' outside option is return to France, rather than deportation to Rwanda. It is unclear why Starmer felt the need to take any French asylum seekers at all, but we have already explored (in Chapter 2) Britain's failed negotiations as part of a more broadly compromised statecraft.

* * *

Britain benefits enormously from what is described as the rules-based international order. This, put as expansively as possible, is the system of legal norms, the acknowledgement and respect for democratic principles, the internationalised markets of open commerce and the subjection of sovereign power to international limits on its legitimate use. There is now an unhappy equilibrium where challengers to that international order, including the BRICS nations (Brazil, Russia, India, China, South Africa, Egypt, Ethiopia, Indonesia, Iran and the UAE), are attempting to undermine the West with displaced populations while simultaneously flouting many of the asylum rules they are notionally committed to. Western nations, including EU members such as Hungary, which have aligned geopolitically with the Russians and the Chinese, have chosen to flatly ignore their responsibilities to migrants under the 1967 Protocol.

Approaches such as Hungary's significantly damage the international order. They come at a time when the Russian invasion of Ukraine, the actions of Iran and the conduct of the Israeli-Hamas war continues to see respect for international law diminish. In a sense, they show how flouting the rules leads to a better national outcome than attempting to comply. Rwanda, in a rather specious way, is testament to the fact that the UK commitment to this rules-based order is unshakeable. That the government could design a scheme of such cost and complexity which meets every requirement of our treaties is, in a sense, encouraging. What is less encouraging is that the courts sought to obstruct it, rather than treating it as our neighbours are beginning to see it – as a policy innovation that helps to restore adherence to international legal norms until such a time as they can be changed.

The UK's internal domestic discourse gets more coverage than any nation on earth with the exception of the US. In large part, this is the result of English being the world's most widely understood language. There are more people worldwide who speak English as a second or third language than speak it as a first language. It means anything conducted in English is possibly conducted under the eyes of the world. This sometimes works against us, as our internal self-flagellation is watched internationally, and gives rise to the unhelpful notion that we are an international pariah on several issues, despite our record as having perhaps *the* staunchest commitment to the rule of law anywhere on earth. But there is a genuine opportunity to lead reform through debate. Britain's current asylum system causes significant vulnerabilities and is not robust to geo-strategic exploitation; hostile states create population movements to sow long-term destabilisation in the West. A reforming agenda and dialogue in the UK domestically would likely be enough to prompt the international treaty-making process. Starmer, given his legal reputation, could do this credibly, if only he were to realise the civilisational scale of the need.

* * *

In effect, forced migration is going to be a feature of the world for some time. Much of this will be local, some triggered by short-term factors, but there is no reason to believe the numbers of those displaced or those seeking a better life will diminish in the near future. All trends are running in exactly the wrong direction.

According to UNHCR, by April 2024 the world had passed 120 million forcibly displaced, with increases year on year without relent for twelve years.[12] Of this 120 million, some 43.4 million are refugees, with the remainder being internally displaced. Together, this is 1.5 per cent of the world's total population. Compared to a decade ago, the number of refugees globally has more than tripled, with Afghanistan and Syria each contributing 6.4 million to the global tally. Myanmar, Sudan and Palestine continue to record escalating numbers of displaced persons. By way of comparison, there are around 300 million so-called 'economic' first-generation migrants in the world.[13]

It is also already clear that the poorest countries in the world bear the bulk of the burden of physically hosting refugee populations. This is mainly a function of geography: Turkey is adjacent to Syria, Bangladesh to Rakhine State in Myanmar, and so on. Equally, as we have seen, the great majority of refugees are still in their country of origin but displaced by civil conflict such as in South Sudan, Gaza and the Yemen (in both of the latter instances it is nearly impossible for people to flee the conflicts). That said, the vast majority of the funding for refugee camps in each of these theatres of conflict is paid for by foreign aid, which comes overwhelmingly from the US.

A superficial examination of the causes of this increase in refugee populations would point to conflict as the main driver of refugee movements. But such an analysis lacks the kind of second-order consideration that would prove insightful. It is necessary to ask: why is there an increase in circumstances that produce displaced persons? Why do so many people wish to leave the places where they were born or brought up?

One unfortunate answer to these complex questions is that nations around the world are being plundered by their own politicians. Rampant corruption feeds an engorgement of the political class, many of whom siphon billions to Swiss bank accounts. Later in this book we will explore several methods proposed for freezing assets belonging to these individuals – something for which we now have precedent in the granting of frozen Russian assets to

Ukraine. Gabon's Ali Bongo continued his father's political dynasty, reportedly siphoning more than $1 billion offshore to the Virgin Islands. The same story is repeated across Africa and the Middle East, and indeed in south and south-east Asia as well as in Latin America. Not limited to recognised governments, it is well known that the leaders of Hamas, Hezbollah and other Iranian proxies are billionaires personally, all with wealth cruelly extracted from the people their sham democracies are supposed to be serving and cynically pilfered into private offshore accounts.

While with a young population and a low capital-to-labour ratio it is almost impossible *not* to see economic growth in the twenty-first century, the countries collectively referred to as the Global South suffer from extractive governments, corruption and election fraud that sustains incredible wealth inequality. This system of extractive, dynastic corruption is common from Pakistan to Venezuela. Any debate about the migration and refugee crisis must come to terms with the fact that theft – at a national scale – is a core element of almost all population movements worldwide. This is most straight-forwardly seen in Venezuela, where a veneer of socialist populism has been used to entrench a rigged electoral system with corruption and economic maladministration creating the largest sustained exodus Latin America has ever borne witness to.

Indeed, social programmes have been accused of intentionally making all Venezuelans dependent upon them for survival; they are used to leverage coercive social and political control. Chile, Peru, Colombia, Brazil and other neighbours have been creaking under the economic pressure of large population movements, but also the parallel importation of Venezuelan organised crime.[14] From the perspective of a country such as Peru, which already struggles with corruption and crime of domestic origin, the cause of population displacement and immigration could not be clearer: corrupt and unstable governments.

A second but more reflective answer to the questions posed above is this: bad foreign policy is enabling conflict, while corrupt extractive regimes are increasingly offering each other support. The ability to collectively develop alternative supply chains of key military, industrial and natural resources in an anti-US coalition reduces the effectiveness of US tariffs and increases the collective ability of such a coalition to launch invasions and adopt disruptive foreign policy stances. This trend has coincided with a protracted sequence of US foreign policy miscalculations. As a matter of diplomatic fact, the US is seen as a less-than-honest broker in the Middle East, whereas China has secured successive diplomatic victories, including treaties between Saudi Arabia and Iran that the US could never have sponsored.

In an ideal world, American foreign policy would see a US fully invested in the international legal order. America's influence might then be forcefully used to increase the payoffs to international cooperation based on law, and by doing so entrench democratic institutions around the world which will themselves trend their countries towards international cooperation. Almost the entire continent of Europe has been secured by means of the Marshall Plan and other aspects of American foreign policy interventionism, and the process has so far resulted in high returns for the US. This is a prosperous market which also, to varying extents, contributes financially to US security goals around the world.

But this is not an ideal world. In this world of second bests, the UK cannot rely on US influence. An extensive literature exists which explores how conflict is likely to rise as the world transitions away from a unipolar order. The war in Ukraine is one early example, which has seen cooperation, to varying extents, from China, North Korea, India, Iran and Syria. Brazil charted a 'neutral' position – something it is accustomed to doing – by refusing to criticise Russia under both Jair Bolsonaro and Lula, showing that even democratic states often find advantages blurring the lines at the edges of the legal order. Is it increasingly permissible both to invade foreign states and to continue relations with those that do. Britain relies more than most nations in Europe on the international legal order.

It would be a mistake, however – given the peacekeeping influence of China in the Middle East – to think that this new international order can solely be a cause of conflict. The retreat of the US could, in some circumstances, result in greater treaty-making room for countries to find non-violent diplomatic solutions. However, this is likely to come at the expense of democratic states and involve undermining or manoeuvring around international organisations. The world is more willing to do deals with strongmen and autocrats when international law loses its teeth. As such, corrupt and power-hungry political parties everywhere can find advantage in allying themselves with the anti-Western coalition. We have already discussed how corruption fuels population displacement.

Unfortunately, the world is trending towards a more permissive environment for international aggression and for corruption. Both have the capacity to drive migrant and refugee movements into the West. Climate change, as discussed in the last chapter, may become a significant driver of population movement in its own right.[15] Institutions must equip themselves with the law and the authority to resolve potential conflicts connected with resource shortages.[16] The wider refugee crisis across the Sahel already owes much to climate change, as previously viable economic systems collapse in the face of new strains and stresses.[17] In the face of such complexities, the UK's role will require a careful balance.

*　*　*

The UK cannot neatly resolve these difficulties. Necessary friends and partners in some theatres can become instigators in another. In a less well-known example, the UK is actively protecting the UAE over its funding for the paramilitary Rapid Support Forces (RSF) in Sudan – a group responsible for worsening the refugee crisis in the country.[18] No doubt those involved see this as a necessary compromise as part of creating an enduring settlement, but the harsh reality is that the UAE's funnelling of arms (in part paid by oil sales by its proxy factions in Libya) is itself a major cause of instability.

Some organisations, like the notorious Stop the War coalition, whose anti-Western bias borders on compulsive, blame every crisis on the West.[19] This analysis does not hold such claims to be true. But there is a need to recognise that our choices, and who we choose to support, can be a cause of state collapse in a fragile environment. Our strategic minds are well aware of this. Iranian drones are being used against the RSF, and Iran have been security partners of the ruling SAF (Sudanese Armed Forces) for more than a decade. Similarly, though much more controversially, Israel is a crucial ally of the UK, and a functioning common-law democracy whose enemies seek not only to destroy it, but the West also. Supporting Israel against Hamas and other Iranian proxies should be straightforward, yet we must acknowledge that Israeli strikes against civilians and civilian infrastructure, even if being used by Hamas as human shields, places severe strain upon the reputation of the West. How and why are we condoning some of the same methods that the international legal order exists to prevent?

A broader question is: in order to secure peace and rights under law, what level of tyranny and use of force is permissible? In a profound sense, this question is one for political theory and has been debated ever since Thomas Hobbes first wrote *Leviathan*, a seminal text in the school of political liberalism. Carl Schmitt – a fascist in Hitler's Germany, mentioned above – perhaps wrote the most provocative and insightful answer, made all the more interesting by the fact that he himself was a great enemy of 'toothless' liberalism. For Schmitt, the preservation of order could never rely solely on the neutral operation of law: the sovereign must ultimately stand above the legal order and decide when it is suspended in the name of survival. There is, it seems, a theoretical and philosophical incoherence with the rule of law as a part of national sovereignty. However, it remains less of a problem for liberalism as a political theory than a problem for liberalism in political practice. Should the UK, which aims above all to protect liberalism and democracy, lend its support to illiberal or illegal acts that benefit liberal states and harm the interests of autocratic ones? Many international leaders, from China and Russia to Iran and South America, and including many in the US and some in Britain, claim to find either insight or justification in the works of Schmitt. Supporters of liberalism ought to set out to prove Schmitt's conclusions untrue by actions, not dismissal of the arguments of these varied critics. Making the world order work is the greatest possible riposte to such thinking. The questions are posed regardless.

The realist school of international relations has dozens of critical insights on this topic. One is that, despite all their ideological, economic and geographic differences, the US and the USSR undertook the same kinds of action, more or less, throughout the Cold War. They both followed the same blueprint of intervention in foreign coups and civil wars, espionage, alliances and nuclear proliferation. In the service of the anti-communist effort, to bolster American economic interests and to prevent the tyrannical model of government seen in the USSR spreading to more countries, the US supported all manner of distasteful and illiberal regimes. When great power competition is at hand, scruples go out of the window in the effort to benefit liberal states and harm autocratic ones.

This debate can also be reframed as follows: should the UK ever allow itself to trade hard power for soft? Reasonable and patriotic people can disagree, naturally, because to some extent they are substitutable goods. The calculation, which must be run at every significant juncture, is this: is the payoff from turning a blind eye higher than the damage done to the UK's 'credibility' and the rules-based international order, particularly in terms of lower payoffs at future junctures? Some recent UK decisions fail this test dramatically. Most notably, as discussed in Chapter 2, the UK's decision to give the Chagos Islands to Mauritius was born from a naive enthusiasm for 'credibility' without an understanding of where it is lost and gained. Put simply, credibility is not about doing *everything* an international court asks. It is about retaining the trust of our partners (and even our enemies) that we'll uphold our end of any bargain we enter into with them. Neither we, nor indeed any nation, promises (or can promise) to follow instructions that we are not required to. Refusing to follow a court's advisory opinion, especially on a matter such as Chagos – which was already settled as a matter of domestic law and with respect to the ECHR – does not cost 'credibility' in any meaningful way, and, given it isn't binding, does no real damage to the rules-based international order. The fact that the issue had been mostly dormant since 2019 testifies to this. Indeed, handing over the islands actively *undermines* the bargains we enter into with other countries – hence the excitement in Madrid and Buenos Aires (where many want to claim British sovereign territory in Gibraltar and the Falklands respectively, without fighting) – even though they may not even have an advisory opinion claim to press. Hence, this would fail the test of being worth trading hard power for soft, and overwhelmingly so.

Applying this realist international relations doctrine to the crises of mass migration and the mass displacement of persons yields an interesting policy prescription. Does deviation or departure from international agreements on migration and refugees harm our credibility *qua* our trustworthiness to uphold the bargains we enter into? The answer is that it depends massively on the context. A departure from the ECHR would have to be handled with tact and openness: a political debate, which Britain could lead internationally, would be required to set out the liberal case for its replacement with modern text that isn't a 'living document', and which doesn't have the power to sap away at political and democratic control or to concentrate power in the courts. Given its uptake on the continent, a policy such as Rwanda has clearly not damaged Britain's reputation in itself, but as above, our self-flagellation in respect to it could be taken advantage of by our enemies to reduce our diplomatic power. Anything beyond Rwanda which shirks obligations written into domestic and international law would be incredibly damaging, given the number of countries grappling with the issue of immigration. Were Britain to undermine the global agreement in this way, it would likely cause a cascade of nations to do the same, fundamentally undermining the UN in a way that would prevent Britain from reaching its other key international goals.

* * *

The link between immigration, displacement and development has been discussed for some time but not really brought together at a policy level.[20] State failure can be linked to internal gang and drug violence, with this largely driving the refugee crisis in Central America. On the other hand, Venezuela is a major source of refugees due to domestic economic mismanagement and rampant corruption.

The idea of liberal interventionism has been ended by the Iraq War and the hubris of its main supporters.[21] There are open questions about the Chinese model of economic development. The main recipients of Chinese development money have not as yet been able to translate that development into political stability. Indeed, the potentially predatory nature of the loans, and the ways in which the political class are able to use Chinese support to entrench extractive practices and deflect from domestic failures, might work in the opposite direction. It should be quite clear that Chinese loans are less predictive of development and stability than loans secured from the West, if for no other reason than Western private capital seeks a competitive rate of return, unlike Chinese state capital, which seeks to entrench pro-Chinese politicians and purchase trading influence and, quite possibly, military infrastructure.

While it may be superficially attractive to link allocation of aid (which remains mostly under the direct control of the donor) to a reduction in corruption, the limited evidence suggests that this only reduces funding for particular programmes. It also ignores that some of the most rampant embezzlement in corrupt nations is the embezzlement of aid money, as in the case of Hamas as well as in several African states. Here, the former colonial powers often play a dual role. They may, as aid donors, wish to promote good governance, but they are also in control of the many avenues by which monies can be extracted from poor countries by corrupt leaders.[22][23] In this respect, concerns both about the UK's network of tax havens and the actions of part of the City of London are long established.[24]

Finding practical examples is not difficult. In 2020, Jordan received around $1.5 billion in aid from the US and $218 million from the EU. It lacks the oil and gas that bankrolls the lifestyles of the rich in the Gulf Cooperation Council (GCC) region but that doesn't stop its ruler matching such profligacy. Jordan's King Abdullah II spent $106 million on properties in the US and UK alone from 2003 to 2017.[25] The cash transfers were disguised by shell companies registered in the British Virgin Islands (BVI). There is, of course, no reason to believe this represents the totality of money siphoned out of a poor country where over one-third of the population are already refugees. (The UK also has very close ties to the Jordanian monarchy and military, notably selling its Challenger 1 tanks to the Kingdom.)

It would be naive to imagine that Britain's government is in a particularly compelling position to close down or even impact the expropriation of foreign citizens by their governments. Britain is nonetheless a major financial hub, as are some of its overseas territories and Crown Dependencies, over which it exercises considerable influence. There are recent examples, including an incredibly successful operation to freeze Russian state-linked assets in Britain, Europe and the US and subsequently set out the legal framework which allowed those funds to be allocated to Ukraine. However, it must be pointed out that these ill-gotten funds were not 'hidden' and were quite overtly held in the names of Russian oligarchs and

Russian state enterprises. It is quite another matter to be able to shut down financial crime when sophisticated methods are used.

The UK's anti-money laundering (AML) strategy and legislation will be a topic that we will explore in much greater detail in Chapter 8. It's worth highlighting here that, no matter how resolute the *intention*, the efficacy of such methods tends to be very low. AML is treated in many aspects of the legal, banking and estate agency industry as a box-ticking exercise. Some 22,000 estate agencies are signed on for supervision by HMRC; the industry spends thousands training staff in how to ensure compliance in order to avoid fines, which often befall small companies that are *not* involved in money laundering but haven't correctly met the compliance requirements. In all, enormous efforts are expended in what many analysts call a 'performance' driven by the need to be 'seen to do something', rather than by any objective evidence that it works. Because, quite frankly, successes from AML are very few and far between: *The Economist* estimated in 2004 that AML was already costing the US $5 billion a year. Anti-money laundering is, in this view, something of a red herring. The ability to confiscate assets as was done in the case of Ukraine is not aided by AML regulations. Our ability to detect hidden cash, squirrelled away by dictators, is also not meaningfully aided.

The good news is that many of the jurisdictions with the most exploitable rules, particularly the BVI, are changing these rules. The use of anonymous shell companies for crime has tarnished the reputation of the islands as a compliant tax haven. There are dozens of options internationally for mobile capital to seek low rates of tax, and those who invest it are keen to avoid any suspicion that the money has been laundered. For reasons of self-interest, legitimate mobile capital shuns regimes that will present difficulties for bring-ing capital back home. This is why the BVI are following in the footsteps of the Channel Islands as well as low tax regimes around the world in reforming shell company law. While AML regulations may be overhyped, real solutions do exist in reforming company and trust law to make it more transparent. Here, the UK can lead by example.

There is much Britain can do to clean up the world of kleptoc-racy and dirty money. Initially, these things may not be popular. Criminals and tyrants the world over would rather have London and British Overseas Territories as havens to hide their ill-gotten gains, but it is in Britain's interests that the world order continues to function. International finance is undermined by corruption and international peace is threatened by theft. Doing the right thing is sometimes costly, but in anti-corruption work, the opposite is true. Britain can clean up its own jurisdictions and help meaningfully not only to improve its own status and finances but to make the world a more honest place. A better place to do business. A better place to perform international politics. All of this is in Britain's – and the world's – interests.

*   *   *

Over two-thirds of the 956 companies that the Pandora Papers reveal have a link to public officials worldwide were set up in the British Virgin Islands.[26] One purely internal reform would be fi-nally to deal with the Scottish Limited Partnerships (SLP) that have been central to money laundering by mafia-related groups and the Putin elite since the early 2000s, similar to the BVI's shell companies. Currently, you don't even need to be a UK citizen to gain access to all the benefits that a SLP offers.[27] SLPs function as a hybrid corporate structure under Scots law, comprising at least one general partner and one limited partner. Only the general partner is responsible for management, while limited partners' liability is restricted to their investment – yet both enjoy the ability to hold property, open bank accounts and contract in the partnership's name. Crucially, SLPs can register overseas partners and conceal ultimate beneficial ownership, enabling opaque financial flows through UK jurisdiction without meaningful oversight. This combination of legal personality, limited liability and minimal disclosure requirements has made them an attractive vehicle for transnational money laundering and sanctions evasion.

In one instance, wealth was stolen from Moldova equivalent to one-eighth of the country's GDP (some $3 billion) and then transferred via SLPs.[28] The result was to undermine Moldova's government and financial system and remove all the financial reserves built up by an already poor country. In 2018, the UK government belatedly declared its intention to crack down on this abuse.[29] The resulting reforms have been ineffective and by 2022 few checks were being made, while the limited fines raised by HMRC are small and often ignored. The criminals who set up the SLPs take advantage of lax rules at Companies House with little concern for the very limited fines they face even if they are caught. Part of the problem is that this is fully confined to the UK government but involves some knowledge of how Scottish law is different to English law. In effect, for HMRC and the UK government it is of minor interest but demands some specialist knowledge – meaning the problem is all the more likely to be ignored.

SLPs are a good place to start in a regulatory sense. We have good examples of bad regulation in the form of current AML. If there is a way to organise these business structures such that they cannot be exploited by criminals, the UK must attempt to find that way. There is no need to negotiate with other Commonwealth states, no need to align to UN procedures and no need to negotiate with the US: it is essentially a matter of domestic UK political and administrative will.

A final question, implicit in these discussions, is whether, should we manage to square the circle in preventing embezzled funds from reaching our shores, this will translate to a meaningful reduction in the rate at which corruption consumes the future of developing nations and drives their young men abroad. It is likely to translate for a variety of reasons, very well explored in the literature. The first and most significant is that the West is the only stable destination for stolen wealth. Not only in the economic sense, but in the sense that many developing countries, or indeed Russia or China, will confiscate assets if you start to become a problem for the regime. The case of Jack Ma stands as a particularly salient example of what can happen if one's assets are kept in reach of an authoritarian regime. Changes which restrict company law loopholes are likely to increase transparency without driving money to hostile shores. Should they be pursued personally for their embezzlement, their assets could then be frozen successfully, but more importantly, the visibility will make it harder to embezzle in the first place. The abuse of international finance is an area where the UK has considerable capacity to reform – we will return to it in Chapter 8.

*   *   *

As noted above, the UK already has a workable framework. It has been willing to produce specific schemes for particular instances, it has programmes to allow people to apply for asylum from refugee camps and it allows people to apply for family re-union. This positive list approach has its advantages for the UK. Specifically, due to the geographic location of the UK, far away from any likely population displacements, the UK can select crises where it wishes to go beyond the pale and offer refuge to those displaced. Unfortunately, it also suffers because it does not vary or diminish the effectiveness of Channel crossings for those who are not on the positive list. In other words, it cannot solve the small boats crisis unless every nation is on said list – equivalent to no border policy at all. There is also the added security problem with this approach: Paris attacker Ahmad al-Mohammad and dozens of others have fraudulently claimed to be Syrian to take advantage of these schemes, something quite difficult to disprove when documents are often intentionally discarded.

Offshore processing is another approach, which may be combined with a right to refugee status in the UK or in a third country (as with the Rwanda scheme). This could credibly involve UK presence at refugee camps around the world, triaging based on need and connection to the UK, to process asylum claims at source. If this is to work to diminish the appeal of the Channel crossing route, it must also be matched with a reinstatement of the Migration and Borders Act clauses which render a refugee ineligible for asylum if they enter illegally. For instance, at the time of this book, Vietnamese is the most common ethnicity of Channel migrant. Any sensible UK approach will not be offering Vietnamese citizens asylum given the relative peace of their homeland. Even supererogatory generosity at every asylum camp in the world would not diminish the incentive for economic migrants to cross by boat. There is, moreover, no visible appetite whatsoever for the Starmer government to reintroduce those clauses of the Migration and Borders Act that eliminate the rewards of crossing the Channel illegally for one's asylum prospects. Taken together, these observations demonstrate how simplistic calls to open 'more safe routes' have no realistic mechanism by which they could stop or even reduce illegal migrant crossings.

As such, the principal role of the UK is to introduce the idea of reform at international institutions and to innovate new technical solutions to mass population movements at the same time, building towards a new treaty on displaced persons which removes incentives to pass through safe countries. While the advantage in terms of solving the refugee crisis in Europe speaks for itself, it is also crucial to ensure the survival of international institutions themselves. Countries across Europe, including Turkey, are exploring increasingly legally dubious options regarding refugees. In an attempt to stem the flow of people through its borders on their way to the US, Mexico has been involved in countless incidents resulting in the deaths of migrants on smuggling routes.

When the law becomes too impractical to comply with, international respect for the rule of law is diminished. As such, a new Refugee Convention for the twenty-first century is sorely needed, not just for the developed world, but for the developing world too. If not, we risk a cascade of countries shirking obligations that they find they cannot meet and killing the international legal order through a thousand cuts.

The impact of a lack of reform on refugees themselves also warrants explanation. NGOs and charities in the West are often guilty of a kind of patronising double-think when it comes to refugees. Those moved by forced human trafficking are victims, often bound for employment or modern-day slavery in illicit industry where traffickers will use coercion and control.[30] Many nations, including the UAE, are hotbeds for what amounts to slave labour.[31] Although noble, the instinct to sympathise with the plight of an economic migrant seeking to better themself overseas has a dark consequence. Permissiveness towards illegal migrants, allowing them to stay, encourages others to follow in their path, providing revenue and organisational infrastructure which traffickers can then use to smuggle genuinely desperate and deserving refugees into exploitative lives in the criminal or shadow economy. Opposition to legislation like the Migration and Borders Act is, in this sense, self-defeating. Repealing it, as we have already seen, drives up attempted crossings and strengthens the business models of traffickers.

*   *   *

Britain must return to a focus on incentives with respect to migration and to reform progress at the UN level regarding asylum law. Incentives, in particular, must be adjusted not just to ensure that migrants are able to pay their own way and support themselves, but that their presence in the country fiscally benefits the Exchequer (after considering all dependants and their eventual retirement and ill health) enough to compensate for all pecuniary externalities (such as on house prices and wages) and for the non-economic social and political costs, particularly on social trust and crime. This chapter has shown that immigration, at least in the way that Britain has gone about it, has damaged the fiscal position of the UK and continues to do so, but not in a way that is irrecoverable. It is the damage to political and social trust, the fuelling of a far-right/Islamist cultural centrifugalism and the dominance of high-status concerns over low-status ones that will have the most enduring effects on Britain's future. Many of Britain's voters will never forget how their fears and concerns were ignored. In our discussion of the rise of authoritarianism, we have already shown how mass migration has pushed many on the Western extremes of politics to see Putin as an anti-woke defender of European civilisation against an external threat. Putin is able to manipulate this role for himself, and he uses it to undermine the West's strategic posture, because Britain and Europe have elevated high-status opinion over national interest. The threat from mismanagement of immigration and asylum goes beyond public finances or a far-right backlash. It undermines the sustainability of Britain's foreign policy and threatens to turn us down a permanent path of illiberalism. Squeamishness about racial or imperial history must be set aside. Immigration must be required to serve the interests of the British people as a whole, and the case for asylum reform must be urgently made at the UN.

CHAPTER 5

INTERNATIONAL
LEGAL NORMS

It is self-evident that Britain needs change at the level of international law. Before the democratic recession began in the mid-2010s, international institutions were the natural way that such change was to be conducted. Particularly during the John Major and Tony Blair years, Britain had remarkable success at this level of diplomacy. Yet as world capitals recede from global multilateralism in favour of bilateral and plurilateral agreements, and as the US steps back, Britain will need to support the international legal order without excluding itself from the opportunities and gains from the new, more adversarial world of bilateralism.

The approach Britian must take to the international legal order requires understanding what we really get out of it. The answer is an economic and geopolitical framework that regulates and, when functioning, sustains the conditions by which freedom, contract and law proliferate and where aggressive, domineering and escalatory behaviour is punished. A strategy for Britain requires a realistic assessment of the ways in which that international legal order is breaking down, as well as the reasons for this breakdown and the limits of what Britain alone can do to sustain it.

* * *

The idea that there are a set of rules that influence international relations has ancient antecedents. Stretching back to antiquity, states exchanged ambassadors and made agreements about borders. These deals were often underpinned by the swapping of hostages (usually nobles or their children) as guarantors that such a deal would be maintained. The resulting treaties were sometimes time constrained, and usually, but not always, designed to end a conflict or secure non-aggression to prosecute a war elsewhere.

Both classical pagan and early Christian thinkers gave equal attention to two related problems. When might war be justified and, if one occurred, what conduct was justified? At one end of the scale was Cicero's claim that 'in war, the law falls silent', but he also set out criteria by which a conflict might commence: 'It may be understood that no war is just unless after a formal demand of satisfaction for injury, or after an express declaration and proclamation of hostilities.'[1] This framing is then extended to an argument that the only reason for a just war is to secure future peace. Later classical authors suggested that what we would regard as civil law has no place in conflict, but that there were unwritten, natural laws that legitimised some conflicts and the actions within them.

Very early Christian traditions tended to adopt some degree of pacifism in response to seeing the Roman army as an instrument of pagan power; the inevitable conduct of a war undermined both social and personal piety. With the adoption of Christianity as the state religion of the Roman Empire, this tradition fell away and was replaced with varying criteria both for what constituted a just war and what, again, was acceptable within it.[2] Similar debates emerged within the Islamic traditions.[3]

A given state was at liberty to decide how it acted in war and it was the state itself that judged whether it met whatever amorphous criteria it was prepared to accept. Indeed, from antiquity to the modern era any such restrictions have been readily ignored in practice. In effect, there really was no concept of an abstract international law that applied to all (and did so evenly) – there was a patchwork of secular, religious, moral and social rules that each state could use to justify its own actions. Indeed, while Magna Carta was the first successful attempt to codify such a view, the counterintuitive idea that there are *natural* laws or laws of God that exist above a ruler – even without being written explicitly – took centuries to take hold outside the Anglo-Saxon world (though Thomas Aquinas's *Summa* arguably contained the blueprint for restrained government from the mid-thirteenth century onwards).

The post-Napoleonic era saw few interstate conflicts in Europe in part due to exhaustion but also because the existing great powers usually exercised diplomatic pressure to avoid, or limit, any conflicts that broke out. The idea of rules within war gained a boost when all the major powers (including the US, Brazil and Mexico) signed the Geneva Convention in 1864. This set out not only expectations for the treatment of the wounded but also those taken prisoner in war. It lacked any formal means of enforcement other than the moral force of it having being accepted by all the major powers. As a framework, it survived both world wars and the various conflicts that marked the period between 1919 and 1939.

Of more importance, the idea of having a valid reason for entering conflict became entrenched after the end of the First World War, though 'just war theory' had first become popularised in the early modern period by Dutch humanist Hugo Grotius. Again, there was no shortage of violations, but the precepts were strong enough to form the basis of the Nuremburg trials of the Nazi leadership at the end of the Second World War. In effect, among numerous other crimes, they were held to have violated the rules regarding when a war could be declared. However, the bigger shift was the adoption of the idea that there were real laws that constrained state behaviour and that these laws could be developed, and applied, by a non-state body.

Britain has the proudest and most consequential legal history of any country. The English and later British common law made immense contributions to justice in many countries. But today, Britain is being strangled by the law. International treaties constrain British interests on migration, refugee flows, self-determination, self-defence and our efforts to control terrorism and organised crime. To take the examples favoured by Britain's tabloids, the British state is so constrained by human rights law that it cannot deport many rapists, murderers and terrorists. The majority of failed asylum applicants are not deported. A foreign court, the European Court of Human Rights, is seen by many in Britain as a final court of appeal, above even our Supreme Court. In international affairs, Britain is signatory to the ICJ and the International Criminal Court. Both of those bodies claim the ability to restrict the conduct of British foreign policy. This is an inversion of the historic pattern, where traditions born in the mother of parliaments in Westminster spread across the world. How did this happen? This chapter seeks to find out.

* * *

The first early attempt at creating an international legal system was the League of Nations. Often now reviled as a failure, it actually managed to set out rules that held around the use of chemical weapons (on the battlefield) and even sustained efforts at disarmament such as the limits on navy size set out in the Washington Treaty in 1922. It also created a framework for conflict resolution; even if this continued to be at the state–state level, there was an overarching framework.[4] The second attempt was the creation of the United Nations; this formed a set of international laws around conflict and human rights and provided the collective tool to maintain these rules as well as a justice system to enable their implementation. In turn, the emergence of entities such as the European Economic Community (EEC) and its subsequent forms all contributed to the idea that an international framework had a tangible existence – though, of course, political and economic union in the case of the EU, and the difficulty in leaving, shows that this organisation can be seen more as a federation than a framework for state-to-state conflict resolution.

Clearly there have been plenty of failures, but the UN as an entity has in the past seventy years fought wars to stop aggression, has intervened in civil conflict to create and maintain peace and has acted to punish those guilty of war crimes. Perhaps the single most decisive success of the UN has been the war in Korea. A free and prosperous nation has been salvaged from the jaws of dynastic communist dictatorship by the sacrifice of millions of men from sixteen nations who fought and died for the freedom of a country they had never seen. The confidence and clarity of the US's moral purpose that defined those early post-war years, and led to such success, was sapped away by subsequent failures. The 'coalitions of the willing' of the Vietnam and the Iraq War, though they had honest proponents, were not the same calibre of moral crusaders that had fought in Korea a generation earlier.

This conflict regarding international law encapsulates the key debate in international relations. On one side, the realist school argues there is no such thing as international law. The argument is that for a legal system to really exist, it must be backed by the power of a sovereign state in its own territory. By definition, this is lacking between nations, so at worst the concept is misleading and at best it only holds so long as power relations are strong enough to sustain support.[5] If this falls away, then the apparent security of international law is no protection at all. On the other side is the argument that international norms and laws and bodies tasked with administering international justice (such as the ICJ) offer a sustainable method that benefits us all.[6] These laws also create a framework to develop legal norms around emerging issues such as AI and the growth of autonomous systems in warfare.[7]

Though the post-1945 convention that there were rules and that they could be applied by an international body to nation states was broadly accepted, there were exceptions. The Soviet Union was a core part of the UN's practical governance and clearly had diverging geopolitical goals to, say, the US. It also had its own view of human rights, among other things. However, it framed these differences around the terms adopted by the wider consensus.[8] In theory at least, its position was one of accepting that there *were* rules while holding that they were gravely flawed.

Since 1991, the world has seen two divergent trends. One was defined by the relatively hubristic view that history was now over and the only future was one of liberalism and free market capitalism. The other saw the return of authoritarian regimes and their re-interpretation of the old Soviet argument.[9] This second trend is exemplified by contemporary Chinese arguments that there is nothing wrong, as such, with international rules, except that the current set are, all too often, wrong and self-serving.[10] The return of (a crude interpretation of) the realist school of international relations as a key part of the mindset of the populist right and, in particular, the rejection of both international rules and of any interference in the choices of a given government in terms of domestic law also mark this second trend.

This fraying of the concept of global rules not only affects human rights but also the wider international trading order. That is covered in the next chapter, but the key here is to consider first the implications of this trend away from international law and then what, outside the EU, the UK can realistically achieve in the face of it.

* * *

Perhaps the key theme in the rise of populist regimes since the mid-1990s has been their rejection of what they see as constraints on their domestic actions. This largely stems from their rejection of US judgement over their systems of civil rights. Quite often, distrust of the US is used to pass illiberal reforms leading to the contraction of civil liberties. Legal frameworks that entrench rights are a significant barrier, whether embedded into domestic law or upheld by international law.

Many on the political right in the UK believe some version of this narrative, with *The Spectator* having run articles detailing the horrors that will be inflicted by the then new Labour government. High on this list is that universal rights 'written into the constitution ... [will give] more power to quangos at the expense of elected representatives' and will be 'put beyond the power of Parliament to abridge ... Starmer will complete the process of franchising out democratic governance to independent watchdogs'.[11] The argument is not that universal rights are in some way undemocratic, but that the UK has done a very poor job in the last twenty years of controlling imaginative judgments in the courts that go beyond political legislation, and that the placement of significant powers in unelected quangos with political biases undermines the legitimate democratic role in lawmaking.[12] It would be a mistake to discard this line of thought or to think it mere populism. We have explored the thought of Lord Sumption – perhaps the greatest legal mind of this generation – who holds that the government has got it very wrong over the prorogation of Parliament, and who supported membership of the European Union but 'reluctantly' backs leaving the European Court of Human Rights because it is a 'very ideological court'. In his words, it has 'given itself a roving brief over large parts of the whole range of social policy in respects which are not covered by the Convention'.[13] He continues, 'If you have an institution which ignores the limited mandates given to it by the states and cuts across the demarcation lines of responsibility essential to a democracy, I think that you should pause and ask yourself whether this is a sensible way to behave.'

Two broad lessons must be drawn from this. Firstly, that international organisations are not intrinsically helpful when it comes to maximally benefitting the cause of liberal freedoms worldwide. Courts or international agreements may be outdated or have run roughshod over their mandate. This weakens them, as their jurisdiction is made increasingly artificial and gives demagogic leaders more substance with which to overthrow them. International courts may indeed be populated by judges from the very states which are most concerned with undermining the international legal order. Second, and by corollary, there is a significant difference between the liberal opposition to a court going beyond its brief and the opposition to the rules-based international order common in countries from Hungary to Putin's Russia. The golden thread linking Xi's China, Russia and the populist right in eastern Europe and beyond is the argument that, in some way, liberalism is decadent. This idea again is voiced in Carl Schmitt's fascist critique of liberalism. This view spreads directly into a perspective on both shared international rules and their basis. Part of the critique is that the liberal order was really only liberal for the powerful who were set to benefit; the other part was the naked self-interests of states such as China and Russia; and finally the somewhat incoherent ideology of many populist movements and ideologies. This suggests that the rejection of the current order is multi-faceted, and builds off real dissatisfaction, rather than being the presentation of a clear alternative. This separates Putin's Russia from Xi's China in many ways (both domestically and internationally), with the latter being a serious player that builds alternatives from the mitigation and avoidance of excessive global warming, as well as rival frameworks of foreign direct investment.[14]

One thing that marks the post-1945 order is it is essentially not coercive.[15] Yes, the dominant powers have at times abused their position, but unlike previous systems it is not a product of power. The Roman Empire imposed a form of order, but it rested on the military power of Rome to maintain. The 1815 Congress of Vienna created an order in Europe that largely lasted a century. That settlement, brokered after the Napoleonic Wars, re-established monarchical rule and a balance of power designed to prevent revolution and maintain stability through the concert of great powers. But any breaches of it, most notably in 1848–9, were dealt with militarily and with great brutality. The emergence of Germany and Italy could be absorbed, but the emergence of significant social change was to be suppressed. The systems proposed by Xi, Putin and the populists are, in their different ways, an attempt to re-impose this model of agreement by coercion. There is no doubt that China uses its Belt and Road Initiative to impose compliance on those who enter into it.[16]

The fraying of a global order has given more importance to regional bodies. Internally, the EU is highly successful and the GCC always has the advantage of substantial wealth, but other groupings, such as ASEAN and the African Union, remain relatively weak and fragmented.

More than China, Russia sits at the core of any move to dismantle the current international order.[17] It has adopted a zero-sum global view in which the disintegration of the current liberal order is an essential precondition for acquiring what it sees as its natural place in the world. In some ways, there is a depressing logic behind this: under Putin, the Russian economy cannot act as a springboard to conventional international influence (in the way it can for the GCC, say) and this also makes conventional attempts to reach compromise solutions (even before the invasion of the Ukraine) relatively pointless.[18] Russia is now fully committed to a process of destabilisation at the core of its state policy – and Russia's talking points are reliably repeated by the populist right.[19]

Also instructive is the case of smaller nations around the world and their need for, or opposition to, the rules-based liberal order. While free people, free elections and free markets have been shown to drive growth, innovation and equality, it does not follow that all rulers are better off. As such, corrupt states prefer the ease of extraction of wealth. Overturning the US-led legal order will entrench the power of corrupt rulers and their advantage at the top of their societies, even if it does keep them poorer. But smaller states, for instance Singapore, benefit so enormously from security and trade access secured under the status quo that they back Ukraine despite having deep and mutually beneficial relations with Russia. The UK must learn that we are a small actor, much like Singapore, that cannot afford the legal order to be jeopardised.

*   *   *

Key to supporting the rules-based order is to back those nations and populations that are victims of any violations to the order. Presently, that means backing Ukraine economically and logistically and targeting Russian actors to the fullest extent permissible under the law. It means ensuring that genocides in Tigray and Myanmar do not go unpunished, and that even our allies like Israel are investigated for the use of excessive force in the presence of civilians. This role for the UK will be different to the role we were once able to play, as successive strategic reviews have found that the UK is not strategically or even operationally independent of the US.

We in Britain would struggle in a conventional combined-arms war if we were to fight it alone. We lack sufficient tanks, fighter planes and military personnel. This is, of course, a frightening prospect, but our position is not altogether unintentional. The UK sees its hard power as situated within the context of NATO and as an extension of US hard power. We have a key role in certain areas of military deployment – with key specialisation in reconnaissance and cyberwarfare – and we have pioneering aerospace development. Developing these key competences is our specialised offering to NATO and secures our long-term utility on deployment.

Supporting the rules-based order means identifying and investing in these key military technologies and fortifying hard power. When it comes to backing Ukraine, and any future nation targeted by the authoritarian states, the UK must aim to provide the quality and quantity of military support where it has key specialisms.

While we have discussed those circumstances where advisory judgments can be ignored, a key performative requirement to strengthen the rules-based order is to abide by its rules ourselves. A rules-based system must be legitimate; the powerful that gain from its existence must also abide by it. In this sense, as in so many others, the US–UK invasion of Iraq casts a long shadow. It must also be championed: a rules-based system did not emerge by accident and will not be sustained by indifference. It is here that the UK – as a G7 power outside any of the main power blocks of the US, the EU or China – perhaps has a unique role that can be specialised to make ourselves as useful as possible to our allies. This opportunity, however, comes with a risk, as we are exposed to the ebbing fortunes of both NATO and the G7 as the US pivots east.[20]

The EU remains a fundamentally rules-based organisation, although, as discussed, it would be a mistake to assume that all internationalism is necessarily supportive of a democratic and free international order. While detailed considerations of this topic are beyond the scope of this book, the EU at once ardently defends key international legal norms while also hitting developing nations with high tariffs and obstructive regulatory barriers to trade. This protectionism is short-sighted and drives cooperation between developing nations and our strategic enemies, particularly in Africa and south Asia.

The relationship between China and the rules-based order could, of course, warrant its own book, and defies simple categorisation. China severely undermines economic rules. Its membership of the WTO could be listed as one of the most calamitous misjudgements the West has made since the end of the Cold War. Within China's business and political culture, rules and property rights are seen as obstacles to be manoeuvred around rather than boundaries to be respected, especially so when it comes to their own market and their own country. Perhaps as a hangover from their 'century of humiliation' from the beginning of the First Opium War to 1945, and perhaps as a straightforward product of their Sino-centric exceptionalist view of the world, China abhors being told what to do in its own house. They do not, at a social or state level, hold individual rights to be particularly important: their treatment of the Uyghurs demonstrates the humanitarian vacuum that can sometimes exist within CCP policy.

But there are many distinctions to be made between China and Russia. Demographically, both countries are in crisis and are at the peak of their military-age populations. But while Russia is irredentist, China is widely understood only to have concrete territorial ambitions in Taiwan and the South China Sea. Unlike Russia, China continues to benefit enormously from the rules-based international order. Indeed, the lip service they continue to pay to the rules, despite rampant IP theft and anti-competitive practices, is what allows them to continue to drive their export-led growth. They cerebrally denounce the rules-based order as American imperialism. Yet they benefit from the rules being there by undercutting the West, which is effectively competing with one arm tied behind its back. They benefit from peace and stability, and they rely completely on the global markets for their goods. As such, to coin a phrase, China is in some respects a fair-weather enemy. When the chips are really down, and Chinese prosperity is at stake, they are not as interested in exporting authoritarianism as Russia is.

When I say 'undercutting the West', that of course includes cut-price, carbon-intensive, low-regulation, mass-produced goods entering Western markets, often under *de minimis* rules. But it also includes cyberespionage and stealing US and UK academic and industrial research. It also includes collecting masses of data on private citizens and subsidising strategic goods exports to make Western production uneconomic, particularly in steel. In this view, China is willing to behave badly when it is in its own interests and especially when it concerns its own territory. Concerns about Taiwan are, therefore, absolutely justified. China is a fundamentally more capable state than Russia but has considerably more to lose from instability. Their interests are often aligned, but not always. Key to the UK's role as a separate actor to the US and EU is to understand the different threat these two authoritarian regimes present.

The American commitment to protecting the global rules-based order is weakened and may weaken still further during this second Trump Presidency. The doctrine of America First is not the only change, however. The US also carries the taint of some of its more self-serving actions from the Cold War era; it has a legacy of hiding self-interest behind global rules (and now, in any case, it has a large isolationist political movement). It can (or at least believes it can) afford to let the rules-based order run into peril. Meanwhile, the EU is often focused on internal matters and economics in international relations and is seldom a coherent geopolitical actor. This creates a role for the UK, either in specific policy areas or as a mode of interaction, to leverage influence and build international coalitions where feasible.

In the latter sense, international relations are still essentially at a state–state level with groups like the EU attempting, with some success, to be a coherent state actor and institutions such as the UN as a facilitator. In some fields, particularly around the COP process, there has been increasing access for what could be seen as non-state actors. These range from distinct polities within states (major cities or specific territories) to lobbying organisations (acting on behalf of existing interests), pressure groups and NGOs. If the concerns about legitimacy of the rules-based system are to be addressed, acting to broaden the range of participants is one tool – and one that fits the UK well. It has the capacity to bring any of three devolved governments into a system. So, on discussions about policy for the North Atlantic or the Arctic, for example, it may make sense to promote a voice for the Scottish government. On the practicalities of trade arrangements with the EU, the Northern Irish assembly may be a powerful voice as it is often more directly engaged than the UK government. Equally, the 2019 COP in Glasgow was seen to be successful, in part because the UK government, as host, promoted a plurality of voices.[21]

In effect, the need for integrated, legally enforced action is as strong now as it was in 1945. The climate transition demands this; the refugee crisis will not be solved by national borders, no matter how well policed; Covid was a brutal reminder that health challenges can move across borders; and terrorism remains a significant problem, as does the risk of further nuclear proliferation. The UN remains compromised by Russian and Chinese membership of the Security Council; the EU by the simple fact that different states have different priorities while NATO is undermined by states not committing the required 2 per cent of GDP. It quickly becomes clear that, with the US in retreat, hope for coherent global advocacy for the legal order rests with the UK and the CANZUK nations.

This leaves substantial scope for us to craft issue-based alliances, and there are suitable bodies within which to do so. The G20 holds 85 per cent of the world's economy, and, like the Commonwealth, captures a wide range of potential actors, ranging from India and Brazil to the US. Equally, bilateral deals still matter: the US–China negotiations in 2014 are widely held to have been crucial to wider agreement at the Paris 2015 COP discussions.[22]

The potential for more integration and cooperation between CANZUK nations is important and exciting. While political to-ing and fro-ing in each of the four nations has prevented a full alignment, all four have been among the most stable democracies in the world. They have each remained committed to climate change policy, and all except New Zealand have direct national interest in a reform of the global asylum rules. The UK is the historical and economic leader among the CANZUK nations and must take the first step in establishing a distinct common foreign policy direction and in defining how close a political relationship the four nations can feasibly have. While the details are beyond the scope of this book, it is worth elucidating two key pillars which must *not* be present in this new association.

First, there must not be a common court between the four nations. Each must retain legal autonomy in order to engage in world legal affairs unencumbered. They should instead engage with the international order individually but with aligned policy, as third nations also would. This is, after all, the key offering of CANZUK against the background of a retreating US and an EU that has legally sequestered itself. To build up yet another legal bloc would further segment the world rather than offering leadership to bring it back together. Second, it must not contain any economic text that involves the creation of a common customs territory, since this would necessitate either a common trade policy or a hefty series of mitigations and exceptions. The justification is that, again, each nation is intended to support the global legal order. Any reform of the WTO must come from nations that have a seat at that table rather than sharing a seat as a customs bloc.

The UK has a great deal to offer when it comes to dealing with Russia, though it cannot act alone. NATO exists separately to the legal norms that govern international relations and acts as their military vanguard under the clear leadership of the US. With the second Trump term, experts and analysts in London and Moscow alike will be asking the same question: to what extent is the US about to withdraw its support from Ukraine? Can Europe possibly achieve a strategic win by continuing in its absence? Figures including John Bolton, who held the first Trump administration in a more conventional foreign policy posture, are no longer in a position to influence the new administration. At the time of writing, it continues to appear that Trump's priority is to end the war and secure mineral rights in the region for the US. He rejects at face value the idea that allowing Russia to win would damage respect for the legal norms internationally. Failing that, he rejects that damage to international norms is a problem for the US: he believes America can survive without them.

Without attempting to anticipate the actions of a fundamentally unpredictable leader, there are some elements to the conflict in Ukraine, particularly regarding the respect for international legal norms, that will likely remain constant. First is that Trump's peace-making style will continue to involve going over Ukraine's head. The US pivot from China – something a succession of US leaders have been promising to do for at least twenty years – has thrown up supply chain issues for rare earth metals, in which Ukraine is rich. It seems likely that Ukraine are being set up to lose the peace, whether or not they can win the war. The idea that the US will prefer to capitalise on Ukraine's resources alongside Russian firms rather than support Ukraine's war effort is less sustainable. Regarding international legal norms, we are again in the territory of the kind of interwar extractive treaties where victorious parties are imposing unfair terms upon those at war. This should make the international community deeply uncomfortable – enough to provoke strong criticism. Faced with no choice, President Zelensky is likely to go along with the minerals deal.

* * *

For Britain, a necessary first step will be to define our enemies. First, we must complete the proscription of the IRGC as a terrorist organisation and cement that Russia is a hostile nation.[23] This will commit Britain to what must be a conclusive vision for Iranian policy: supporting regime change with no countenance for terrorist forces operating with state sponsorship across borders. This should also involve defanging Russian propaganda outlets by alerting viewers to their relationship with the Russian state. Addressing the pervasiveness of Russian influence in our media would quickly result in a reframing of the public's views on Russia and, downstream of that, our politics. Australia, for example, put in place a series of laws to challenge Chinese disinformation in 2018.[24] This not only widened the definition of espionage, but also required those acting as lobbyists for foreign governments to openly register themselves as such. In so doing, it has shed light on undue foreign influence and started to tame it.

The same approach is sorely needed with Iran. The IRGC and its proxies are dangerous and rejoice in criminal activity and sponsoring terrorism on a global scale, including in London.[25] Even public broadcasters like the BBC have done a poor job in reporting on this conflict, such that polarisation has been fuelled and has fed rampant anti-Western sentiment throughout Western nations. Pro-Iranian and pro-regime signage features prominently in marches and protests on the war in Gaza, and 'mistakes' in reporting echo Iranian propaganda.[26] While attempting to control the media is a medicine often worse than the disease, it is vital that guidelines are set up appropriately. The recent scandals involving the BBC manipulating footage of President Trump and giving voice to Hamas propaganda via its former BBC Arabic service and BBC World News proves this point.

A fair reporting of the facts does not mean giving a voice to talking points from the Iranian regime or treating statements from Hamas – a proscribed terror organisation – with reverence. Calls for an 'intifada' in the West, and violence against Israelis and Jews in Western cities, weakens nations and is partly traceable to the proliferation of Iranian state broadcasts through their many channels, including social media – a strategy known as guerilla broadcasting.[27] While obvious, it is not a trivial point that informing Western societies about who our real enemies are will make us more resilient to propaganda and more willing to spend resources upholding the international legal order against them. A media compromised by high-minded cosmopolitanism is not fit to identify state enemies since it has no concept of 'us and them' in the context of the international liberal order; it cannot identify which groups are pushing to bring about a new authoritarian global order and which groups protect it. It sees only victims and perpetrators.

In the most expansive sense, to protect this global order is to rebuild respect for the body of law that governs sovereign nations. In many cases, as with refugee law, it may be necessary to weaken language in order to ensure compliance. Attempting to stick to language (or rather, reinterpretations of it) written more than half a century ago is driving away cooperation. We need to reinvest in global institutions including the WTO, to offer our market access more freely to those who follow the rules and close it more robustly to those who do not. At the macro scale, the unipolar world dominated by the US is in its final years. As such, the payoffs to cooperating with the legal order established and hitherto maintained by the US are decreasing.

One area of international law with significant importance for Britain is nuclear non-proliferation. One of the central dilemmas of the modern order concerns the erosion of arms-control regimes. The collapse of long-standing agreements and the revival of great power nuclear competition have placed unprecedented strain on the non-proliferation system. Russia and China are expanding their stockpiles and diversifying delivery systems, while new aspirants such as Iran and North Korea continue to defy international censure. In such an environment, Britain's traditional restraint risks appearing naive rather than virtuous. The Strategic Defence Review argues for the creation of an independent tactical nuclear deterrent – an argument this book endorses.

Any move towards a British tactical nuclear capability would, of course, raise questions about compliance with the spirit of the Non-Proliferation Treaty. Britain remains legally entitled, as one of the treaty's recognised nuclear states, to modernise its arsenal, yet it has long taken pride in gradual disarmament. Renewed development would test that reputation and could invite criticism that London is fuelling a new arms race. Still, there is an argument – rooted in realism rather than idealism – that maintaining deterrence may be the most effective way to preserve peace and, ultimately, the institutions that safeguard it. When autocratic powers, most recently Russia, openly threaten nuclear use, refusing to adapt out of legal fastidiousness may in fact hasten the collapse of those very norms.

If Britain proceeds down this path, it must do so transparently and in tandem with renewed diplomatic leadership on arms control. The message should be clear: a limited tactical capability is not a repudiation of non-proliferation but a necessary response to its breakdown. By coupling deterrent renewal with intensified advocacy for responsible nuclear stewardship, Britain can reconcile its moral authority with the demands of security. The task is to adapt the rules without abandoning them, with a balance of pragmatism and principle, towards a compromised reduction in the scope of the international legal order so that it remains agreeable and workable to the largest possible number of nations.

Making cooperation compelling for a country of Britain's size means orientating domestic and trade policy to make Britain a home for global finance and a customer for global products. It also means choosing our battles in line with a coherent sense of our own national interest. When the US and the UK failed to enforce the law in Syria regarding the use of chemical weapons, the effects of that destabilisation – and the entrenchment of the belief that legal norms no longer applied – lasted a full decade. To pick our battles means to identify which elements of the international legal order sustain peace, democracy and trade, and which ones under-mine them or can be exploited by our enemies. We need not be prescriptive, except to say that Britain must reopen the case at the international level.

In Chapter 10, we will give a full assessment of our soft-power strategy. Britain has inherited sources of cultural, legal, moral and intellectual influence more profound than any country on earth be-sides the US. Yet these many sources do not automatically work to-gether to make countries wish to cooperate with us when it comes to supporting the rules-based international order. There must, in brief, be intentionality and design if we are to exert influence. We must have a doctrine that leverages unrelated sources of influence – from language to law, ideas to innovation – to push in the same direction to bring about our desired outcomes. We cannot expect disparate sources of soft power to negotiate for us: we must organ-ise them and deploy them to secure our interests. That doctrine, the Knowledge Power Doctrine (discussed in the final chapter), has a role to play in bringing countries back into the international legal order.

The costs of cooperating – including on climate change and ref-ugee law, on sanctions against Russia and on refusing authoritarian investment – are increasing. Success will require increasing the payoffs of cooperation while decreasing the costs. In short, we must make it easier for nations to do the right thing. This ties together our need to innovate new finance, to pioneer new technology in key growth areas, to help reform refugee law and to invest in specialised military capabilities which remain critical to our partners. Global Britain must be the essence of this strategy writ large, and key to this is the subject of international trade, to which we'll turn now.

CHAPTER 6

INTERNATIONAL TRADE

Britain must leverage its market to encourage global cooperation on issues from climate change to security partnerships.
We are seeing the emergence of a world in which carrots and sticks
are tempting third nations into the authoritarian orbit of our new
rivals. Access to Western markets, still the wealthiest in the world,
is mutually beneficial, but should now be given on condition of
cooperation with British and democratic goals. Moreover, trade is a
crucial tool for making our GDP stretch further. We can specialise,
trade and consume more than we would be able to do without free
and expansive trade.

Beneath the top-level discussions about trade rules is a strategic
battle over the setting of rules and norms in the most innovative and
promising industries of the future. There are some industries where
Britain is poised to become a major player, and where regulatory
influence will be valuable in helping our firms gain a competitive
advantage while securing reasonable protection for the consumer
or the environment. Nuclear fusion power and financial regulation stand out as two such industries. Elsewhere, in areas where
the opportunities are less compelling for Britain specifically and

where the logic of influencing global standards is less sound, we should not overlook the advantages of being an open 'rule-taker', by recognising EU, US and any other trustworthy developed nation's standard as being acceptable in the UK. International trade, including our network of free trade agreements (FTAs), gives post-Brexit Britain unrivalled flexibility and access which we can use to become as open as possible when it suits us. Trade, and the laws and regulations that govern it, present Britain with immense opportunities to influence, grow and secure key strategic interests.

*　*　*

As a species, we are richer and better off today than at any point in history. Indeed, our prosperity far exceeds even the wildest dreams of most humans who have ever lived. Yet the British political zeitgeist rejects the mechanism that has brought us this unprecedented prosperity: market capitalism and free trade. No matter how successful free trade has been, however, the unfortunate fact is that the system is so deeply counterintuitive. Our mammalian brains are hardwired for self-sufficiency and stockpiling and we deeply distrust (or, in most cases, fail to even *understand*) the 'invisible hand'. Hierarchy and autocracy are a reflexive form of government for our species: we demand the control and reassurance that free trade is far too decentralised to give. There is certainly a story to be told regarding why free trade as an economic and moral imperative is still deeply unpopular, despite living in a monument to its achievement.

In any event, the UK remains one of the most valuable economies in the world and a highly attractive partner for FTAs. Yet free trade itself is increasingly unpopular, both domestically and globally. This trend has been exacerbated by China's accession to the WTO, a move which, alongside the accession of India, has contributed to the stagnation of meaningful WTO reform. Over the past two decades, efforts to update global trade rules have stalled, leaving no effective institutional response to the rise of non-tariff barriers or the widespread use of Chinese dumping practices.

Brexit is one of the most significant alterations in British trading and foreign policy in the last century. We no longer belong to a protectionist trade bloc which seeks to maintain higher prices for producers through the exclusion of goods from the East and Global South, as well as from the US. Simultaneously, we no longer belong to one of the rule-making blocs, and trade rules, standards or legal structures which we create may push up prices more than standards implemented at a continental scale. It is not my intention to rehearse the problems and opportunities caused by Brexit but instead to look for ways the UK can craft an optimal foreign policy in light of it.

We have noted that there are fields – from finance to nuclear fusion – where the UK can have real global influence through the creation of networks that suit our global standing. Our trade in services is among the most advanced and valuable in the world, and the City of London, along with our legal firms and consultancies, have sculpted industries the world over in their own British image through law and self-regulation. Especially in the US and across the Commonwealth, British commercial and legal practices have been widely adopted. As discussed in the third chapter of this book, British best practice could afford us the opportunity to institute changes to legal and banking services in the fields of AML and climate finance. We also remain the most popular destination for foreign legal cases to find their resolution, as companies located as far away as Singapore and Hong Kong seek resolution in British courts, whose judgments then hold significant legal and academic weight across the world.

However, trade in goods is one of those areas where the UK has no real regulatory power projection. Even within the EU, it was far from common that British standards would become continental ones. If we could not arrange the standards we wanted as a leading member of Europe's regional bloc, there is no prospect at all of us exporting standards or frameworks to any developed country when it comes to trade in goods as 'global Britain'. This does not mean that the UK is not able to create its own standards.[1] Rather, it means simply that we should abandon hope of influencing the regulatory environment in other states. The EU's single market remains the largest slice of international trade in services – something the UK specialises in – so any substantive trade frictions will impact UK service exports.

The elephant in the room is Trump's tariffs. From a British perspective, Trump's 25 per cent tariffs on imported cars represented a serious risk: the US accounts for 27 per cent of the value of Britain's car exports. The early UK–US deal has not undone all the risks from these tariffs. British-made vehicles (often higher-end models like Jaguars and Bentleys) were especially vulnerable to being priced out of the US market. This not only threatened jobs and investment in UK manufacturing but also appeared to narrow the country's post-Brexit trade prospects at a time when diversifying beyond the EU is a strategic priority. The deal struck with the US solved the acute worries: in the short run, the worst thing Britain could do is start to engage in tit-for-tat tariff wars of its own. While protectionism harms the imposing country in the long run, the political pressures driving it can force partners into retaliatory measures that are economically damaging to all.

The UK had an opportunity to position itself as a voice of restraint and pragmatism and it took it well. Strategically, Britain demonstrated global leadership in resisting protectionism and promoting open, rules-based trade. By taking the initiative, the UK can protect its own economic interests, strengthen ties with its most important trading partner and model a trade posture that is both realistic and principled in an era of rising economic nationalism.

Rising above the instability of current events, Trump's tariffs, though enormous in scale and global scope, are part of a global decline in openness to trade which has been ongoing since around 2012. From that year onwards, the number of rules and acts, on a global level, that sought to reduce trade barriers began to be outnumbered by those seeking to erect them. Protectionism was already entrenched in Beijing, Brussels and New Delhi years before it was loudly adopted in Washington. Ironically, by bringing the trading system to its knees and then doing a partial backtrack on the changes, Trump has made global trade more popular than ever among his political enemies. Erstwhile allies like Elon Musk were ultimately unable to stomach the damage.

* * *

A core element of British trade policy decision-making regards regulatory divergence. At the highest possible level, all states with independent customs policy have production standards within which its producers must operate, and a set of safety standards which all products must meet, including those imported from abroad. Having identical standards to one's neighbour minimises the frictions and costs associated with international trade with that neighbour. But it is not the only way to minimise frictions. Mutual recognition of standards – declaring that whatever is good enough, say, for Europe, the US or Australia is also good enough for us – means that we can accept foreign standards as being equivalent to our own and reduce trade frictions that way. Mutual recognition of standards is a superior strategy for Britain, not least because there is more than one potential trading partner in the world.

There is, unfortunately, a certain tendency among politicians to veer towards simplistic interpretations of regulatory divergence. UK regulatory divergence since Brexit's formal completion in 2020 has been significant in some areas. The Financial Services and Markets Act 2023 is most instructive as an example. The Act put into practice the outcomes of the Future Regulatory Framework Review, giving a further competitive and innovative advantage to UK firms in the sector. The UK market had already been significantly more dynamic than continental counterparts, particularly on fintech (financial technology) and new digital banking, with companies like Revolut and Monzo. While in theory, access into the EU's market is now negotiated via mutual equivalence (which can be withdrawn) and is reliant on maintaining regulatory alignment, the reality is that the UK can and has diverged significantly. Substantive trade frictions *do* exist, but it is wrong to assume that divergence will always result in trade friction.

We have not followed the EU into their Digital Services Act, have made our own Data Reform Bill and have made provisions to allow for self-driving cars on our roads, for instance. But we have stayed in alignment where it suits us, including determining that European Economic Area (EEA) regulation of investment funds is equivalent to our own, allowing EEA-based investment funds to access the UK market on the same terms as pre-Brexit. Without getting lost in the detail, new UK regulation – for instance the

Digital Markets, Competition and Consumer Bill – goes *further* than EU regulation in many aspects of market and trade regulation, in this case by introducing measures against fake online reviews and against misleading 'drip pricing'.[2] As we have discussed, in May 2025, Starmer completed a rather unfortunate negotiation with the EU as part of a 'reset' of relations. This involved a pivot away from mutual recognition and requires adopting on a rolling basis whatever SPS rules the EU should create.

This is an inferior position in more ways than one. First, EU SPS rules are designed to perform a protectionist function. That is not compatible with Britain's economic and geostrategic direction as a trading nation (and a net exporter of services and importer of goods). Second, it makes it more difficult to agree trade agreements with other nations, because we cannot make commitments about our own rules, since we no longer control them. Trade disputes between Britain and a third country from outside Europe could, quite bizarrely, have their SPS case settled in a European court.

One might imagine that, given the UK has less influence in the regulation of goods, we would have diverged *less* in these areas than on services. However, this would be to forget that the EU's trade and customs rules were and are largely designed to prevent foreign goods, particularly agricultural ones, from reaching the EU market. We have made it easier to use UKCA marking, the mandatory mark that confirms that certain products conform to Great Britain's regulations (I say Great Britain because, of course, Northern Ireland to a significant extent remains inside the EU's regulatory sphere). We have also refrained from following the EU in announcing new restrictions on chemical usage and have lifted barriers, including those against Japan, which were introduced following the nuclear power plant disaster at Fukushima Daiichi in

2011. We have not followed EU requirements to introduce a 'right to repair' for electrical goods sold, nor have we adopted their (rather damaging) anti-deforestation regulation. To reiterate, Britain absolutely can and does diverge. There are costs and benefits to doing so, with efficiency being the most common benefit and market frictions being the most common cost, since many markets will often use differences in regulation as a non-tariff barrier. Starmer's commitment to align on SPS is therefore of real consequence. It reduces our capacity to act in these kinds of ways to prevent the over-regulation of our market.

In theory, the WTO can prevent this becoming a form of market protection, but the relevant disputes procedure is slow and flawed.[3] This leads many to believe that Britain's best post-Brexit route is to shelter beneath the regulations of a larger bloc. But this is emphatically the wrong approach. The UK can, has and will continue to diverge from the EU, but has maintained closer trade access than any nation except Switzerland. This approach would also ignore two important dynamics in international trade. The first is that divergence can be in the form of wider mutual recognition. For instance, the UK Medicines and Healthcare Products Regulatory Agency (MHRA) has recognised not just the EU standards as equivalent to their own, but also those of Australia, Canada, Japan, Switzerland, Singapore and the US. This means medicines approved for use in these trusted nations are automatically approved for use here. The second is a corollary of this: while to *export* to the EU requires meeting their production and safety standards, to import from them clearly does not. Even if we were to diverge so far from EU rules on a certain good that they no longer consider our standards equivalent, there is nothing stopping producers from meeting those standards anyway to continue access to the EU market. If they find greater opportunities ignoring EU rules and exporting elsewhere, then the deregulation has succeeded. It is, on this view, a fallacy to believe that divergence decreases trade access.

The key for the UK, then, having abandoned any pretences of being a leading rule-maker in the trade of physical goods, is to diverge strategically in those areas where we have key advantages in which to specialise. We can and should recognise trusted foreign standards to ensure cheaper and frictionless imports from overseas, and we should not be afraid to remove costly or burdensome regulation on our producers, since if the benefits of market access outweigh the benefits of deregulation, then industry will continue to comply with foreign standards.

*   *   *

The UK has traditionally been an open economy with a long-standing trade deficit, importing far more than it exports. It formally ceased being a member of the EU's single market and customs union on 31 December 2020, with its open access being replaced by the UK–EU TCA.[4] While there are substantial problems in calculating such flows, the EU reports that UK service exports have grown since 2021. They may have grown more significantly had the UK remained fully within the EU market, but this trend shows that at the very least UK exports have, after a period of painful adjustment, continued to grow.

Any UK strategy will have to involve nurturing and continuing to allow innovation to flourish in the City of London. The financial sector is already, and must remain, a vital source of fiscal revenue, employment and global influence. But the over-reliance on the City of London has, some argue, distorted the UK economy since the early 1980s. If the UK is to rely on it to offset other weaknesses in its international trading position, then governments will find themselves under more pressure to pander to its demands and pick up the pieces when regulation fails. The bailout following the 2008 financial crisis – when the banks were prevented from failing – casts a long shadow. One of the most important features of the City has long been its capacity for self-regulation among competitors; a growing school of thought holds that a greater capacity for innovative and risk-taking behaviour, invigorated by a revamped regulatory regime, would help the UK compete with financial centres in the US and Asia.[5] Separately, the UK's stock market, the London Stock Exchange, and its FTSE index have a lower capitalisation than rival exchanges in France, Canada and Australia as a percentage of GDP.

The UK has separate ambitions to drive free trade access for its exports and drive cheaper imports, but also to push investment in key climate technologies and push forward new financial products to the world. Britain should aim to retain its position as a major capital market for the world. We remained the world's biggest exporter of financial services in the two years after leaving the EU, although our market share is declining. Our own pension fund providers find themselves allocating savers' capital to investments outside the UK, due to low rates of return. It's a problem that goes beyond Brexit: it's one that speaks to an overall contraction in entrepreneurialism and risk-taking. Each year, more British businesses are relocating to the US, and new listings of British-born start-ups also find themselves being listed overseas for a more ambitious capital-raising market and more competitive tax environment.

How best to combat this pernicious risk-aversion and over-regulation – particularly of pension funds – is a question complicated by the long legacy of the 2008 financial crisis. High taxes and rules on bankers' pay are unfortunate and, most recently in the case of private equity, have proved incredibly destructive to the UK's financial sector. The fateful decision to bail out the banks has cast the financial sector as a leech on the public finances. Although it is the single largest contributor, the fact cannot be avoided that taxpayers' money bailed banks out of their own reckless decisions, and that most of the people who made those decisions made it out rich. It is important that the British government does not do this again. An ambitious and risk-taking financial sector cannot be allowed to expect government bailouts, or else innovation and strategy will give way to recklessness. No other area of British economic policy is more important than that of our financial sector: placing it front and centre as the first key pillar of our economic model, and moving on from the moral hangover of 2008, is crucial for our long-term success. Getting it right will facilitate advances in climate finance and leadership in particular specialised technologies, as well as driving signatures on more FTAs and improving our reach when it comes to tackling extractive financial crime from authoritarian regimes. It will also secure our fiscal future for our foreign policy and aid objectives.

The second key pillar must be principled and expansive free trade policy. The FTAs of old are being replicated, as with countries like Mexico and Morocco, or revamped in the case of countries like Japan, Switzerland and Australia. These new deals approach what are referred to as DTAs, deep trade agreements, which not only include services but also address non-tariff barriers including air travel, legal and educational recognition of qualifications and more. The continued improvement of our FTAs delivers more benefit than first analysis reveals. For instance, the UK's new

Australia FTA was projected to increase GDP by just 0.08 per cent per annum. First, this disguises the lower prices and higher quality made possible by importing foreign goods, since Australian production and British consumption does not contribute to GDP figures, but meaningfully improves our standards of living. Second, it is calculated pessimistically, simply by evaluating the cost of the current tariffs and stating the benefit of the policy is the cost saved by avoiding tariffs, indexed against static growth forecasts. However, trade does not really work this way. A small improvement in the terms of trade can make certain enterprises viable that previously were not. Previous high tariffs and tariff-rate quotas inherited from the EU on Australian beef are gone: this meaningfully increases the viability of Australian beef in our market, and our products in their market, which over time will shift entire supply chains to benefit from lower costs and higher diversification. Legal and educational changes will make new British offices in Australia suddenly more logistically and legally feasible.

In short, the goal of an FTA is not just to make current trade cheaper, but to make entirely new and valuable supply chains viable. That the UK government takes no account of this when forecasting (and indeed, almost *no* government forecasts dynamic changes in decision-making to reflect new profitability) means that the impact of FTAs and other liberalising policy changes are always structurally underestimated with a bias towards the status quo.

* * *

Britain remains one of the most valuable economies in the world and a more-than-worthwhile partner for an FTA. The problem, as discussed above, is that free trade is not a popular doctrine. The situation has been worsened by the influence of China following its admittance into the WTO. Together with India, it has been instrumental in preventing any meaningful developments at the WTO in the last two decades, meaning that no institutional response from international organisations has yet been implemented for the changing nature of non-tariff and tariff barriers, nor of the proliferation of Chinese dumping. Attempting to 'win' the argument over free trade is a lost cause.

The British politician and historian Lord Macaulay writes, 'Free trade, one of the greatest blessings which a government can confer on a people, is in almost every country unpopular.'[6] Yet Britain, quite peculiarly, has both major political factions united in their understanding that free trade brings prosperity and that protectionism reinforces the advantages of incumbent producers. This is a political opportunity to be taken advantage of, but not one which will be reciprocal among many of our negotiating partners. India and the US, in particular, offer enormous upsides for an FTA, but both will seek to extract their pound of flesh in terms of protectionist clauses. In a static sense, it of course makes sense to allow trade partners to exclude certain goods if it means dropping barriers across the board. But dynamically, it weakens the long-term negotiating position as other countries will consider they have a chance to secure exceptions of their own.

In particular, the initial negotiations for a UK–India FTA became muddied by insistence on visas for Indian businessmen and a refusal for India to take back several hundred thousand Indian citizens who have overstayed their tourist visas. Signing DTAs with Australia arguably emboldened India to make unreasonable requests. There is also the higher-level observation that India, after all, is not overly keen on free trade. The election of Donald Trump changes matters significantly: he is at once a protectionist (not unlike Joe Biden) but also a self-confessed friend of the UK. He flaunts his photographs with the Royal Family, embellishes his Scottish heritage and aligns his political project with the UK and its exit from the European Union. Signs suggest that he and Starmer, against the odds, share positive personal diplomacy. Trump's rather strange assertion that he was known in the UK as 'Mr Brexit' speaks to a long-standing sympathy for Brexit, at least in so far as he sees it as a socio-political rejection of centrism and embrace of an unabashed national project like his own. His 'Brexit' is by no means the same as the one we have discussed in this chapter – the Brexit of 'Global Britain' – nor is it even the Brexit of Nigel Farage. His conception of Brexit is a narrowly nationalistic one that rejects immigration.

This book rejects the idea that nationalism and isolationism is the solution to Britain's twenty-first-century woes. As Peggy Grande, former adviser to Ronald Reagan, claimed, Trump wants to see a 'successful Brexit' and so he spared the UK from his tariffs; not even Starmer could look a gift horse in the mouth a second time. In May 2025, Trump and Starmer signed the first UK–US trade deal since the Marshall Plan, but a full DTA is unlikely to follow. American professional associations are notoriously protectionist, and Trump would not be minded to cross them.

Over the coming months, side deals to make the UK–US FTA deeper and more expansive will continue behind the scenes. It has already produced a crucial breakthrough: alongside the trade deal, the two governments announced a landmark partnership covering civil nuclear energy, quantum technologies and aerospace collaboration, coupled with new frameworks to streamline customs procedures and align regulatory standards across advanced manufacturing and digital services. The UK–US Tech Prosperity Deal will help the UK technology and research and development sectors stay close to the only serious, free and democratic locus of innovation: the United States. It was a prerequisite for any serious British attempt to stake a claim to these crucial industries of the future, and as such, it is a very welcome development. In many respects, this agreement begins to realise several of the ambitions set out in this book, by reasserting the UK's role as an outward-looking, technologically driven economy, and pragmatically identifying those industries where the fullest possible alignment with the US will pay the highest dividend.

Several years ago, the Heritage Foundation, which commands considerable influence throughout the MAGA movement within the Republican Party, joined forces with British right and centre-right think tanks to hash out what an ideal DTA both for Theresa May's Conservatives and Trump's America would look like. In the end, it was May's (and briefly Boris Johnson's) hesitation to get into the detail of the agreement before formally leaving the EU that stopped it from becoming reality. Much would need to be changed from the original text (compiled by the Institute for Free Trade) to reflect Starmer's different political stance, but the core of the deal would not present problems for either country to accept. Starmer would probably insist on insulating the deal from the NHS and from blocking chlorinated chicken specifically, both of which have become tinderbox issues in the UK.

Expanding our new US deal must be a key goal of any UK government, but we must recognise that it runs contrary to the general trend of increasing American isolationism and has only re-emerged as both a necessity and possibility due to the unlikely return of Trump as President, compounded by his quirky internalised sense of British exceptionalism.

Britain's FTA strategy should involve revisiting the rollover deals agreed since our formal departure from the EU. Some of these details include tariff schedules that impose tariffs on goods that we don't actually produce, such as oranges (their inclusion is a hangover from the days when our tariff schedule was designed to protect the interests of southern European fruit production). We also have quotas for olive oil from producers like Morocco and Tunisia, despite having no capacity whatsoever to produce olive oil here. Even protectionism does not justify it, especially in light of very high consumer prices. These agreements should be replaced by full FTAs, to the great benefit of Moroccan and Tunisian exporters and to the great benefit of British consumers. Similar opportunities exist the world over, including through the potential expansion of CPTPP.

It is worth noting that the inclusion of services in such deals will mean enormous advantage for the British service sector, which will find that it is the only G7 nation routinely signing such deals for access to countries like Morocco. Interestingly, the other G7 nation to have a FTA deal with Morocco is the US itself (if Trump does not cancel it), although it does not afford the same access for educational and legal services that an updated UK deal would. At any rate, the UK will find great advantage for the City of London and for the UK as an accessible destination for foreign direct investment. There are, in short, great advantages to being one of the only G7 nations in the market buying goods tariff-free from developing countries, and gaining access for our services there.

One will notice a familiar pattern emerging here. As in previous chapters, the conclusion is again that Britain must specialise and work on incentive compatibility: to offer access to our market (particularly for those goods, from tomatoes and oranges to olive and palm oil, that we don't produce) in exchange for access to services.

* * *

The wider international trading environment is changing at a time when the WTO is slipping further into irrelevance.[7] It is undeniable that more and more states are turning their back on international trade, with some shifting to correct what they see as too much globalisation in domestic economies.[8] There is increased regionalism (such as in Africa), with regional organisations from ASEAN to AfCFTA stepping in to do the job that the WTO should rightly be doing.

The issue with the WTO revolves around several key failings. One is that China has been willing, quite simply, to accept any fines imposed upon it because they are too low to discourage breaking trade rules. While the US almost always wins their cases against China in court, by then, so to speak, the damage has been done. Many, including those who advised Donald Trump the first time he was elected, have proposed booting out nations which repeatedly breach WTO rules. The drawbacks, however, are that Chinese trade would be so severely impacted from their ejection that the entire world's supply chains would be affected.

The story would not be complete, however, without acknowledging that to some extent, the world had no choice but to admit China. US policy documents from the time show that the US was aware that China would likely fail to meet all of its WTO obligations, but others from the USTR (United States Trade Representative) seemed to take for granted that the system would work.[9] If nothing else, it is a testament to how confidence in international institutions has diminished so spectacularly in the last few years. If America continues on its current path, transitioning from an exceptional liberal pluralist power to a garden-variety self-interested great power, this will likely come to be seen as the decade which ushered in that change. Staying idle with respect to China and the WTO is not an option at all. But engaging in naive and simplistic posturing towards China is foolish.

China's leaders have a profoundly different conception of the state. They consider their country exceptional. China does not wish to consider itself dishonourable, and its leaders are primed to reject any notion that they are morally bound by the diplomatic creations of the US. Indeed, China is also increasingly shifting focus to drive domestic consumption and focus on expanding their own consumer base. Posturing against the Chinese over the last two decades has *not* significantly damaged China, but it *has* almost fatally wounded the WTO. This is especially true of Trump's interventions. Ideally the US would recommit to the WTO and push for the introduction of new disciplines alongside the current set of multilateral rules. But Biden wasn't ideologically minded to do this, and Trump certainly isn't. This is the sphere of international governance that Britain must find a strategy for.

*   *   *

Despite some signs that globalisation was again moving in the right direction, at least prior to Trump's tariffs, the big movements in international trade are now overwhelmingly negative.[10] Domestic spending in green technology has become a source of tension, with the US Inflation Reduction Act (triggering a state spend of $369 billion) becoming a focus for US–EU disputes. The EU has responded by adapting its own state aid rules and proposing its own 'Green Deal Industrial Plan'.[11] Equally, China's policy of subsidising the manufacture of electric cars has led to increasing trade tensions with the EU.[12] This is, of course, an area where the desire to meet climate goals runs straight into an old-fashioned trade dispute over domestic subsidies.

Encouragingly, it is a trade dispute that Britain has so far opted out of. From this perspective, the most important dynamic in terms of international trade regards relations with China and the stance China adopts. China now sits at the core of international trade; it is the largest partner for manufacturing trades for the EU, with this pattern repeated in other global regions.[13] The US may still be the biggest trade partner for most states if the focus is on services but, partly driven by US protectionism, some 70 per cent of states now trade more with China than the US. China's electric cars, for example, are subsidised by the Chinese taxpayer. The Chinese government have spent $5.4 billion to incentivise the production of 3.7 million cars, or almost $1,500 per vehicle.[14] Another study suggests $231 billion has been spent on Chinese subsidies for the EV industry.[15] Especially considering demand for vehicles continues to outstrip supply, and Britain imports some $40 billion of cars per year anyway, ensuring these vehicles are cheaper can only be a win. If that is the price of involvement in the subsidy race, Britain is right to duck this fight entirely. When it comes to the subsidy and industrial strategy side of international trade, Britain should, again, pick its specialties rather than attempting to go toe-to-toe with blocs with deeper pockets. In this case, it should also pocket subsidised goods paid for by foreign taxpayers. The transition to green and digital economies may lead to shifts in the relative importance of some traditional economies and trade routes, but this should not be as dramatically overstated as it sometimes is.

Efficiencies in long-distance shipping have flipped the script on 'eating local' due to the CO_2 produced in transport. Yet even before new green fuels began to power our container ships, it was still found that New Zealand lamb produces 2,000 kilograms *less* CO_2 per tonne than Welsh lamb, even when accounting for the food miles.[16] The same logic continues to apply that *production* produces more CO_2 and consumes more energy than transportation. To return to the example of Welsh lamb, slower growth rates in colder Welsh climates, higher fertiliser and feed use and the need to overwinter animals indoors all compound the carbon cost per kilogram of meat. By contrast, New Zealand's year-round pasture grazing, faster finishing times and lower input intensity mean that even after the long voyage to British ports, its lamb still carries a smaller overall carbon footprint. There is no sense in using energy, no matter how it is generated, to heat greenhouses in northern Europe in order to grow tomatoes and summer berries when they could be imported from southern Spain and Morocco, where artificial heating is not required.

A more realistic vision of how the green transition affects trade is by placing a much finer emphasis on those scarce resources, including lithium, cobalt, silver, uranium, plutonium and others, that will power present and future energy technologies. Trade will also reflect green outputs, not only green inputs. Morocco, due to its massively different weather to the UK, is one of the most efficient places in the world to place a solar panel; the UK has less than half the solar productivity of Morocco. One company, Xlinks First Ltd, is developing an enormous solar farm, the size of Greater London, which will be linked to the UK grid via an undersea cable thousands of miles long.[17] The sale of green energy will see money flow from the energy-poor but cash-rich northern hemisphere to the energy-rich Global South, just as we saw with oil investment in the Middle East and North Africa.

The current trend is for G7 nations to 'friendshore' production and supply chains away from China and its allies.[18] In key security sectors, this is starting to happen as the enthusiasm for Chinese investment drops away and security considerations take priority.[19] Returning to an overly optimistic era of China–UK cooperation, as Starmer seems intent to try, would be dangerous to our national security, would undermine our allies and serve the interests of an uncooperative, if not actively hostile, rival. Under the aegis of the WTO, coexistence with China will be feasible only if new disciplines can be added.[20]

The dispute settlement system has not functioned since the US blocked appointments in 2019. The US seems to have abandoned a global focus via the WTO (and its predecessors) in favour of other mechanisms such as the US–EU Trade and Technology Council, where the intention is to improve cooperation and coordination.[21] The focus is on laying the groundwork for agreement and dialogue around emerging disputes, rather than the traditional approach of creating detailed trade rules. Despite his wider isolationist intentions, Trump does not appear to want to interfere with this cooperation.

Considering these trends together, Britain has an opportunity to take advantage of the moves towards friendshoring and nearshoring without making the protectionist mistake that the EU and US are making. To pull this off, we should seek trade deals with countries underserved by Western competitors, like Morocco and those in Latin America and Africa, as well as a long-term plan to sign deals with Pakistan and Bangladesh to supplement that with India once political instability and corruption (in the case of Pakistan and Bangladesh) show concrete signs of improvement. In each case, Britain will be able to offer world-class services at a fraction of the cost of our competitors and generate significant foreign currency reserves with which to buy in foreign consumer goods and capital.

* * *

It has been suggested that Britain's historical role as an open, service-led economy means it can be important in shaping data governance. Quite clearly, e-commerce is of growing importance and, again, the WTO has failed to adapt to this change.[22] The new EU–Japan deal enshrines European rather than US norms around data privacy, at least in so far as it governs EU–Japanese data flows. While there could be a role for Britain to play in this area, it is not clear at all what we would seek to gain by seeking to export our approach to data management. Companies can very easily choose to domicile here if they wish to take advantage of our data laws (as many do to take advantage of our commercial law expertise, for example), but currently there is scarcely any reason for them to do so. We have not diverged significantly from the rather Luddite tech and data rules of the EU. As with other standards (excepting those on nuclear fusion and banking where we should seek to take a major market share), the best approach is a maximalist recognition of foreign data governance rules, in so far as they do a sufficient job guarding against privacy threats. There is no compelling case that attempting to set global standards on data rules is realistic for the UK.

It is worth exploring here what makes nuclear fusion power a key *regulatory* (as well as economic and environmental) opportunity for the UK, where data management is not. Anu Bradford's book on the power of the EU, *The Brussels Effect*, has done much to shape our modern understanding of power within democratic societies. States project power through regulatory capacity and market forces as well as through traditional means. A state's consumer base, for example, is used as leverage to bring about substantive productive changes overseas, where military force might once have been used.

That, in essence, is the litmus test for whether power is just for show, or whether it can be used to effect change abroad. So far, EU disputes with the US on digital law have not been particularly productive. The EU's desire to chart its own path and to centralise regulatory power (and project it extraterritorially) has earned it lawsuit victories against several US tech companies. But referees, as they say, do not win the game. This could only be considered a win if the process resulted in innovation, growth and opportunities for Europeans. The evidence still seems to suggest that almost all digital innovation comes from the US. If the regulatory power the EU has undoubtedly secured in digital law, such as GDPR rules, has *hampered* the digital economy, then that regulatory power fails to pass the litmus test as a useful alternative to hard power.

A second distinction must also be drawn. Nuclear fusion power, being actively developed at the Culham Centre for Fusion Energy and by private enterprises such as Tokamak Energy (both in Oxfordshire), requires hard and immovable capital investments. Data involves flows. Successful fusion regulation achieves *safety* but also a dominant market position, commercial export opportunities and contracts to bring technology overseas. In other words, the British fusion industry, and by extension British interests, would benefit enormously from being at the centre of decision-making on fusion power. The same is simply not true of data management. Successful data management regulation achieves safety (again) but also permits the maximal possible flow of data. The maximal possible flow of data is achieved by the maximal recognition of acceptable foreign standards, not by insisting upon one's own standards. This is why Britain must have a clear plan regarding international institutions. It must keep an eye on international trade and industry at all times, to ensure that we're not seeking power in international forums which can't easily be used to benefit us. Again, we must learn to identify those opportunities where regulatory leadership is appropriate and specialise in them.

French economist Frédéric Bastiat was the first to remark that 'when goods don't cross borders, soldiers will'. The peacekeeping power of trade cannot be ignored, as isolationism can breed poverty and grief. Short-term economic relief is traded for long-term instability regionally and globally. Getting trade right is key if we are to help develop the Global South, keeping it in our orbit while securing a world with fewer anti-Western grievances. Without offering the same opportunities for export-led growth that the West offered east Asia, we continue to face the growing prospect of violence spreading back home.

Money is power. Britain's refusal to specialise – to let those inefficient parts of its legacy fade away – is currently costing us our role in the industries of the future. Britain is therefore becoming poorer compared to other nations that understand that the future is built and not inherited. A trade policy that secures a high degree of access to both the US and the EU is crucial. The service-led and productive realities of our economy mean we are uniquely able to sign deals with developing countries without upsetting domestic production. One of the few silver linings to having very little low-skilled industry left is that trade with low-cost producers has very few 'losers'. A regulatory model will become appropriate in those industries where Britain can still carve out a competitive advantage for ourselves – and where we might still create and retain those high-value, high-export companies of the future.

CHAPTER 7

INTERNATIONAL TERRORISM AND STATE AGGRESSION

Terrorism is one of the greatest threats Britain and many other countries face. Britain's intelligence agencies are second to none, but politically, our leaders are asleep at the wheel. The relationship between international terrorism and state aggression is closer today than it was at any point in the twentieth century, and Britain must adapt to the new realities of terrorism as a tool of authoritarian regimes to destabilise liberal democracies. In the twenty-first century, states do not only suffer terrorist violence; they aid and abet it. The UK will seek to remain an active member of NATO, but the organisation itself is weakening, in part due to US decisions but also because the EU seeks to create a more robust foreign policy capability beyond NATO. In terms of terrorism, the UK has much to offer and much to gain from international cooperation, and how it uses this ability to help others could be a key indicator of how Britain comes to be seen in the wider world.

It is unlikely that hostile states such as Russia will take overt military action against a NATO member (tensions with Turkey over Syria being a different issue). Russian expertise in using hybrid warfare, including information warfare and state-sponsored terrorism, is used to undermine the main pillars of the Western economic, legal and military systems. Deep in our human psychology is a clamour for disciplined, authoritarian rule when we feel our safety is at risk; a fearful world is an authoritarian one. At its best, the UK can offer much to its allies in challenging this authoritarian threat; at its worst, its passivity is seen by some as enabling Putin's agendas. Indeed, combating terrorism and the exploitation of it by authoritarian powers starts with cultural change at home. In short, we must be willing to proscribe terror organisations even if they frame themselves as freedom fighters; something that cultural relativism inherent in postmodern thinking has made increasingly uncomfortable for Britain's leaders. This vulnerability produces the tactic known as 'salami slicing': using proxies and stopping just short of an escalation which would force weak leaders to respond. Confidence and clarity of purpose is essential, but it is currently scarce in most of Europe.

Combating international terrorism and its destabilising effects also requires a focus on regimes around the world which extract and embezzle government funds for their own private enrichment. The resultant loss of economic growth and rise of refugee movements matters profoundly to Britain's interests, as does the simple reality that failed states and their rotten money feed terrorism around the world. The universality of the threat of terror – common among almost all nations – makes it a fertile area within which to deepen international cooperation and draw in more engagement from the US. Britain must leverage its specialised strengths, particularly in finance and cybersecurity, to build resilience against economic warfare and disrupt the clandestine funding of terrorism. This includes reforming company law to eliminate anonymous corporate structures and improve transparency in financial transfers. With adversaries like Russia, the UK's trade diversification and sanctions must align with the strategic goal of eventual regime change. In contrast, relations with China require a more nuanced approach: disengage and divest on sensitive national security matters while remaining economically pragmatic. Strategic openness – such as accepting subsidised Chinese electric vehicles or engaging in climate cooperation – can offer leverage, particularly in encouraging US-led action on IP theft and cybercrime via multilateral institutions like the WTO.

Despite growing instability, the West's intelligence-sharing frameworks and defence cooperation remain robust, with initiatives like AUKUS signalling meaningful alignment. The UK's efforts to elevate issues of terrorism and hostile state actions at international bodies such as the UN and WTO not only reinforce global norms but also create diplomatic channels to sustain US engagement.

Counterterrorism is an area where the UK has much existing expertise, making it an important member of groups such as Five Eyes. To some extent, this expertise is something an independent UK should seek to offer as widely as possible so as to both help our allies and gain further experience. This chapter will consider the aggression demonstrated by the Russians, the Chinese and the Iranians towards the states and institutions they perceive to be a barrier to their goals. The threat from terrorism is not just measured in the risk to British citizens and the citizens of our allies. It is measured, perhaps primarily, in the influence that acts of terrorism have on our populations. The goal of terror is to weaken hearts and sow fear – the consequences of terrorism therefore permeate societies.

They damage democratic and social institutions, they harm public trust and often bolster support for irrational policies, including isolationism, that push politics to its extremes.

*　*　*

The UK currently faces persistent threats from both Islamist and far-right terrorism. While groups like ISIS and Al-Qaeda are no longer capable of large-scale attacks in Europe, they remain active in exploiting failed states, using extortion, smuggling and brutal violence to fund and expand their influence. Domestically, radicalisation continues via online platforms, often with transnational funding and ideological support. The far right similarly exploits digital channels and cryptocurrencies to finance their activities, with leaders like Tommy Robinson highlighting how foreign support and online anonymity enable destabilising actors. Cryptocurrencies have become a key vulnerability, offering unregulated, anonymous financial flows that are increasingly used to support terrorist and extremist networks.

To counter these threats, the UK must reinforce its strengths in intelligence sharing, counter-terror finance and international legal cooperation. This includes tightening company law, closing loopholes in overseas territories and improving regulation of cryptocurrencies. While there is some blockchain tracing capability, the current regulatory framework is insufficient to effectively disrupt terror finance. The UK should also press for realistic, collaborative action to reduce online radicalisation, but must be careful not to undermine free speech through overreach. A recalibrated balance is needed, one that defends national security without empowering censorship or chilling legitimate public discourse. Importantly, such an approach reflects the myriad ways that terrorism has changed since the twentieth century.

In the 1970s and 1980s, domestic terrorism in the UK was mostly connected to Irish republicanism. If there was a foreign power directly involved, it was Libya rather than the Soviet Union. The Libyan regime engaged in direct terrorism (the worst, of course, was the bombing of a US plane over Lockerbie) and re-armed the IRA, leading to a major upsurge in violence in the mid-1980s. Since then, there have been episodic attacks by the far right and since 2001, a sustained, if inchoate, sequence of attacks by Islamists inspired by Al-Qaeda and ISIS. These various strands have killed and maimed many, but at no stage have they posed a direct threat to the British state or broader social structures.

The same era also saw a well-defined and serious threat from the Soviet Union and its satellite states. There is no need here to rehearse arguments as to whether the Soviets intended to invade western Europe or whether they had the capacity to succeed, without recourse to nuclear weapons, if they did so. What was clear was that they had the capacity to *start* such an enterprise and, in response, there was a clear commitment to conventional military deterrence via NATO. Many column inches have been given to whether or not NATO had the means to stop the Soviets without resorting to nuclear weapons. Fortunately, this was never put to the test.

Now, however, NATO planners face a similar dilemma regarding Russia's growing arsenal of short-range nuclear weapons. Moscow's explicit threats to use low-yield 'battlefield' warheads in Ukraine have exposed a dangerous gap in Western deterrence. If an adversary can employ a limited nuclear strike to force political surrender without provoking full-scale retaliation, the logic of deterrence begins to unravel. Britain today possesses no non-strategic nuclear capability; its last tactical warheads were retired in the 1990s. The United States still maintains such weapons in Europe, but London's reliance on Washington to authorise their use means the United Kingdom lacks a truly autonomous deterrent below the strategic level. In an age of renewed authoritarian coercion, that absence is a serious vulnerability.

The latest Strategic Defence Review recognised this problem by calling for a 'full spectrum' deterrence posture and opening the door to re-examining shorter-range nuclear options. Such weapons would not replace the strategic deterrent at sea but would complement it by filling the credibility gap between conventional and intercontinental responses. A limited, low-yield capability – delivered by US-manufactured F35-A aircraft or cruise missile – could serve as a warning shot that Britain retains both the will and the means to respond proportionately to nuclear intimidation. In this sense, tactical nuclear weapons are less about actively fighting wars and more about preventing war through restored deterrence. In the context of rising authoritarian threats, reviving a modest tactical capability would strengthen NATO's deterrent coherence while ensuring Britain's voice can retain independence from the US – the only NATO power to maintain tactical nuclear options.

The sudden collapse of the Soviet Union after its well-ordered retreat from eastern Europe left a considerable vacuum.[1] Every member of NATO cut their military spending in the decade that followed. The UK had been spending around 5 per cent of its GDP on defence up to the mid-1980s, but this had dropped to 2.1 per cent by 2000. These cuts mainly fell on what can be termed conventional forces, due to the lack of a clear threat and ongoing debates about the purpose of the UK's armed forces and of alliances such as NATO. The 9/11 attacks on the US reinforced a view that conventional military forces were increasingly irrelevant in an era where likely threats were deadly, but scarcely warranted substantial numbers of tanks. At the same time, under Boris Yeltsin, the Russian Federation could not have offered a sustained threat even if it wanted to, and all the evidence suggested it was sincere in seeking partnership, not competition, with the West.[2]

We now face a very different world. As discussed earlier in this book, the climate emergency itself is a major security threat, destabilising nations and increasing the numbers of refugees. China has established itself as a serious conventional military power and, under Putin, Russia is now a committed threat to the West. Equally, in a development that would be scarcely believable pre-2014, Europe now has a major conventional war ongoing within its borders. In addition, while the threat of Islamist terrorism may be much reduced in western Europe, the perpetrators are certainly making sustained gains in Africa and parts of Asia.

If earlier chapters of this book suggested a downsized but specialised assessment of the UK's role, that is not really the case here. The UK may no longer be a great power and may no longer be able to field conventional forces in its own right, but it has much to offer its partners in the fields of security and wider defence issues.

* * *

The nature of non-state terrorism has changed over time, both in terms of underlying ideology and the tactics in use. It is useful to draw a distinction between a few key points. First, not all uses of violence by political movements can be described as terrorism. Second, while terrorism clearly has the capacity to kill and disrupt, it only rarely actually threatens a state. Third, there is a distinction between groups that use terrorism for very specific aims and those with a much wider focus.[3]

These dynamics tend to be repeated throughout modern history. The end of the nineteenth century saw the prevalence of leftist, usually anarchist, assassination attempts and Irish republican groups increasingly relying on bombs. The years leading up to the First World War were marked by a substantial degree of violence (even in the UK) connected with political groups and in relation to industrial disputes or land ownership. Irish republicanism had, by 1918, made the jump from terrorism to a generalised revolt that could indeed threaten the British state – or at least its hold on Ireland. If they had wished, the British government could have negotiated with Irish republicans over the future governance of Ireland, as the late Liberal Party had sought to do for decades (in the end, the government did so). It could settle industrial disputes; it could give crofters in Scotland some degree of security of tenure. In these cases, a shift of political stance also saw an end to violence. What was impractical and thus difficult to theorise was how to negotiate with the more amorphous, internationalised anarchist movement.

The end of the Second World War demonstrated the variety of forms non-state terrorism could take. The dominant form was connected to the various anti-imperialist struggles across the colonial empires held by European states. By the late 1950s, these had mostly precipitated the independence of those polities, with the principal exceptions of South Africa and Rhodesia, where colonial rule morphed into the local rule of a domestic population of whites, with a white supremacist legal rule behind them. By their nature, these struggles were local and mostly pragmatic. As some nations gained independence, they tended to offer support to their struggling neighbours. This meant the Algerian FLN was able to operate from independent Tunisia, and the ANC was able to base itself in independent states in southern Africa. In the main, they did not generate terrorism within the borders of the colonial power. Algeria was the partial exception, but in that case the terrorism in France came less from the FLN and more from those on the French right opposed to any negotiations and to Algerian independence.

Meanwhile, there was the growing importance of Palestinian terrorism as a response to the expulsion of much of the local population from Palestine in 1947–8. This in turn spawned tactics such as hijackings of aircraft as well as attacks on perceived Israeli targets, both domestically and internationally. While, in the main, Palestinian groups did not attack targets in western Europe, various leftist and nationalist terrorist groups made common cause with their more radical comrades. In turn, this gave them access to training camps, arms and cash that were used to sustain terrorism in nations including Italy and the UK.

There was some degree of state support for these movements. Ideologically, almost all the anti-colonial movements found common cause with the Soviet Union, China or both. In turn, both powers were prepared to send arms and funds, but their direct control was limited, in part due to the more pragmatic goals of their clients. By the 1970s, Libya played an important role as a sponsor of terrorism and a facilitator of links between the extreme left internationally and parts of the Palestinian movement. It also carried out terrorist attacks itself, including bombings and shootings in Europe as well as the state-sponsored murder of critics of the regime. In 1972, Palestinian group Black September carried out the Munich massacre during the Summer Olympics in Munich, Germany.

By the early 1990s, it could be argued that most of these

movements were burnt out or irrelevant. Extreme leftist violence had long become dormant in Europe and that of the far right remained episodic. The collapse of the apartheid regime in South Africa completed the process of decolonisation and offered a more peaceful consensus model going forward. Long-running nationalist movements such as the IRA and ETA (the Basque separatist organisation) had mostly come around to the idea of a peaceful end to their violence.

But this optimism was premature. Al-Qaeda emerged out of the war in Afghanistan with a fusion of previously fragmented Islamist ideologies.[4] Its fundamental intention was to restore what it saw as the golden age of Islam from the seventh century and to do this meant defeating the 'far enemy' (basically the US) and any near enemies (Israel, but also the rulers of the current states across the Islamic world). It had developed its model during the war with the Soviets, with safe bases in Afghanistan and in other fragmented states. Throughout the 1990s, Al-Qaeda made a number of murderous attacks within Islamic countries and against Western (mainly US) targets.

The next stage, of course, was the 9/11 attacks in the US. It cannot be overstated how deeply 9/11 cut into the American psyche. Terrorism shot up to the most critical national security issue. The US–UK invasion of Iraq, allied with conventional Arab nationalism and antisemitism, and galvanised by injustice in Palestine, gave these terrorists a wider audience of those who felt that Western hypocrisy justified terrorism. Over time, these attackers have increasingly come to rely on suicide bombings, driving trucks into large crowds or knife or gun attacks.

Individuals inspired by Al-Qaeda or its ISIS offshoot have carried out almost random killings. The evidence suggests that the larger attacks have all had some degree of external support and organisation but, in effect, any disaffected person can use a knife to attack someone in the street. Given the nature of their motivation, the overwhelming majority of such attacks are undertaken by those from immigrant backgrounds. This makes the terrorism additionally destabilising – in the first case due to the physical threat, and then by entrenching the view that such violence is a necessary consequence of hosting immigrant communities from troubled parts of the world.

I have argued in the past that Islamist fundamentalism and far-right extremism are best examined side by side, a matter which deserves fuller treatment. They are, of course, radically different in character, and each threatens Britain and the West in different ways. Yet both share a deep contempt for the liberal values of tolerance, diversity and individual freedom. Each embraces a narrative of in-group supremacy: the belief that only their community (be it the faithful of a certain puritanical Islam or the ethnic/racial 'nation' of the far right) is virtuous and deserving of power, and that this community must purify society of corrupting outsiders or ideas.

Fundamentalist Islamist movements such as Al-Qaeda, the Islamic State, Boko Haram and others emerged in recent decades partly as a violent reaction against modern liberal culture and a variety of geopolitical grievances. They advocate a return to an imagined early Islamic order, implementing an extreme form of Sharia law and rejecting governance by democracy as impious. These jihadist groups have perpetrated terrorism on a global scale: from the events of 2001 in the US to bombings and shootings across Europe, Asia and Africa and the establishment of a brutal 'caliphate' in parts of Iraq and Syria in 2014. Their actions aim to terrorise and polarise, often deliberately seeking to trigger backlash against Muslims, which in turn they use to recruit more followers, all as part of their endless 'holy war'. While these groups do not represent Islam as a whole, they claim justification from selective religious texts and fatwas. I have previously explored, for example, the Mardin fatwa, a historical religious ruling that jihadists have distorted to endorse violence against any government not adhering to their doctrine. By twisting theology, fundamentalists like ISIS provide their adherents with what amounts to a totalitarian ideology wrapped in religious language – one that demands absolute obedience, glorifies martyrdom and dehumanises all outside the fold. Under such regimes (as briefly seen in ISIS-controlled territory), there is no room for liberal concepts of individual rights or pluralism: women and minorities are subjugated, dissenters are executed and any cultural artifacts deemed un-Islamic are destroyed.

On the opposite end, far-right extremists in the West have been reawakening, driven by fears of demographic change, the political sidelining of their concerns, economic displacement and anger at liberal social norms. These include neo-Nazi and white supremacist groups, militant ethnonationalists and self-styled 'patriots' convinced that their nations are being betrayed from within by multiculturalism or globalism. They propagate conspiracy theories such as the 'Great Replacement' – the false claim that elites are intentionally replacing native-born Europeans or Americans with immigrants – to justify hatred and violence against immigrants, Jews, Muslims and other minorities. This milieu has produced its own share of terror attacks: for instance, the 2011 Norway massacre by Anders Behring Breivik (who killed seventy-seven people to ostensibly fight multiculturalism), or the 2019 Christchurch mosque shootings in New Zealand (where the attacker explicitly cited white supremacist talking points). Like the jihadists, the far-right violent fringe often seeks to spark broader conflict – some fantasise about a race war or civil war that will overthrow current liberal governments and bring about a homogenous, authoritarian order along racial or nativist lines.

These two extremes feed off each other symbiotically. Each time jihadists commit a heinous act of terror, far-right demagogues seize the opportunity to generalise blame to all Muslims and push an-ti-Muslim policies; this persecution and demonisation then bolsters the jihadist narrative that the West is irredeemably hostile to Islam, helping them draw in new recruits from alienated Muslim youth. It is a vicious cycle of hatred that undermines the liberal vision of coexistence. Both extremes also thrive in polarised environments saturated with fear and conspiracy thinking – conditions very much abetted by social media echo chambers. For example, ISIS recruiters masterfully used online platforms to disseminate slick propaganda videos worldwide, while far-right agitators exploited forums and imageboards to spread manifestos and live-stream their atrocities for maximum psychological impact.

Historically, the moral frameworks of these extremists are akin to those that fuelled twentieth-century totalitarianism and geno-cides. The jihadist conception of a divinely sanctioned, puritanical caliphate bears resemblance to other utopian totalitarian projects – brooking no dissent and enforcing ideological purity through violence. The white supremacist ideas on the far right revive the poisonous notions of racial hierarchy and eliminationism that led to the Holocaust. In both cases, an in-group's supremacy is asserted at the expense of the fundamental liberal tenet that all humans are equal in dignity. Thus, whether they invoke God or blood and soil, fundamentalists and fascists arrive at a shared destination: a world of absolutism and intolerance, the polar opposite of a pluralist liberal order.

The presence of these radical movements forces liberal democracies into a delicate balancing act. On the one hand, they must defend against and defeat violent extremism to protect their citizens – which can require robust security measures, intelligence operations, even military action overseas (as in the campaign against ISIS). On the other hand, democracies must be careful not to overreact in ways that betray their own values or fuel the extremists' narrative. For instance, policies that indiscriminately target Muslim communities, or draconian surveillance laws curtailing civil liberties, can themselves erode liberal norms and validate the claims of both jihadists and the far right that democracy is hypocritical or weak. This implies that understanding the grievances and psychology driving these extremes is also key to countering them. Liberal societies will need to address the root causes – whether it's the alienation of second-generation immigrant youth in Europe that jihadists prey on, or the economic and social anxieties of rural working-class whites in America that populist demagogues exploit – while not compromising on the rule of law and human rights.

In recent years, the US and European far right have become more dangerous, seeking to carry out violence, and in some cases murder, to (in their view) protect European civilisation. Outside the US, these have mostly remained the acts of individuals, but individuals able to draw on a carefully curated set of arguments put forward by notionally respectable figures. The fusion between these ideologies and the populist right is in turn spawning yet more political violence.[5] The 2025 foiled far-right coup attempt in Germany (using ex-military personnel to storm the Bundestag, in an echo of a similar attempt in 2022) should crystallise for our governments that these ideologies are not confined to fringe online spaces or isolated acts of violence, but can metastasise into organised efforts to overthrow democratic institutions.

The cycle of immigrant crime prompting far-right violence is firmly established now in the UK. The 2024 Stockport stabbing, which occurred shortly after Keir Starmer became Prime Minister, saw three children killed and another eight wounded, as well as two adults, by Axel Muganwa Rudakubana, then seventeen years old. The tragedy produced false reports and social media posts claiming Rudakubana was a Muslim, or that he had arrived by small boat. These facts were instrumental in sparking the riots which followed and in determining their Muslim targets. The government, media and police attempted to be vigilant by withholding details of the terrorist and his motives in a naive attempt to deflect public anger about the attack. There were perceived attempts to disguise Rudakubana's family background through the use of euphemisms such as 'he was from Cardiff' and that the incident was 'not being treated as a terror attack'. In the time since, Rudakubana has been sentenced to fifty-two years in jail under section 58 of the Terrorism Act 2000. In his possession was *Military Studies in the Jihad Against the Tyrants: The Al-Qaeda Training Manual*. In hindsight, it is clear that the euphemistic approach of the government, media and police aggravates public anger more than honesty would.

Such equivocation lends credence to the far-right narrative that Britain has an egregious two-tier policing system stacked against ethnic Britons. Such a narrative has its origins in the failure to prosecute Muslim perpetrators of rape and sexual violence against young girls in Rotherham. Reports, including the main commissioned report written by Professor Alexis Jay OBE, found that

1,400 children were groomed and exploited from 1997 to 2013, predominantly by British-Pakistani men, and that authorities failed to act to protect the children for fear of being seen as racist or of upsetting racial relations in the area.[6] With this trend repeating throughout the decade, the phrase 'two-tier policing' was coined, when the perceived special treatment was at its most notable. There have, so far, been 1,280 arrests, nearly 800 charges and more than 200 convictions in relation to the events in Rotherham. Dishonesty, euphemism and cover-ups over terrorism therefore only serve the interests of the terrorists. They stir up more anxiety and fear and turn people against their institutions and governments, who they (not unreasonably) accuse of lying to them.

Meanwhile, some who 'retweeted' false information about Rudakubana's background were jailed: Lucy Connolly, the wife of a Conservative councillor, was sentenced to thirty-one months after calling for hotels housing asylum seekers to be set on fire on social media. She had no prior convictions. So-called counter-riots organised by Muslim communities also turned violent, including with deadly weapons, but by contrast only a handful of convictions have been made.[7] Gabriel Abdullah threatened the public with a knife while shouting antisemitic abuse in Golders Green, but was handed a suspended sentence. Julie Sweeney, a 53-year-old carer from Cheshire, is to serve fifteen months in jail after posting online that someone should 'blow the mosque up with the adults in it'. Haris Ghaffar, wearing a balaclava, attempted to smash his way into a pub in which terrified punters had barricaded themselves, and was sentenced to twenty months in jail – almost a full year less than Lucy Connolly got for her incendiary tweet.

Another facet of the negative and destabilising feedback loop created by reactionary responses to terror attacks concerns community policing itself. Videos have emerged during riots of officers telling minority community leaders that they would not be arrested but should discard their weapons in the mosque. The force admitted that public confidence had been significantly undermined by the video, which again vindicates the idea that 'critical legal theory' – or the idea that the law is political and should be applied differently when dealing with diverse groups – is being applied in the UK and results in two-tier policing.[8] Research oriented at improving the police force consistently shows that engagement with communities and being seen to be fair promotes faith and confidence in procedural justice.[9]

These findings and recommendations, which are the product of diversity, equity and inclusion (DEI) initiatives, should arguably be used among white British communities to improve relations and end the destabilising loop. The College of Policing's community guidelines for 'solving problems' speak of 'using evidence-based and innovative responses that target the underlying causes of problems and are tailored to local context'.[10] In practice, this often means turning a blind eye to crime and instead supporting local 'leaders' and mosques to self-police, while guidelines on 'engaging communities' suggest 'engagement that is tailored to the needs and preferences of different communities'.[11] Dealing with the social destabilisation in the fallout of terror attacks and immigrant crime requires that justice is seen to be applied equally. Whether or not two-tier policing exists does not diminish the fact that the perception of it is massively destabilising, pushing people to the far right where their concerns are given voice.

This book therefore calls for robustness in policing and recognises that reducing the anxieties of citizens is a prerequisite for effective counterterrorism. A politics of denial or trickle-truthing is not an optimal strategy and plays into the narrative both of the far right and of foreign hostile actors. One central theme in British statecraft repeats itself: vulnerability over race and the network effect of high-status opinion accelerates the anger and instability caused by terrorism. To be perfectly clear, neither the far right nor Islamic terror are single, static political features. As such, the number of citizens attracted both to the far right and to Islamic terror grows and wanes. At present, the single biggest recruiter for the far right is woke institutions and police, with totemic issues like the ongoing Rotherham rape gang scandal and cases like that of Rudakubana driving political radicalisation. The single biggest recruiter for Islamic extremism and sectarianism is the Israel–Palestine conflict.

The emergence of far-right ideology and its symbiotic opposite, Islamic terrorism, in the US, Britain and Europe has particular consequences. Through social media, both have become do-it-yourself, pick-and-mix ideologies. Both can see people move from vague approval to full acceptance at worrying speed. Both promote acting alone as an approach and both blur the line between rightful gathering and intimidating or politically violent protests. That they are related and feed off each other means both must be tackled, domestically, simultaneously. It will not do to coddle and insulate minorities who harbour terrorist risks if this provokes many to turn to far-right politics.

* * *

These strands of Islamic extremism and far-right violence affect every Western state, and the UK is no exception. In some respects, the UK already has clear expertise, including a criminal justice approach to terrorism and the robust use of security services. These security services produce material that is already shared with other Western states regardless of links to either the EU or NATO. Indeed, it would be unusual were we not to engage in international collaboration in this respect. Even with the retreat of the US, there is no realistic prospect of Five Eyes security cooperation ending.

However, there are things the UK could do that would contribute more widely. The sharing of intelligence with third parties, to the extent that it does not compromise our trust with our security partners, is one way to provide significant value overseas. Preventing the flow of funds to terror cells is also key; this is a vital competence of the UK now and will become even more so in the future. We have suggested earlier in this book that company law be tightened to prevent anonymous accounts, and that the UK should use its influence over places like the British Virgin Islands to ensure that they close their own loopholes which prevent transparency in global money flows.

Preventing corrupt and extractive governments in aggrieved parts of the world from embezzling their own nation's wealth and siphoning it via the West is a key foreign policy objective. We have already explored how this corruption fuels the poverty and despair that drives migration and refugee flows. We have seen how it complicates international aid, including climate aid, which ends up serving the interests of extractive elites. But we must also recognise that terrorism breeds in failed states, and that corrupt money funds terrorism. Iran and the IRGC generate enormous funds by extracting oil wealth, particularly from Syria and their own nation, as well as through smuggling, and use it to fund terror and hostile state action, including orchestrating murders in the UK. In this case, the acceptance of funds from corruption causes multiple problems. Just as this makes those states more vulnerable to the impact of climate change, it also makes it easier for groups such as ISIS to take hold. Currently, neither ISIS nor Al-Qaeda seem to be able to mount significant attacks in Europe or the US. But they are not vanquished: instead, both are assiduously exploiting local conflicts across Africa, Asia and the Middle East. Any corrupt state with a significant Muslim minority is of interest to them – not to resolve the conflict but to turn it to their advantage. Their playbook involves controlling resource production; extorting governments, civilians and officials; and murdering religious and political enemies though brutal terror attacks.

Related to this, running a terrorist group is an expensive business. ISIS may have lost access to the oil wells of Syria and Iraq that funded it between 2012 and 2016, but it remains a wealthy organisation. Each of its affiliates now largely undertake their own fundraising, but there remains a network of transfers to and from the core of the organisation.[12] In terms of cash transfers, while the organisation still relies on physical movement of funds, it is increasingly exploiting the various forms of online currency, including cryptocurrency.

In 2023, the US found that Binance (the world's largest virtual assets service provider, based in the Cayman Islands) had been enabling money laundering for both terrorist and criminal groups. The company enables trading in cryptocurrencies and is not currently registered in the UK (but can be accessed by anyone based in the UK), having been effectively banned in 2021.[13] The US remains the centre for both the innovation and regulation of cryptocurrencies; the EU has not been involved in significant innovation but hosts governmental debates about the ethics of cryptocurrency and AI. This points to a wider issue: a given platform may be banned or limited in certain jurisdictions but there is always an alternative, including virtual private networks. Even the removal of anonymous companies, as well as the banning of the use of fiduciaries by anonymous owners, would not stop money being sent over the blockchain and then sold where it is wanted to fund terror and destabilise the West. Anyone can set up a cryptocurrency wallet address, and while most major Western exchanges require ID, there are always clandestine grey-market exchanges that don't. Anywhere from 5 to 20 per cent of global militancy and terror is estimated to be funded through cryptocurrency, which also provides options for extractive regimes to siphon wealth to Swiss banks.[14]

Another problem is that crypto assets remain largely unregulated in the UK.[15] Even the Financial Conduct Authority (FCA) blithely notes that 'cryptos are developed and run by groups, individuals or companies. Publicly available information about some of these groups/individuals can be vague, and, as crypto activity is not regulated yet in the UK, there is no safety net if things go wrong'. What can 'go wrong' is not just individuals losing their investments but that such funds then become key to funding terrorism and criminal activity. That said, regulating crypto assets is by no means as simple as some other forms of asset regulation. Not only is the technology specifically designed to be almost impossible to trace (though there are some tools available to police forces, and some information left on the blockchain), but there are additional steps including using 'mixers' which disguise transactions through a web of wallets and allow illicit payments to submerge themselves in a sea of anonymous transactions.

The far right also increasingly make use of cryptocurrencies. The violence they inspire may often be cheap and low technology, but they need income – not least to fund their own lifestyles. The UK far-right agitator Tommy Robinson relies heavily on transfers of cryptocurrency for this reason, with funding mainly coming from the US (with Putin's Russia allegedly contributing, knowing how destabilising Robinson can be to British democracy).[16] Robinson has been arrested for terror charges under Schedule 7 of the Terrorism Act 2000 for refusing to provide his phone number to police. Rather than as a means of siphoning money, the far right use crypto in an attempt to protect their assets from government seizure or freezing.

Arguably there is no practical value to cryptocurrencies: their production wastes useful energy and microprocessors, contributes substantially to climate change and their usage enables clandestine funding that would be hard using conventional currencies. They do not function well as a low-cost means of exchange. They do not hold a stable value. It seems that they are primarily held in speculation on their future valuation – a valuation in turn supported by a belief that their fixed maximum supply, their scarcity, assures their value. When bought and sold, the effect is purely distributive and creates no gains from trade. There remain opportunities and applications of blockchain technology more generally in medicine, data management, banking and elsewhere, and the US is at the forefront of developing these applications. In medicine, distributed-ledger systems have been trialled to secure clinical records, trace pharmaceutical supply chains and manage research data while protecting patient privacy. In finance, tokenised assets and central bank digital currencies promise faster settlement and could lower (or, perhaps, increase) fraud risk, while in data management and public administration, blockchain technologies offer tamper-proof audit trails and more transparent governance. At the moment, the UK's official regulator seems relaxed at the lack of regulation over organisations for which there is – at best – vague information.

This problem has more in common with the other key strand

– social media – than might appear to be the case. This is not the place to rehearse the wider harms done by the current model of social media, but it's important to stress one point.[17] If someone posted something illegal (in terms of discrimination laws) or incited violence on the *Telegraph* or *Guardian* websites, both the poster and the newspaper would be liable. Do the same on Facebook or Twitter/X and you retain some degree of liability (though often can hide behind anonymity), but the very rich publishers of those sites carry no responsibility.

Social media regulation is far beyond the scope of this chapter, but it bears mentioning that while there have been numerous well-intentioned requests for companies to improve their internal regulation, the medicine is very often worse than the disease. Treating them like other news organisations is often advocated by those who would want any public speech subject to the same standards as journalism, but this only empowers those institutions and elites who are most able to reach the required threshold to enter public discourse. Twitter/X, we cannot allow ourselves to forget, succumbed to public pressure to ban a sitting President, Donald Trump, from its platform, and 'shadowbanned' (or algorithmically supressed) right-wing discourse more generally. Meanwhile, external attempts to police social media in the UK have bordered on absurdity. In a well-publicised case against *Telegraph* journalist Allison Pearson, she saw police at her door on Remembrance Sunday for a post allegedly made a year before that had been recorded as a 'non-crime hate incident' (NCHI). She could not be told what she had said, or who had accused her, but it is hard to disagree that her experience was 'Kafkaesque' and does indeed have a 'chilling effect on free speech'.[18] A quarter of a million NCHIs have been recorded, each punctuated by visits from the police. The balance between counter-extremism and free speech is important, and it is clear that the UK has got this balance massively wrong.

In the end, it is all too easy to find the sort of material online that encourages radicalisation either to Islamist or far-right terrorism.[19] The UK cannot individually control the murkier parts of the internet, but many believe it can cooperate with like-minded states to limit the reach of such material. How to filter legitimate social commentary from genuinely dangerous radicalisation is obvious in the abstract. 'Regular people' should not be worried about knocks on the door for expressing themselves, and especially not journalists. But, in practice, how to write the law such that radicalising material becomes hard to find is *incredibly* difficult without riding roughshod over personal liberties.[20]

The proliferation of these attacks on personal liberties strengthens the rhetoric of authoritarian states. That the state is at once unable to prevent terror attacks while it is cracking down on non-violent and non-incendiary speech again does severe reputational damage to the UK. Bilateral dealings with Donald Trump have reflected a concern within the US administration that the UK has got this balance wrong. It is hard to escape the conclusion that the British cultural moment has left democratic confidence and humility lower here than in the US, which has proved itself – ironically, considering the state of the executive – more resilient to terroristic radicalisation, precisely because it has a more confrontational, liberal and responsive attitude to free speech. Britain's failure here plays into the hands of our enemies.

* * *

Despite their claims of a close alliance, in practice there are substantial differences between Russia and China.[21] They may sit at the core of the wider rejection of the post-war US-led international order, but they do so with very different pasts and future goals and substantial differences in relative power. As we have seen, they share an (increasingly brazen) approach of using non-military means to undermine governments they see as hostile.[22] Both have built up their military power to the extent that they now represent serious threats, at least to states in close proximity (it is unlikely that either has a global reach) and, as in Ukraine, have made steps towards engaging in conventional warfare. They have both, thus far, stopped short of Iran's overt sponsorship of terror overseas, while China has actually proven useful within the Middle East, where it is seen as a more honest and consistent broker than the US.

Their framing of their future goals varies substantially. China sees itself as the centre of a revised international order, having supplanted the US, but one that actually repurposes many of the world's existing structures. In effect, it is not a zero-sum approach where the only way that China can benefit is by existing powers losing out – even if that is the broad direction of travel envisaged in their wider strategy.[23] Putin's Russia has taken a decidedly different approach. It remains, notionally, part of many international bodies, but often flouts their norms and rarely cooperates. More fundamentally, Russia's international outlook suggests Putin feels his only means of regaining great power status is by undermining what he sees as Russia's opponents.[24]

Russia's lack of economic power to compete and undercut in the way China can pushes it towards asymmetric warfare, in particular by seeking to undermine the US, the EU and any stable Western democracy. At the same time, Russia is seeking to exploit various conflicts in Africa (in many ways as the mirror image of

ISIS) to build a network of client regimes.[25] These Russian- and Chinese-aligned third world countries are headed largely by authoritarian leaders who run extractive governments prone to embezzlement. Russia's permissive (we might even say encouraging) attitude towards this bribery and theft aligns these states with the authoritarians as they attempt to preserve their power and make their embezzlements more politically sustainable. More generally, backing one side or the other in various civil conflicts has the secondary advantage, from a Russian perspective, of generating more refugees. This, in turn, creates another fissure that it can exploit to undermine western Europe and the EU.

By contrast, China can be seen to be acting as a challenging power, quite prepared to engage in subversion if that helps it reach its goals. It is using the wider Belt and Road Initiative both to create a network of client states and to offer a different economic model to that traditionally sponsored by organisations such as the World Bank. China is revisionist and wishes to be the centre of the world in order to make up for its centuries of humiliation; it seeks to put democracies in their place and reap the rewards of their collapse. It has reintroduced the idea of great power competition into international relations, something that was meant to be mediated through multilateral bodies such as the UN. This creates numerous tensions, especially as China is a reliable partner on many issues, and on others is amenable to diplomacy and compromise. However, under Xi it is reducing its role in the global economic order and is clearly being more aggressive in pursuing what it sees as its legitimate demands.

Russia feels it has little to gain from cooperation. As far as the regime is concerned, given they are already sanctioned, they are largely correct in this view, though the Russian population has the world to gain from global integration. A powerful Russia is deemed impossible alongside a powerful and successful West. This framing has some roots in late Soviet ideology, but has come to the fore over the last twenty years in the form of extreme nationalism and disdain for what it sees as decadent liberalism.[26] While Putin publicly disdains the Soviet Union, seeing communism and the creation of the various Republics as a historical error, his regime has inherited its expertise in subversion. The upshot is that Russian opposition is more ideological but less durable. It is less clear how long Russia can continue, particularly with its demographic issues and lack of a state surveillance panopticon.

Nevertheless, shorn of any former need to promote Marxism-Leninism, the Russian Federation has found its mission easier than its predecessors through an emphasis on hard power and pragmatism. Russia has proven willing even to work with North Korean troops, completing their transition to a fully rogue state. Some strains of the populist right in Europe and the US are reflections of Russian claims about the dangers of liberalism, diversity (both religious and sexual) and the need to restore what are seen as traditional values.[27] [28] This is not particularly true of the UK, whose right-wing parties support Ukraine against Russia, though quibble about how much money we can afford to send. The riots in the UK in August 2024, however, echoed some of these traits; the arguments, such as they are, share similar forms, and Russian media is often the source of the false claims used to provoke unrest. Putin's regime has no interest in who wins, or the cost: merely fragmenting the target polity is enough. A West weakened, both collectively and individually, means a stronger Russia.

*　*　*

China is engaged in a competition to become the dominant economic power and to engorge the prestige and wealth of its ruling class. To do this, it needs to repurpose existing institutions to fit its preferred model; it is willing to engage in aggressive actions where it feels this is appropriate. At a fundamental level, the Chinese mentality explored in the previous chapter views sovereignty over matters they consider to be intrinsically Chinese to be outside the remit of Western interference. Any UK protests were ignored when the political arrangements around Hong Kong were unilaterally altered. Similarly, the protests of some UK politicians over the persecution of the Uighurs are readily dismissed, even if they do trigger retaliatory action against individual MPs, who are blacklisted from entry to China. This realism matters: there is nothing to be gained from posturing or from declaring that China is an enemy, a threat that needs to be directly challenged. The UK doesn't have the requisite dominance in a single area for China to lose any sleep over. While we do have the capacity to project military force into east Asia, it is only through our US alliance and through our partners in South Korea and Japan. Making ourselves valuable to the world, whether it be through an unleashed financial sector or through technology, might give China pause for thought.

It's clear that, despite their rising challenge, China's claim to the global future will not be granted on its own terms. China has an enormous problem with capital flight, meaning being wealthy in China is incredibly dangerous. One wrong step could find you firmly out of the graces of the CCP, perhaps even disappeared for citizen re-education, much like (former) billionaire Jack Ma. Wealthy Chinese citizens go to extreme lengths to outmanoeuvre the personal controls which prevent money being easily brought out of the country. Similar capital controls applying to businesses have been relaxed slightly, showing China's need to reassure foreign capital that capital controls will not stop them returning their profits home.[29]

London is a major destination for Chinese wealth, including CCP money. It flows via complicated, high-commission foreign transfer agencies, particularly into London properties and funds held in the UK. UK-based Chinese students are sometimes used to facilitate this process. Many high-net-worth Chinese individuals are very conservative with this money – it is hidden from the CCP but not from the UK Treasury. Ensuring we remain stable in our relationship to China, compared to the US and EU, will solidify the trend that successful and powerful Chinese earners continue to store and invest their wealth in the UK. This is not principally an economic policy, nor is it a moral one (indeed, such a policy includes storing the wealth of CCP elites who may have a hand in genocide against the Uighurs). Rather, it is a *security* policy. If more senior CCP members continue to keep their nest eggs in the UK, leadership in China will continually face internal resistance to, and personal disincentives against, destabilising China's relationship with the UK.

We can ensure that, at least in the realm of security, the same is not true in the opposite direction. The Cameron-era goal of seeking direct Chinese investment into core infrastructure has, thankfully, been reversed, but under Starmer we risk returning to a naive policy where China is concerned.[30] Under Xi, China is becoming more aggressive, more insular and more prone to taking risks. Xi's recent economic reforms have largely failed and the economic growth that was such a feature of the nation from 1990–2020 is now stalling.[31] China has particularly struggled to develop a resilient domestic market and to wean its economy off a house-building (and house-buying) binge. The economy cannot survive the property bust that appears imminent. This in turn may make it more prone to risk-taking, especially around Taiwan, posing the danger of open confrontation with the US.

Britain must criticise both the persecution of particular minority groups and the wider expansion of the surveillance state in China; both require a full investigation, to which the UK can contribute as an ally. When states such as Australia face a direct digital attack from China, they need support. Some of this is moral, some technical. Equally, developing the skills to detect and deter Chinese online spyware, corporate espionage and IP theft activities is also something that the UK should be contributing to. As long-standing members of the Five Eyes intelligence grouping, the UK already has close links to states that face direct Chinese actions.

Many of the same actions that can diminish the ability of terrorist organisations (and terrorist states including Iran) from operating unimpeded can also apply to state hostilities from China. The difference, and it is a positive one, is that with China there are additional multilateral approaches which can and must be leveraged. As explored in the previous chapter, new WTO disciplines must be added if we are to reform global trade. In the absence of US re-engagement, the WTO cannot be used to implement global restrictions on the trade in goods and services derived from stolen IP and stolen research. But much remains to be uncovered about Trump's new trade doctrine, even if we accept that it changes over time. The desire to protect US advantage and research from theft should speak directly to Trump, who is a protectionist at heart. The well-founded speculation that Britain would be largely spared from his tariffs came true, and we may have a better hearing with him and his advisers than any other nation on the planet. Among all the potential avenues to prompt US re-engagement with the WTO, pushing for tougher rules and sanctions for IP theft could be presented in the US as a major win.

If there is one thing the UK can do, it is resolve its 'confused' approach to China.[32] The UK has tended to stress its closeness to the US in its dealings with China, while other EU partners tend to focus on where they have specific shared issues. The US is currently tending to economic confrontation, driven as much by growing domestic protectionism as any need to challenge Chinese aggression. The EU is not innocent of this: the proposed ban on electric cars, discussed above, has much more to do with protecting domestic manufacturing as challenging Chinese subsidies.

In contrast, Russia, at least in theory, offers a simpler set of options. Russia is no longer a great power and is in demographic decline, while the war in Ukraine is even calling into question the extent to which its military can punch above its economic weight. As states have found alternative energy sources since 2022, it is becoming less integrated into the Western economy and is being forced to find less profitable markets in east and south Asia. Its leadership are clear about their ideology: liberal democracies must be undermined so that Russia can regain its proper status. There is little of the Chinese balancing of assimilation, cooperation and aggressive competition in this framing. Frankly, this irredentism makes regime change a key security priority for NATO. Russia, in a sense, has very little to lose from destabilisation and has the world to gain.

There is, however, a sense in which China could follow in Russia's footsteps. At the turn of the century, Russia could conceivably have become a more liberal democratic state. The New Labour administration was arguably far too willing to allow London to act as the centre of money laundering as the new breed of oligarchs looted the assets of the old Soviet Union, but this situation also allowed us to seize enormous quantities of Russian assets at the start of the war in Ukraine. The vulnerability of these assets to our seizure could very easily have stopped the war from ever starting, given how many powerful Russians lost much of their fortunes. Historians will debate the extent to which Putin considered mass seizure of assets (and their subsequent provision to Ukraine) as a possibility, given that he also believed his 'special operation' would be over in a matter of days. Put another way, would Europe really have pressed ahead with blocks on Russian oil and gas, sanctions and seizures from oligarchs, if Putin's desired regime change in Ukraine was already a *fait accompli*?

The infamous Scottish Limited Partnerships, discussed in Chapter 4, still enable Russian money laundering, and the UK's libel courts are still available for Russian oligarchs to try to silence inconvenient journalists. The Conservatives, after the Brexit vote, did their best to stop any investigation of Russian interference in UK elections even after it was clear they had carried out similar actions in the US.[33]

The far-right riots in the UK in August 2024 offer a case study in how Russia attacks liberal democracies. Russian-sponsored media will invent or amplify the type of false claims that cemented the anger of local communities that give rise to the riots. The Russian-owned Telegram social networking system is the place of choice for the disparate far right to organise. Far-left and populist-right politicians repeat Russian talking points either as facts or as 'legitimate questions' that need an answer. And this can be achieved without identifiable Russian funding or direct links: the toxic combination of venal populist politicians, unregulated social media and people all too ready to blame outsiders for problems is all that is needed. Some measures were taken to prevent this – Russian TV channels such as Sputnik and Russia Today have been severely restricted across Europe since the invasion of Ukraine – but Russian funding still flows to populist movements across Europe.

The EU has largely failed to find a common voice regarding the Russian invasion of Ukraine. It did enable the transfer of military equipment as part of its funding package, though opposition, in part from Germany and France, as well as Viktor Orbán's Hungary, has failed to generate the necessary level of unanimity. Russian influence may no longer act through a formal network of ideologically aligned communist parties, but it has morphed into a network of individuals, politicians and movements who take its funding and act in its interests. Making public any evidence of an individual's receipt of Russian money, once it passes the threshold to establish it beyond reasonable doubt, will be key to cleaning up our information and media environment and weakening the grip of authoritarian states to wage information warfare.

The UK should capitalise on specialisation of skills within the Five Eyes, as well as specialisations covered in other chapters, particularly in banking. This will build resilience against cyber and economic warfare and clamp down on the clandestine funding for terrorist organisations by reforming those company laws that allow for anonymous registrations and opaque wire transfers. Sanctions and diversification of trade must support a broader foreign policy objective of regime change in Russia. With China, disengagement on matters related to our national security is essential; we must not repeat those errors which allowed Russia to turn from an adversarial and corrupt state into a fully destabilising and hostile one.

We must be ready to meet so-called 'salami slicing' – using

paramilitary proxies – by fully aligning with the US before China has the chance to become bolder, potentially launching an invasion of Taiwan. But we also must not hasten to disengage where it is not necessary or where we can seek advantage. We should not reject cheap imports, particularly of subsidised EVs. We should remain open to Chinese money to hold collateral against any potential Chinese escalation. We should continue to maintain a productive trading relationship if we are to have any hope of cooperation on climate change, where China is poised to be the largest producer of electro-voltaic panels, or of negotiating deeper access (with security exemptions) in exchange for expedited climate cooperation. We can encourage Trump to target Chinese IP theft and cybercrime via re-engagement with the WTO.

Beijing's 'salami slicing' strategy is visible in its incremental militarisation of the South China Sea, the steady normalisation of PLA flights through Taiwan's air-defence zone and the quiet installation of surveillance infrastructure in partner ports acquired under Belt and Road debt deals. Moscow applies the same playbook in Europe: the creeping absorption of Abkhazia and South Ossetia, the passport handover scheme that turned eastern Ukrainians into 'Russian citizens in need of protection' and through cyber-provocations in the Baltic states. Each slice is small enough to avoid triggering a full allied response, but cumulatively it alters facts on the ground; meeting it requires an early, coordinated pushback rather than reactive sanction packages issued after the new status quo is already in place. Since 2016, dozens of Western diplomats and intelligence officers (first in Cuba, then in China, Russia and even Washington) have reported sudden vertigo, tinnitus and cognitive impairment consistent with directed-energy exposure, which came to be known as Havana Syndrome. Whether the culprit is Russian experimentation, rogue actors inside the Chinese security services or a mix of the two, the episode showed how hostile states now probe Five Eyes personnel directly, below the threshold of open conflict, with tools that leave scant forensic trace yet can result in operational degradation. In the event of a formal war, which is no longer beyond the realm of possibility, Britain will need to be prepared for significant disruption, including of a terroristic nature.

Unless terrorism is radically counteracted, it will continue to shake the world and drive it to authoritarianism. It is hard-wired into our mammalian genetics to turn to disciplinarian order when our safety is threatened, and authoritarian states use this fear for massive strategic gain. Yet counterterrorism and opposition to hostile state action is one aspect of the Western order which remains relatively intact. AUKUS cooperation is groundbreaking and serious. The UK's elevation of these issues to the UN and WTO level is helpful for soliciting US re-engagement; gains here can compound and accelerate gains elsewhere. The issue of large population displacements should again be raised at the level of international forums to coax the US into staying at the table. Responding to global terror is, in many ways, the area where the West remains most resolute and can begin reasserting its moral authority. We should seek to contextualise our ambitions for trade, climate, migration and international law on the foundation of cooperation against hostile states and their terrorist proxies.

CHAPTER 8

INTERNATIONAL FINANCE

The UK is a major global player in finance. It has deep capital markets. It has extensive foreign reserves. Even after years of downward pressure on sterling, it is still a world currency and a significant reserve holding for many foreign institutions and central banks. In terms of financial services, Britain exports more in this sector than other global leaders, including the US, generating a trade surplus of well over £60 billion.[1] As such, this is one field where the UK already has the capacity to insist upon our own standards rather than following our larger neighbours. Progress has already been made in this regard, for example with the UK–Switzerland Global Financial Partnership, covering both regulations and emerging issues such as cybersecurity, AI and digital financial services.

Financial regulation is an immensely complex topic. It is particularly badly understood in the UK, where despite large changes since the financial crisis, significant parts of the financial system still self-regulate. While at first this may sound like a recipe for corruption, checks and balances and state involvement keep the process functional and, on the whole, result in regulations designed by those with knowledge rather than by politicians and their advisers. The British system is also more transparent than more top-down regulatory models which often suffer with a revolving door between regulators and industry, where regulators that are assumed to be independent are actually staffed by people expecting senior positions in industry later on. Often the appearance of independence is a telltale sign of a lack of it.

The financial system is the engine room of 21st-century economic activity. Britain's success in particular rides on the City. It operates at the forefront, too, of changes in AI and in digital technology. If there is technological change in the world, it will sooner or later be applied to the architecture of world finance. The potential for corruption is high and the rewards are great, which is why very few countries have managed to create a trustworthy banking system. Almost all those that have done so have common law with origins in Britain (New York, London, Singapore, Hong Kong). London's stable currency, unrivalled legal prowess from corporate law to banking, liquidity, time zone and market access has played to its strengths since the 'big bang' deregulation of the 1980s. Each major financial centre has been built by understanding the same fundamental principle: capital goes where it is treated best. That means robust law, high rates of return net of taxes, sound regulation and innovative offerings.

The UK's financial system is tarnished by the extent that it enables corruption, both domestically and in various tax havens. This is not just the view of those critical of current policy. According to the National Crime Agency (NCA), 'the UK, and especially the London property and financial markets, is a favoured destination to launder and invest the proceeds of international corruption, posing significant reputational and financial risks to the UK'.[2]

The financial system is so integral to the economy that the pro-liferation of bad money can spread throughout the country. Again, according to the NCA,

> the ease of opening UK companies means they are often used to enable corrupt activity. UK-registered companies pay bribes overseas in order to conduct business while companies based in large financial centres are used to disguise ownership and to conceal corrupt payments. The involvement of UK nationals or companies in financial sanctions evasion damages our interna-tional reputation and undermines the foreign policy goals of the UK and our partners.

In total, the NCA has estimated that money laundering costs the UK £100 billion per annum.[3] [4] There are some problems with that figure, particularly because it imagines that ill-gotten gains would still pass through the UK financial system were loopholes closed, rather than skipping the British economy entirely to be laundered in a different jurisdiction. Nonetheless, it is instructive considering the sheer scale of the laundering believed to be happening here.

Political will when it comes to dealing with this has often been lacking. Gordon Brown and New Labour were all too willing to see the City of London as a convenient source of revenue, enabling public expenditure without matching public taxation. UK govern-ments from 1991 did not only turn a blind eye to the money flows from the former Soviet Union, they actively encouraged it.[5] This led to the view that London was a centre of corruption, the laundro-mat where dirty money was converted into property, football clubs, British newspapers and an opulent lifestyle for those favoured by Putin.[6] Individuals from this world have ended up using the UK's legal system to silence critics, been ennobled to the House of Lords and have had close relations with UK politicians of all parties.

In theory, the UK now has a full property register, but a 2023 investigation found some 52,000 properties owned anonymously via shell companies in tax havens, with these concentrated in the richest corners of London. It is worth exploring the difference between shell companies and tax havens when it comes to money laundering, since they are often conflated. Tax havens have low rates of tax. Shell companies are a highly exploitable structure with anonymous company directors which are used to hide money siphoned from illegal sources. While tax havens give the rich options to park their assets overseas to avoid domestic tax (or, at least, to postpone it until they repatriate the profits), opaque company structures give terrorists, cronies and corrupt politicians options to make themselves billionaires by stealing on a national scale.

Some efforts have been made to address this. Both the Economic Crime (Transparency and Enforcement) Act and Economic Crime and Corporate Transparency Act have closed loopholes, and the post-2022 sanctions aimed at named associates of Putin have also made a difference. The problem is in part that the nature of financial crime mutates: if some forms of cryptocurrencies are caught by new legislation, then other forms emerge. In effect, cryptocurrencies may be attractive to some as an alternative form of finance, and to others for the notional libertarian ideology attached to them, but they provide a constant opportunity for criminals and those evading sanctions.

To some, this suggests a need for a different and less permissive regulatory form domestically and internationally. Europe tends to take this approach, as a digital variant of its precautionary principle. Unfortunately, Europe still suffers from rampant financial crime, and they sacrifice the useful components of their precautionary innovations, leaving the US to develop them instead. At the moment, the FCA continues to detect massive regulatory failings even among the established banks, and every time there is exposure of illicit money flows, UK institutions are heavily implicated.[7] In effect, a relatively clean system can, paradoxically, harbour substantial flows of dirty money.[8] Many surveys indicate that well-run economies operating within the rule of law paradoxically harbour more frauds (as the history of the Vancouver stock exchange, a well-run exchange in a prosperous, decently governed country, shows).

Even for the UK, it may well be that the size of financial crime actually outstrips the export earnings of the UK financial services sector. But it is not principally a cost borne by the UK: the money extracted and laundered from poor countries leaves them unable to develop, to adapt to climate change and makes them all the more vulnerable to state failure and the emergence of serious civil unrest and terrorism. The ease of corruption pushes developing nations to despair, driving immigration and increasing the payoffs to authoritarian regimes.

There is a quiet school of thought that holds that the UK actually profits from money laundering. That we should allow it to continue to 'take our piece of the pie'. Almost all money being laundered here is in transfer: a house sale or a football club changing owner that displaces capital elsewhere. It is not meaningful investment, so even the most cynical of leader should prioritise the minimisation of enormous damage done domestically and internationally over the illusion of capital coming to the UK. The costs of the global destabilisation it causes are incredibly high – and as the US withdraws – may prove too high for the UK to ignore.

* * *

Financial services are a major contributor to both domestic GDP and domestic taxation. New Labour in the late 1990s saw the financial sector as a ready source of funds to invest without the need to use general taxation. The Liberal Democrat–Conservative coalition undid most of these changes to 'do good by stealth', quite simply as the case for the social programmes had never been properly made. In turn, all too many UK politicians can foresee a future for themselves in the financial services sector when their political career ends.

However, this book's focus is on how the UK's financial services sector can be used to bolster its international standing. This has been a theme in earlier chapters, including how to use it to improve investment in both mitigating and reducing the impact of climate change. Generally, the UK's financial services score well domestically in terms of transparency, the single most important element for the prevention of financial crime – but this masks serious problems.[9]

The issue of Scottish Limited Partnerships has been discussed in Chapter 4, especially as they have been a favoured tool for money laundering from corrupt states. The UK government has often indicated an intent to reform this, but action is slow.[10] This is partly because legislation is so complex – the English version has some problems but is nowhere near as widely abused as the Scottish form – and there is the additional problem that it relies on Scots law, yet the Scottish Parliament can play no role as this type of legislation is reserved to the UK Parliament. It is complex both to understand the problem and to construct a response, thus action is glacial, and the corruption carries on.

A further issue is the systemic difficulty the Serious Fraud Office (SFO) encounters in bringing successful prosecutions of complex financial fraud. Sometimes, as with its investigation into BAE's alleged bribes to the Saudis, it has seen cases dropped on government instructions. The case concerned the Al-Yamamah arms deal, in which BAE was accused of paying illicit commissions to Saudi officials to secure lucrative defence contracts – a probe ultimately shut down in 2006 after Saudi threats to end intelligence cooperation. In other instances, their own errors undermined prosecutions. Recent revelations about its failed prosecution of the Eurasian Natural Resources Corporation (ENRC) form a classic case study of all the problems in dealing with corruption.

The ENRC was first listed on the London Stock Exchange in 2007, run by a group who has acquired valuable mining assets in Central Asia. The nature of the firm, and its backers, indicated close links to the many front companies created by the KGB in the 1980s, designed to acquire foreign currency (and much of this was kept off the books even from the Soviet regime).[11] In effect, this was part of the wider move of post-Putin Russian money into London. An early accusation of corruption opened the door to a predictable deal with the SFO. In effect, the company would hire a City law firm to investigate the allegation and, depending on what was found, would come to a financial settlement with the SFO (well away from any public knowledge).[12] At the time, the previous chair of the Audit Commission, Sir David Cooksey, was on the board of directors. He had also been a director of the Bank of England.

In this case, the SFO itself found evidence of further corrupt dealings connected with acquiring mines in Africa, and by 2013 the SFO had decided that ENRC was unlikely to produce an acceptable internal review. By 2019, the SFO had evidence that the original backers had illegally extracted capital from the public company to fund their own lifestyles. In turn, ENRC sued both the lawyers they had originally hired and the SFO. The SFO's case unravelled, and in 2023, it decided it no longer had the evidence needed to move to prosecution. However, this has not ended the saga: at some stage in 2025, ENRC will expect to be *paid* by the SFO in compensation.

A combination of the British government welcoming Russian money (and not asking questions), notable names in the City being prepared to take well-paid board positions and the simple ability of money to influence the dynamics of a court case has led to a situation where a company that has used opaque internal mechanisms escapes paying tax in South Africa and is now expecting to be compensated by the UK taxpayer.[13] As with other similar instances, at the core of the issue is both the UK's willingness to be seen to be important globally and its far-too-complex legal system. In combination, this seriously undermines the ability of the UK to stem the problem of global corruption, given its own systems enable it (for those able to pay).

The more conventional failure to prevent money laundering in the UK arises by accident. Fines are common, with both Metro Bank and Starling Bank receiving fines from the FCA for failures to make their automated transaction monitoring system completely watertight. Investigations found that the 'serious deficiencies' meant transactions weren't monitored the same day an account was opened, and that they wouldn't be until the account record was updated some years later, in 2022. When looking back at what the system had missed, it was found that 6 per cent of transactions had gone unmonitored and that forty-three account closures followed suspicious activity reports. Junior staff had noticed the issue in 2018, two years after the system was launched, but even after the 'fix' in 2019, there were still vulnerabilities with the automated monitoring. The challenge is that vulnerabilities like these can exist for two years even in a regulated system. Then there's the issue of the relatively manageable fines – £17 million for Metro – which are often treated merely as part of the hazard of doing business.

* * *

Corruption is not just a matter for the UK to deal with domestically. The UK's global past has left it with a network of British Overseas Territories (BOTs) that are independent of regulation but share elements of the UK legal system. Some of these are of no particular concern in terms of their finances, but a cluster of BOTs in the Caribbean are frequently implicated in money laundering. Bermuda, the British Virgin Islands, the Cayman Islands and the Turks and Caicos Islands come up time and again. Closer to the UK, the Channel Islands and the Isle of Man (which are Crown Dependencies, not BOTs) are often painted with the same brush, even though, especially in the case of the Isle of Man, AML and anti-terrorism funding rules via their Financial Services Authority are every bit as rigorous as our own.

Tax havens impact the legal international economy in two ways. There is a net loss of tax income (as it is transferred to a more suitable jurisdiction) and there is a net loss of potential capital if it is then invested somewhere other than the UK. Clearly, even if all these havens did was to enable tax avoidance (which is perfectly legal), they represent a problem for the wider international economy – but they also enable both tax evasion and the secret acquisition of illegal funds.

Other former colonial powers, especially the Netherlands, are linked to some tax havens, while others are conventional states with unusual tax and financial services legislation (Ireland, Luxembourg,

Malta and Switzerland). Equally, there are oddities such as the US state of Delaware, with its banking secrecy laws and permissive approach to the incorporation of firms. Delaware has to some extent been captured by its role as an onshore tax haven. The state makes so much money from the easy incorporation of thousands of legitimate businesses that little effort is put into closing loopholes for potentially illegal activity happening via shell companies there.

For the UK, the network of tax havens presents some practical problems. In each case the actual legal and constitutional link reflects very specific circumstances, and for the Caribbean states there are the additional issues of colonialism and slavery which have considerable popular resonance. In other words, doing little is often the path of least resistance, and this has strongly influenced UK actions. If the problem was simply one of tax avoidance and the loss of critical capital from the global economy, this approach might just be acceptable, but it is not. Every major leak of data on financial crime implicates the same jurisdictions. Lack of transparency in terms of company ownership is a core part of financial corruption. Also, every implicated firm of lawyers has been either based in London or one of the BOTs.[14] These firms not only create the corporate structures that allow money laundering but make full use of the UK's libel laws to ensure that criticism is suppressed.

An analysis of 237 money laundering cases (where the evidence was strong enough to trigger some form of criminal action) found that 1,200 corporations were named and their net value was £250 billion. Of these, 92 per cent were registered in the BVI.[15] Both the UK and BOTs are notionally committed to open registers of companies, but actual progress remains limited. Presently, in the Turks and Caicos Islands it is a criminal offence to disclose information about companies registered there, and this includes their true beneficiaries. This is more far-reaching than it first appears, as it is also a penalty to 'attempt to obtain confidential information'.[16] The consequence is predictable: bribes and the proceeds of embezzlement flow into banks based on the island. With past changes and new regulation, financial fraud has been able to adapt, with cryptocurrency becoming an increasing concern.[17]

The key building block to progress must be the establishment of beneficial ownership registers to end the myriad problems caused by secrecy. The UK can help directly here – and indeed force progress – through its legislative position. Such registers must be open to UK authorities to enable effective prosecution of fraud. In part, this will also help the BOTs pay for the new legislative regimes if some of the burden of policing and prosecution could be eased. The US has historically been aggressive in taking actions against individuals and companies it believes are involved, and the EU is also likely to be supportive. Only the Netherlands and France have a similar network of territories, and both have been historically lax in dealing with the issues. But, given the bulk of the financial flows go through UK territories and no one gains from the current secrecy, this is an area where the UK can lead. The structures of the Commonwealth can be effectively used to arrange summits and debates among many of the relevant states at short notice.[18]

A second key building block must be the creation of payment disclosure laws on oil, gas and mining. While not directly related to money laundering in areas where the UK has influence, this is the origin of large quantities of stolen money. In 2014, ONE (Bono's anti-poverty organisation) estimated that $1 trillion is stolen by elites from their own countries every year and siphoned out overseas. This is only a drop in the ocean compared to the many trillions in corrupt business practices and dodgy contracts common throughout

Asia, Africa and Latin America. These funds are awarded to the same elites, but here the wealth doesn't go offshore because there is little chance of repercussions without regime change – these elites *are* the regime. The most prolific theft concerns natural resources, where corruption affects every stage from the acquisition of mines and oil wells to the relationship with government – who often turn a blind eye and ensure special treatment.[19]

The perpetuating feedback loop of deeper corruption undermines economic and political freedom, since elites benefit from command economies where they control resources and extract economic rents. Elites benefit from higher tax rates since they control government spending and shelter their gains from tax overseas. Low economic freedom entrenches lower growth rates, keeping countries poor and driving immigration to the West. In many nations, these elites are often the leaders of groups like the Taliban, Hamas, Hezbollah or members of state-affiliated groups including the IGRC. Their position, and the desire to maintain it, produces electoral interference and corruption, including the election-rigging behaviour seen in Pakistan by its military government. It makes leaders less willing to sign agreements with the West on trade and cooperation, since Western rules could force open their monopolies, expose their corruption and reduce their power. Hence these countries trend towards dealing with China, who have no scruples doing business with crooks.

The UK financial system is by no means at the centre of this calamity, but the capacity to launder and hide money is a major artery that gives blood to the whole system. By cutting it off, we reduce the incentive to carry the crime upstream and so deliver outsized benefits to developing countries. Fixing this issue is the key to bringing these countries back on side with the West.

* * *

The desire to deal with financial crime is clear and shared, but the problems include a lack of both regulatory clarity and wider global adherence. In terms of cryptocurrencies, the risks of the coins are well known, and the intergovernmental Financial Action Task Force has set some key requirements for the 200 states and international bodies it counts as members.[20] It demands that crypto providers should hold full records of any clients with whom they interact, with a particular focus on regions that are subject to sanctions. Part of the problem is there is no shortage of good intent, but a lack of a clear structure. It wasn't until 2023 that the Russian Federation was removed as a full member and the BVI are still not members (nor are they members of the wider Caribbean Financial Action Task Force). In addition, the Cayman Islands and the Turks and Caicos Islands sit outside the framework. This is an issue, since voluntary adoption and self-regulation is not working in every jurisdiction. As noted, every major leak that exposes financial corruption points to the same regions as being at the core. In the case of the BVI, the UK must look beyond any sensitivities around colonialism and slavery in order to ensure Parliament's robust legislation can be made applicable to the islands. The technical process for achieving this would involve adding a clause to a statute specifying that the law applies to the BVI; alternately, an existing Act could be extended either by subsidiary legislation or by an Order in Council.

Crypto is valued in terms of central bank currencies. It lacks the backing of a state and even its most ardent believers would accept it does a very poor job as a means of exchange. It has high transaction costs and no protections against fraud or theft. It fails in the very basic test of holding a steady value, which suggests that, despite the name 'cryptocurrency', it is principally seen and valued as a new asset class for investment purposes. Its appeal is broadly based on two things: its ability to make payments that are very difficult to trace, and the widely shared story about how the finite number of coins means their value will increase exponentially. That story is largely based on psychology rather than economics, since nothing is valued only for its scarcity. The production of Bitcoin is actually a major contribution to the climate emergency, due to its high water, land and power demands.

In economics, the scarcity theory of value suggests scarcity enhances the value of anything that can be possessed, is transferable from one person to another and is *useful* to its possessor. This does not necessarily apply to Bitcoin, which has no inherent use. Psychology, however, defines the scarcity principle as the notion that humans intrinsically place a higher value on things that are perceived as rare, while devaluing things that are seen as common or abundant.[21] It is, in other words, pure animal spirits in the first order; in the second order it is a measure of how many other people we think might buy into the story. Even if that story is less than convincing, speculating on the tale and how it might spread or become so normalised that it starts to seem true is a legitimate and fascinating enterprise.

Crypto is complex; indeed, it is designed to be so. There are, however, ways to simplify the problems. Currently, the guidance works by checking the chain to ensure it meets the expectations of information retention and presentation. One proposed solution is to refuse conversion to central bank money unless this can be proved, in effect shifting the regulatory burden from having to prove there is cause for concern to expecting the *provider* to prove there is no cause for concern.[22] The UK's FCA takes a very fatalistic approach to all this. It has created rules that catch some fraudsters, and it does its best to ensure that sanctions are applied, but to prosecute it must show that regulations have been breached. The situation is worse for states like the BVI, which sit outside the voluntary international regulatory bodies. Significantly, the UK's importance as a financial centre creates the means to enhance the global approach to cryptocurrencies, especially in conjunction with the US and EU financial authorities.

The UK can shift the regulatory weight from having to *prove* fraud to demanding that those trying to convert crypto into real currencies are not actually engaged in money laundering. A softer and more agreeable approach to this would be so-called Know Your Customer (KYC) checks at both ends of a crypto transaction. The UK could, and should, add a requirement to this effect and ensure it applies in the BVI and other BOTs.

*   *   *

As with other themes covered in this book, there is an intersection between UK domestic policy and its ability to influence wider trends. An important distinction is that due to the size (and spread) of the UK financial sector, this is an area where we can directly influence the international rules. We may not be able to act unilaterally, but the UK's stance matters, and it influences that of both the US and the EU.

Across several fields, we have seen systemic regulatory failure in the UK. While Gordon Brown once celebrated the implementation of a risk-based approach based on 'trust in the responsible company', the direction of travel in British banking law has instead been to cement an overly cautious sector that does not take the required risks for the financial sector to function efficiently, let alone grow. We are less able to use technologies and innovate new applications for them than our competitors in the US. Getting regulation right could help money laundering on the periphery, but growing the City of London to its full potential would also purchase immense influence on the global financial system. We would then be better equipped to export our best practice around the world. A dual approach of increasing regulation on shell companies while broadly freeing up the City to grow and innovate is the winning combination which will do the most good in the long run.

The UK's AML strategy is riddled with inefficiencies; as we have seen, it is more about ticking boxes than tackling crime. Despite thousands of estate agencies being supervised by HMRC and millions of pounds spent on compliance training, the system overwhelmingly penalises small businesses for paperwork errors rather than catching real money launderers. The truth is, AML regulations often fail to deliver meaningful results, functioning as little more than a costly exercise in optics – *The Economist* estimated back in 2004 that global AML efforts were already burning through $5 billion annually with negligible success. Worse still, AML laws do little to address critical issues like seizing the hidden wealth of corrupt dictators or recovering stolen assets, as seen in cases like Ukraine. Yet there's a glimmer of hope: jurisdictions like the BVI, once synonymous with shady shell companies, are reforming their laws to protect their reputations. Legitimate investors increasingly shun opaque regimes, forcing tax havens to embrace transparency. Instead of clinging to ineffective AML strategies, the UK should focus on leading by example, pushing for global reforms in company and trust laws that dismantle the structures enabling financial crime.

In opposition, the Labour Party acknowledged that removing

the link between the UK financial system and corruption was of benefit to the UK and would help it achieve other key goals.[23] This builds on the Economic Crime Act of 2022, which sought to improve registration of companies, force individuals to explain how they acquired their wealth and make it easier to impose sanctions. Despite the good intentions, these measures are limited. Unexplained Wealth Orders were first introduced in 2017, but by 2022 only nine orders had been issued, and there is little evidence that they have much impact in isolation.[24]

There is now recognition of a clearer link between the problems of the domestic financial sector and the issues of overseas shell companies and tax havens. But the tone is one of evolution and reform in consultation with the sector, with the government committed to enhancing the international competitiveness of UK financial services. In terms of money laundering, the government is committed to expanding the register of assets and backing an internationally based anti-corruption court. Legally, the intent is to build on the new offence of 'failure to prevent fraud' and extend corporate liability for crimes committed by employees. While an anti-corruption court would be a strong asset in this field, new duties to collect yet more information, to ensure more corporate liability and to impose more fines for failure to prevent fraud are simply unlikely to work.

Collectively, the UK financial sector contributes somewhere around 3.5 per cent of the UK's gross value added and attracts foreign investment to the UK of over £1 billion annually.[25] In addition, if the financial sector is to be used to drive the response to the climate emergency, then the existing skills and reach of the City of London remain critical. These are genuine advantages to the UK domestically and can be used to promote the importance of the UK internationally.

But we cannot turn a blind eye to the consequences of corruption. David Cameron may have noted that corrupt states attended his anti-corruption summit in 2016, but he ignored the role of the UK as central to enabling the illicit money flows that result from corruption. Corruption is not carried out solely by specialist banks or firms (although some of those who gained from the influx of Russian money meet this definition): mainstream names such as Lloyds, Barclays, Santander and HSBC – each diligently meeting their requirements – come up time after time when corruption is exposed. Nor does it happen in unexpected places, as in addition to the UK itself, the network of Overseas Dependencies comes up in each and every exposure.

What is needed is a regulatory system that emphasises openness and permissiveness. Restrictions on practices prevent growth and divert capital, but are also corrosive to the downstream economy. Five times more capital can be raised *for an identical company* in New York compared to London. A philosophy that maximises our wealth, wellbeing and the amount of good we do in the world is one which focuses on allowing the expansion and value creation of an innovative and growing financial sector. Without it, aims of influencing allies and rivals and of designing the finance to fund the climate transition are, frankly, for the birds. But transparency must be the watchword of this new industry. Anonymity and business structures that allow corruption should be excoriated from UK corporate law and that of our oft-exploited territories. This is the balance we must strike in the future if Britain is to remain a global financial centre and a hub for world commerce in its own – and not the oligarchs' and criminals' – best interests.

CHAPTER 9

GOING FOR GROWTH

Slow economic growth is the consequence of bad policy and is the single greatest threat to Britain's pretensions to global influence. Economic output, the result of our competitive industry, fuels our defence spending, represents hard power to trade for the resources we need to develop our projects and ensures we can deliver a good standard of living to our people. The Labour government, which communicated effectively during the election that it intended to grow the economy in order to fund public services, has chosen to pursue a constellation of policies broadly categorised as 'tax and spend'. The economic core of its project is formed of two key objectives: increasing government investment to offset suggested underinvestment by the private sector, and providing wider political and fiscal stability. These two umbrella goals provide the motivation for historically large tax rises, house-building goals and revived industrial strategy.

The single biggest recent factor in Britain's high-tax status quo is the Covid pandemic. The virus, and the lockdown in response to it, cost the government around £410 billion in public spending, a figure that does not include private sector costs, lost growth or the resultant lost revenue.[1] Attempting to factor in these cumulative costs might put the total bill for the lockdown period up by another £727 billion, meaning a rough total of £1,140 billion.[2] [3] For context, Chancellor Rachel Reeves claimed the previous government left her a 'black hole' of £22 billion. Explaining this policy direction and why, with a few exceptions, Britain has spent a decade increasing taxes and crowding out investment, requires a deeper analysis of the Treasury as an institution and the incentives it faces.

The growing threat posed by authoritarian states to Western economies is not limited to military or diplomatic manoeuvres. These states increasingly operate using economic levers: from weaponised migration and cyberattacks to price manipulation and the quiet consolidation of strategic resources. These tactics undermine national resilience not with tanks or missiles but through rent extraction, supply shocks and the discrediting of institutions. China and Russia have demonstrated a deep understanding of how economic fragility can be used to degrade Western cohesion and diminish the operational freedom of liberal democracies. In response, the West must treat economic security as national security. Defensive capabilities – from rare earth metal procurement to offensive cyber tools – must be integrated into a broader strategy that sees supply-chain resilience, regulatory coherence and energy independence as central pillars of economic defence.

But this is only one side of the coin. Long-term strategic advantage will be won not by retreating from global competition but by leading it. This means advancing policies that enable compounding growth in critical sectors: energy, artificial intelligence, cyber infrastructure, biotechnology and financial services. It also requires diplomatic alignment with like-minded allies to build parallel systems of capital, trade and technology standards, in effect building a liberal counterweight to authoritarian integration. The core insight is that economic growth is not just a by-product of strategic security, but its engine. When correctly understood, it becomes clear that foreign policy, if intelligently designed, can yield economic dividends, just as economic strength can project enduring strategic influence. Without this synthesis, the West will continue to respond tactically to threats that require a generational strategy.

Britain's present economic strategy, set out in the 2024 Autumn Budget and then doubled down on in the Spending Review of June 2025, is a calamity. A high-debt, low-growth future has two dangerous consequences: high energy costs that will block us from serious involvement in the data and artificial intelligence industry, and high taxation that will harm prosperity, cause our bright young professionals to emigrate and jeopardise any chance we have of maintaining global leadership in finance and nuclear fusion power.

The scope of this chapter is not limited to a discussion of the economic direction of this new government. It includes a wider discussion of UK economic policy post-2008, and a consideration of state bureaucracy and the incentives it faces, with the goal of illuminating the wider trends and biases across British statecraft which continue to suppress economic growth. Against this backdrop of low and declining growth, our state capacity, security and foreign policy is woefully exposed.

* * *

In parallel to postmodern cultural ideas infecting public discourse, 'popular' new ideas about economic growth, some of which entered the mainstream, are increasingly coming under strain due to poor outcomes from those nations which have adopted them. Growing low-wage immigration from outside Europe has failed to pay the same economic dividends that EU migration once paid, and in 2018 represented a £9–15 billion yearly cost to the Exchequer.[4][5] Modern Monetary Theory (often called MMT) – the belief that monetary sovereignty means that nations can safely ignore fiscal budget deficits and increase money supply with low risk of inflation – has been shown by Covid to be quite dangerous, if highly fashionable.[6] Even policymakers who rightly identified a key issue – for instance that investment in the UK is low – failed to confess that high taxes were required for such public spending, and they could not foresee that those taxes would depress private sector investment yet further, as they have now done.[7][8] Record-breaking capital outflows and hiring freezes are punctuated by calculations showing that supposedly revenue-raising policies like a rise in inheritance tax could in fact have a net cost to the taxpayer of around £1,260 million due to associated job losses.[9] Meanwhile, Bank of England surveys show that inflation and redundancies will return due to the incoming tax rise on hiring labour.[10] All of this means business confidence has fallen to a new two-year low.[11]

The fallout from the 2024 Autumn Budget raises many important questions. As Deutsche Bank predicts 100,000 job losses[12] and the service sector petitions against tax hikes,[13] the most fundamental question is this: how could a government (and a historically bloated civil service[14]) committed to growth pursue such a policy? One clue, of course, is that this issue of anti-growth policy and practice predates the incumbent government, meaning it could be due in part to structural issues within the state bureaucracy itself or other affixtures to it, including academia. A second clue, however, is the way government talks about growth. Writing in the *Mirror*, Rachel Reeves argued that her National Insurance rise would increase employment and 'crowd in investment'.[15] There is no theory in economics that would justify such an expectation, let alone provide evidence for it. The Office for Budget Responsibility, by contrast, wrote that 'the employer NIC rise is estimated to reduce labour supply by 50,000 average-hours equivalents, while the net fiscal loosening would crowd out some private investment in an economy with little spare capacity'.[16] More interestingly, Reeves couches her desire for economic growth in terms of pay for minimum-wage workers, and uses 'investment' as a euphemism for general increases in public spending, rather than its true meaning of forgoing some of today's consumption for the promise of more consumption in the future. This speaks to a weakness in our political culture: growth is fundamental for Britain's role in the world and is the essence of the future wellbeing of our people, yet many of our politicians only have the courage to argue for it in reference to the minimum-wage worker.

This second clue as to why we are taking this foolish path indicates that not only is there a lack of understanding of where economic growth *comes from*, but also what it is *for*. Indeed, modern economics makes neat assumptions in order to avoid confronting this question. It expresses welfare gains from growth in terms of gross national income per capita, yet this accurate but abstract term fails to capture the imagination of politicians. In the minds of many of today's leaders, economic growth is not properly understood as the fuel of statecraft and the bedrock of any foreign policy platform. In some circles, growth in the size of our economy is not seen as having the capacity to solve problems, including climatic problems, and is even seen as the primary *cause* of such problems. The myriad ways in which growth – and the economic conditions which give rise to it – buys influence for Britain both statically and dynamically are woefully underappreciated both in Whitehall and in Parliament. So too are the ways in which compounding growth can quickly create huge differences in our standard of living.

* * *

Britain's departure from the EU means we can do more to promote growth, but we also have more freedom to pursue policies which actively prevent it. Growth, in a dynamic sense, is biased towards the industries of the future in developed economies. Semiconductors, batteries, AI, drone technology, nuclear energy and hydrogen have all failed to mature in the UK due to government failures, most notably due to regulatory matters and the crowding out of investment in competitive energy.[17] Giving up on growth today also means ceding ground in the key technology-driven value chains of the future, each with significant military and economic implications. In forgoing growth, we lose strategic independence in these future industries and diminish our bargaining power with security partners. The case of Taiwan's outsized global influence speaks to the immense importance of delivering this forward-looking growth. Britain's historical rise to become the dominant global superpower was due to its economic institutions more than its diplomatic or military prowess.

Even as large parts of the world deepen their ties with authoritarian states, the West's key asset has remained its large consumer market and productive base. Yet the declining share of world GDP, combined with US protectionism and increasing global isolationism, is changing this. Chinese production of solar panels, EVs and soon its semiconductor capacity will outstrip the West. Sanctions will become less impactful as authoritarian states can remain economically stable in the orbit of Moscow, Beijing and Tehran. What has always made the West more innovative and richer than our authoritarian rivals is the incredible economic power of free people and free markets. This chapter makes the case that Britain must return to that vision.

* * *

At its base level, diplomacy is the ability to get others to do what you want. There are many ways to achieve this, but throughout history economic influence has proved to be one of the most enduring diplomatic hooks that a nation can possess. As we noted in Chapter 6, French economist Frédéric Bastiat is credited with saying, 'When goods don't cross borders, soldiers will.' Economic prowess has been more consequential than any diplomatic or military victory (and has underpinned such victories). A prosperous, growing and technologically advanced West was assumed to be the natural order, as it sought to pull third nations into an economic *Pax Americana*. But with low growth in Britain and an isolationist US, this is an assumption of economic advantage that's dangerously close to collapsing.

There is a specific economic role that Britain must seek to play which is peculiar to its position not just as the fifth-largest economy in the world, nor only because of our role as leader of the Commonwealth, but due to our fundamental economic strengths. We are a global research heavyweight; a large, free economy situated between North America and Europe, with a powerful financial centre; and we are home to perhaps the most robust and competitive legal industry, particularly for corporate law, in the world.[18]

From that base, we must bulwark ourselves and our allies in

order to project influence over third nations. This includes leading in research and development for key future growth industries. It means maintaining our role as a trade facilitator, separate from a protectionist US and outside the customs territory of the European Union. This leading trade role – via CPTPP in Asia, Australia and Pacific Latin America, and via the Commonwealth in Africa – can provide a Western market for key rare minerals. It means assuming a dual role in climate change, as both an innovator and as a seller of green investment products, including through the raising of internationally tax-exempt debt for green projects from the City of London. We must become a safe place to raise capital for overseas foreign direct investment, to provide alternatives to Chinese finance. Finally, we must be an international provider, second only to the US, of legal, technical, educational, university and consulting services, projecting cultural and business influence globally.

On the steps of No. 10 following his election victory, Starmer reiterated his commitment to growth, claiming wealth creation was 'the number one priority of this government'. Modelling from the UK Growth Commission (UKGC), however, projects that – with the exception of planning reform, which they expect will raise growth – Britain remains on a path of economic stagnation, preferring short-term gratification over expansion in the supply side of the economy.[19] Politicians and the public tend not to understand how quickly inhibitors to growth can stack up. Productivity has been growing at 0.2 per cent per year from 2007–2019. If it had instead continued to grow at 2 per cent, the average worker in the UK would be £5,000 a year better off. As the UKGC points out, this explains our having fallen behind the US, Norway and Switzerland in terms of growth, and why we are projected to have a lower income per capita than Poland by 2030.[20]

Indeed, growth rates of between 2 per cent and 4 per cent per year are achievable, while unrealised productivity gains leave yet more potential for UK growth. Cumulatively, growth of 3 per cent per year would see the economy grow by 65 per cent by 2040, translating to higher spending of £15,000 per person per year and raising £670 billion in additional taxes to fund public services and public investment projects, and to drive foreign policy influence. But if we fail to solve the institutional, regulatory, ideological and state capacity challenges, there is no limit to how far we can slip behind. UK GDP per capita has fallen from around 77 per cent of the US figure in 2017 to about 70 per cent today.[21] For a typical family household this represents a difference of £24,000 per year in pre-tax spending power. Given tax rates in the US are lower, this difference may be even more dramatic post-tax, depending on the US state in question.

* * *

Britain is failing to grow because we're getting our incentives wrong. It is widely understood that taxing a thing discourages the doing of that thing. Directly raising the cost of a good reduces the total gain from buying it while raising the relative attractiveness of alternative goods. This will lead to less consumption of the taxed thing, provided that its quantity is sensitive to price. (Taxing a thing whose supply is not sensitive to price, for instance something in fixed supply such as land, doesn't 'distort' the economy to reduce consumption and so is called a non-distortionary tax.) The perhaps slightly counter-intuitive insight I wish to get across is this: if the point of a tax is simply to raise revenue, then a lump-sum tax is most desirable since it doesn't affect decisions or consumption. There may be other goals with taxation – perhaps you *want* to reduce consumption of polluting cars or cigarettes – but for revenue-raising, changing behaviour is a bad thing: it means producers producing less and consumers consuming less (or consuming alternatives). Hal Varian, one of the great economic educators and the chief economist at Google, measures this as the value of the output not sold due to the presence of the tax, called deadweight loss. As a result, in a headline: the economy gets smaller.

Nowhere is this dynamic of taxation more familiar than with income taxes. Taxing the income of labour discourages earning income from labour. Let us imagine a worker is deciding how many hours to work per week. With each hour he works, he is trading off his leisure time for additional pay. He doesn't want lots of pay with no leisure time, and he doesn't want lots of leisure time with no pay – ideally, he wants a high degree of both. He will keep working more hours until the marginal benefit from more pay is equal to the marginal cost to him of an hour's lost leisure. In other words – he'll keep working until he prefers the leisure to the extra pay. Say chooses to work forty-five hours. If an income tax comes into effect and reduces his pay by 40 per cent for those last ten hours (because they put him into a higher tax bracket), that point when he prefers leisure to pay will come a lot sooner. So the economy gets smaller.

What if we instead tax this worker 40 per cent (or 100 per cent!) on the *first* ten hours he works (and then nothing on the rest)? We've already seen that he will maximise his welfare until he prefers the leisure to the extra pay at forty-five hours. The tax in the first ten hours *doesn't* affect his marginal decision to work subsequent hours, in so far as he's substituting leisure for pay. So, economists would say the *substitution effect* is zero: the tax doesn't affect his decision to work and you've raised some tax without distorting the economy.

In fact, there is also an *income effect*. With less income due to the high tax on his first ten hours, he may find it worthwhile to work a forty-sixth or forty-seventh hour. Just like with consumption taxes, organising an income tax schedule so that it only minimally affects decisions is crucial. Not all taxes are a significant drag on growth if they are designed with an eye on the incentives and disincentives they cause.

Of course, a policy which had a 40 per cent tax on the *first* few thousand pounds earned per year would affect some decisions. It wouldn't affect the decision of our 45-hour-a-week worker, but it may affect a part-time worker or underemployed worker who only works eight hours a week. They may drop out of the labour force entirely. Other policies may aggravate the effect even for someone working more than the ten hours. We mentioned that taxes push people towards alternatives. At the low end of the income distribution, taxes could push people into out-of-work benefits if they are badly designed. Not only can benefits take people out of work, but they also discourage work (known as the 'welfare trap') further up the income distribution, as the removal of benefits sees effective tax rates rise, in some cases by as much as 600 per cent.[22] Discouraging labour at the higher end of the income distribution causes the highest economic and fiscal costs.

What is true of taxation is true of benefits. As businessman and investor Charlie Munger used to say, 'Show me the incentives and I'll show you the outcome.' The proliferation of so-called 'sickfluencers' (individuals who monetise coaching others on how to exploit welfare eligibility) exemplifies the deeper systemic failures embedded within the UK's benefits framework. The emergence of a marketplace for benefits consultancy, where sessions can rival the hourly fees of top legal professionals, reflects how lucrative and normalised these practices have become. The benefits system, shaped by flawed incentives and weak enforcement mechanisms, has created fertile ground for exploitation. Particularly concerning is the shift to remote assessments, a pandemic-era contingency that has persisted, which has significantly reduced the rigour of claim evaluations and facilitated abuse. With the number of incapacity claimants projected to rise by 800,000 during the current parliament, and with over 3,000 people daily being signed off as unfit for work, the system is patently unsustainable. Yet so unserious are Britain's parliamentarians that attempts to cut welfare under Starmer have so far been thwarted without exception.

This institutional permissiveness carries profound fiscal and social implications. The total cost of benefits has ballooned from £244 billion pre-pandemic to £303 billion today (an increase that makes us a distant outlier compared to peer nations), while the number of individuals *reliant* on the state nearly equals those *funding* it through taxes. Despite historical precedent in controlling welfare expansion through caps and tax reforms, recent policy inertia has allowed unsustainable trends to harden. Indeed, in cities like Birmingham, one in four working-age adults is now economically inactive – a statistic more severe than at any point during the Great Depression. This widespread disengagement from work not only squanders human potential but threatens the long-term viability of the welfare state itself. Attempts to reform the system, such as those outlined by Kemi Badenoch, propose aligning legal definitions of disability with common understanding and eliminating foreign national claims, which cost the government £1 billion monthly. In the context of rising public debt and economic contraction, such measures are not only fiscally prudent but politically necessary. If unaddressed, the current trajectory risks precipitating a full-scale crisis of confidence in both the economy and the state's capacity to govern effectively.

Restoring fiscal control sits at the heart of a nexus of British strategic policy, from cheaper energy to cheaper welfare to cheaper imports to cheaper business. Getting incentives right – by avoiding subsidising expense and inactivity, and avoiding taxing productivity and economisation – is a prerequisite. Efforts by the incumbent government, from winter fuel payments to welfare cuts, all quashed by backbench MPs, testify to the fact that even the most spend-thrift government since the pandemic has realised the need to cut spending – they just don't have the ability. Reeves will have to enact austerity, if indeed she remains in her position long enough. But she will have to do it with the votes of MPs who spent a decade and a half disingenuously arguing that austerity is a choice. Until this unserious attitude changes, Britain will be unable to dislodge the keystone in the wall holding back growth.

* * *

What we have made here is an argument from first principle for tax reform. Even very popular elements of our tax system, like the personal allowance, are inefficient. It would be better to abolish it and lower marginal tax rates, which would encourage more work. We should, by the same token, take efforts to avoid high marginal rates from the withdrawal of benefits.

Optimal taxation theory results from a serious analysis of how to raise revenue with minimal distortion to the economy, while assuming the ultimate goal of maximising social welfare (social welfare is modelled as a function of consumption and leisure and prefers equality to inequality). One alternative to our distortionary welfare system would simply be a negative income tax, or NIT, which would, as the name suggests, allow taxable income to become negative through deductions while keeping the rate flat, keeping distortion relatively low with a 20 per cent flat tax.

Another non-distortionary tax – favoured by the Georgist movement – is concerned with economic rent from land owner-ship. They propose a land-value tax on the *unimproved* value of the land. It's worth briefly explaining why the incentives of a land-value tax (LVT) work well. An LVT would create a strong disincentive to leaving land unimproved, since making improvements to land would not incur a higher tax bill. It would not be distortionary, since land is in fixed supply and quantity is not sensitive to price. It cannot affect the decision to supply land, but it can positive-ly affect other decisions, such as how the land is used, as there is a strong disincentive to holding land for unproductive purposes. Again, a tax can help unlock inefficiencies in the British economy, particularly concerning house-building and infrastructure. Gains from building public infrastructure would accrue to owners, but the taxpayer would receive a higher tax take from the increased unim-proved value of the land. While Georgists once believed in LVTs as a 'single tax', it is clear that an LVT alone cannot generate sufficient revenue to fund the modern British state. It does, however, show that pro-growth, efficient taxation is perfectly possible. Pro-growth tax policy should encourage the maximum and most efficient allo-cation of each input: land, labour and capital.

To explain the third input, capital, optimal taxation theory sug-gests capital income should not be taxed, at least in expectation. Distortions on capital depress savings motives, while decreasing capital accumulation and investment (and Britain has very low cap-ital employment compared to all other G7 economies).[23] The UK's capital-to-GDP ratio was just 17 per cent in 2022, one of the lowest of any high-income country.[24] The problem cannot be confined to tax rates alone, as the UK has many other causes of low investment in this area. It is much harder to raise capital in the UK than in the US, with a much thinner venture capital market. Research and development projects often go unfunded, move to the US or resort to government funding, since they lack the tangible assets that a traditional property plant and equipment (PP&E) investment would hold as collateral. Immigration is another key cause. Low-skilled labour kept artificially cheap through immigrant workers (who, crucially, are also cheaper to hire as they avoid punitive employment taxes) leads to lower investment in capital and little to no investment in skills for long-term workers. During the election campaign, Starmer signalled his awareness of exactly this phenomenon affecting British skills and capital investment.[25]

There are structural reasons why high capital gains taxes (CGTs) are particularly bad for growth. One is that capital is *the* most internationally mobile factor input and can very easily go where it is treated best. A tax paid by just 369,000 taxpayers each year, with 38,000 paying 80 per cent of the total amount, is most sensitive to changing decisions in an adverse way. This is because such revenue from a CGT can, and most often does, move in the opposite direction to headline CGT rates.[26] Capital can move overseas. Capital (including houses) can be held instead of sold in order to leave the gain unrealised, readily causing massive distortions. It fundamentally disincentivises making improvements to property. Consider how CGT is levied on the entire gross gain, not the true net profit post-fees. After purchasing an investment product – and after stamp duty – management fees, performance fees and interest on any leverage are paid post-tax. Hence, multiplicatively, a 24 per cent capital gains tax can quickly represent even a 50 per cent decrease in investment profitability. Corporate taxes and the Air Passenger Duty (APD) are perhaps the only taxes that can claim to be more damaging to growth.[27] They are intensely internationally mobile and directly affect the profitability of investments.[28] The lower the rate of return, the less capital we can retain in Britain, with disastrous effects for growth downstream.

What is perhaps most concerning is not the worsening of our position, day by day. It is rather that the government seems concerned with exporting its failed model of economic management as widely as possible.[29] Starmer was instrumental in the signing of an international agreement at UN level, known as the 'Sevilla Commitment', which calls for greater environmental levies and 'gender-responsive taxation'. The idea is that if all countries discourage growth equally, then would-be innovators will have nothing to gain from leaving the high-tax country. The problem, of course, is that not only will nations (particularly the US and most Asian nations) refuse to sign up, but removing the incentive to emigrate does not suddenly make it worthwhile to innovate and invest. It is the politics of shooting everyone else in the foot so we don't get left behind.

* * *

What is the upshot of all this for Britain? Under successive Conservative governments, the UK's tax competitiveness fell from eleventh in the world in 2015 down to thirtieth in 2024.[30] This set us far apart from New Zealand (third), Australia (thirteenth), Germany (sixteenth), Canada (seventeenth) and the US (eighteenth). Despite conventional wisdom, the UK even lags significantly behind countries like Norway (nineteenth) and Sweden (twelfth), with the French (thirty-sixth), Spanish (thirty-third) and Greek (twenty-seventh) economies being our true opposite numbers. This, critically, was all true *before* Chancellor Rachel Reeves's Autumn Budget of 2024 and her upcoming Autumn Budget of 2025. Personal income tax thresholds continue to be frozen and therefore shrinking in real terms given inflation. Capital gains taxes have increased from 10 per cent to 18 per cent for basic-rate taxpayers and 20 per cent to 24 per cent for higher-rate taxpayers. Stamp duty surcharges add to what is already among the highest burdens in the OECD, making the housing market less liquid and yet more dysfunctional.[31] National insurance hikes for employers function similarly to a personal income tax hike, except they affect the demand for labour rather than the supply. The size of the distortion to the economy is similar, but when employers cannot afford to hire workers, the state is obligated to pay out-of-work benefits instead.

Other non-tax interventions can be similarly distortionary to prices and therefore hit growth. The rise in the national living wage raises the costs of employment. The damage is particularly strong among under-twenty-ones whose hourly pay will increase 16.3 per cent year on year. These workers are most likely to be in part time employment alongside education. They are also likely to have the least experience and therefore be able to command only the smallest wages. Combined with the fact that the NI threshold on an employee's salary now starts at £5,000 for the employer, the total cost of hiring an under-twenty-one on minimum wage will multiplicatively increase by around 30 per cent at the margin. UK hospitality estimates that in a realistic worst-case scenario, a part-time worker on fifteen hours a week will see their NIC bill increase by 73 per cent. Mercifully, corporation tax has been left well alone.

The UK also faces a worklessness crisis of its own creation.

Personal Independence Payments (PIPs) and other health- and sickness-related benefits are on course to pass £100 billion a year by 2030, according to the OBR. Politicians have benefited from being able to claim falling unemployment, when in reality the unemployed were being removed from statistics because they are deemed unable to work for health reasons. Politicians have no incentive to address this, as it would make statistics worse under their watch. A Resolution Foundation report shows that those close to the government are well aware of the costs of long-term unemployment, particularly of the young and physically healthy, many of whom have been university educated at the taxpayer's expense.[32] Unfortunately, alongside convincing the Treasury and the OBR that reforms would be cost-saving, the challenge is so immense that playing 'pass the parcel' is deemed politically savvy.

Tax rises can cause economic losses exponentially higher than the amount of revenue raised. For instance, the economic benefits of abolishing Air Passenger Duty (APD) were modelled by PwC, which predicted a UK-wide productivity gain and a 10 per cent increase in business travel. Modelling showed more flight purchases, 7 per cent more tourism, more fare competitiveness, more investment and, downstream, higher tax receipts from households, indirect taxes (VAT) and businesses. PwC have found that the abolition of APD would lead to a net revenue *gain* for the Treasury and a boost to GDP of 0.45 per cent in the first twelve months. Yet the October 2024 Autumn budget increased it further.

* * *

The government itself, and not just politics, is a major part of the problem. Central government staff costs are up 15.1 per cent *on the year* to £18.3 billion in November. Temporary staffing increases during Covid have become entrenched and permanent. Spending on benefits increased by £1.2 billion.[33] Following a string of pay rises to nurses and teachers, the OBR forecasts that spending will rise by £239 billion by 2030 (the government still claims it intends to see borrowing *fall* over the period). There is no sign, however, of public pay demands relenting after this payout.[34] The government has announced £21.7 billion of funding for carbon capture and storage (CCS) projects – paid for by higher taxation and through levies on energy bills for households and businesses. It is fair to say that, disregarding export potential for any technology created, these industries will be viable only because of government subsidy for removal and storage of carbon, since they produce little of saleable economic value to the private sector. This ongoing funding, as with solar and wind projects, will come from taxes and levies on the ever-shrinking productive and competitive part of the economy. As if to prove the point, the North Sea oil investment allowance, which allowed companies to offset some of the windfall tax by reinvesting in British production, has been abolished, and replaced by a 'decarbonisation allowance'.[35] This cheap energy and fuel is crucial for Britain's pretensions to be a major player in the AI and data revolution, but our leaders prefer to leave it in the sea bed and instead import gas at a higher price.

There are some reasons why our tax system has got this bad. The Treasury prefers taxes that raise money *reliably* over taxes that raise money *efficiently*. For example, the energy levy is immensely damaging to growth, especially manufacturing, computing and other energy-intensive sectors; like APD, it almost certainly costs more to the Treasury elsewhere than it raises directly. Yet because it raises a reliable stream of income, it becomes built into future plans and is therefore very difficult to repeal.

Traditional analysis tends to ignore institutional design. But in reality, institutions are imperfect. Their workers face personal incentives which tend not to perfectly match the mandate of the institution. They are often inefficient and constantly evolving. What is best for the career of a civil servant – a larger budget, more influence and reputation across Whitehall – is seldom best for the country. The challenges with the Treasury, however, run deeper than a simple principal–agent problem. The power dynamics between No. 10 and the Treasury leaves the Treasury in the driving seat of government strategy. If there is an institutional bias, as there is, towards spending control and sound money, then this will be reflected, almost unavoidably, in government policy. The centralisation of spending decisions in the Treasury presents its own inefficiencies, while a total lack of transparency sees the same 'favourite' Treasury ideas (including inheritance tax on farms and means-testing the Winter Fuel Allowance) to come up again and again.[36]

There is merit to *some* of former Prime Minister Liz Truss's criticisms. While it is unlikely, as she claims, the Treasury is 'ideologically' anti-growth, their modelling and processes certainly are. Government modelling, for instance, does not allow tax rises to spur economic growth, while it *does* apply a so-called multiplier effect downstream of public spending. In other words, the benefits of government spending are treated dynamically, but the benefits of tax cuts are only treated statically. The main *static* effect of a tax cut, of course, is to straightforwardly reduce government revenue. As discussed at length in this chapter, the whole point of a tax cut is to change decisions and to allow new transactions to take place that were not otherwise happening. These will not appear in a static analysis. In her column, Truss describes, quite accurately, how this 'inevitably puts pressure on a higher-tax and higher-spend outcome

– hence the inexorable tax rises we are now seeing.'[37] This goes some way to explain why taxes like APD have been allowed to increase even though *decreasing* them would most likely raise revenue and growth.

Indeed, governments are also expected to make decisions according to five-year forecasts about government spending and revenues. These forecasts are, without exaggeration, *always* wrong, but not adjusting policy to satisfy them results in an 'uncosted' budget. It works both ways, of course. Analysts are expecting that inheritance tax changes, and the application of VAT to private school fees, will both raise considerably less revenue than Treasury estimates. This is a leading reason why gilt yields are rising.[38] Hugh Gimber, a strategist at J.P. Morgan Asset Management, opines that 'at a time when yields are rising everywhere, global investors are looking at the UK like the weakest link in the chain'. Much of this analysis suggests that revenues will, in the event, be negative, due to the dynamic decisions of parents and farmers in the face of these changes (parents pull their children out of school and farmers will close down their farms).

The Treasury and OBR are, to put it bluntly, no good at dynamic analysis. Reeves even less so. The effect of this is that 'forecast' deficits often prove illusory – meaning that higher taxes were insisted upon when in fact they were unnecessary or even counterproductive. On the other hand, the overestimation of tax revenues and of the benefits of public spending lead to a budget like that of October 2024, which superficially 'funds' extra government spending, but, in the event, is unlikely to raise anywhere near as much as these static models predict.[39] The UK civil service should also consider, when undertaking technical economic research, that it has a duty to be transparent in the methods it uses and to discuss with outside economists the strengths and weaknesses of the analysis, as is customary in academic debate.[40]

It is quite remarkable how bad Treasury modelling really is. One report from the Cass Business School, memorably titled 'Measurement without theory: On the extraordinary abuse of economic models in the EU referendum debate', detailed the assumptions that went into earlier pre-referendum predictions. The Treasury assumed, without any particular reason, that leaving the EU would cause an economic shock equivalent to 50 per cent of that seen after the 2008 financial crisis. To be clear, this was an *input* into their model, not an output. They also assumed that the UK would, by 2030, have achieved *zero* FTAs, not with the EU nor with the rest of the world. These Treasury modelling errors – if we may call them that – are by no means limited to Brexit, though given the department, and most of the civil service, was intractably opposed to it, some of the most recklessly fraudulent analysis came from that period.

The final piece of this puzzle concerns what the government is more or less forced to do with the analysis supplied. They are to treat these erroneous five-year forecasts as if they are not just indicative, but perfectly accurate. This means forecasts have caused market chaos before now: perhaps most recently, the energy package to households following the outbreak of war in Ukraine, costed by the Treasury at £160 billion, turned out to cost under £78.2 billion, because the Treasury assumed no improvement whatsoever in the wholesale price of gas.[41] Similarly, Reeves was made to design her budget's tax rises based on farcical predictions about how much they would raise, farcical predictions about how large the economy would be and farcical predictions about how much she was going to spend over the next five years. Each highly dubious calculation fed into the next. The result amounts to little more than a performative, hoop-jumping fabrication, and is therefore completely short-sighted and cannot be allowed to promote growth dynamically and is fragile to even slight changes in forecasts – forecasts which are always wrong.

One Institute for Government report points to the Treasury's outsized and unbalanced power and its arrogant secrecy and in-group clique, who export its own engrained biases and low-expectation stasis onto other departments (since 'departments are expected to subject their workings to minute Treasury scrutiny, while seldom enjoying a reciprocal right over Treasury deliberations over tax initiatives relevant to their own policy area').[42] The Treasury is far from the only instrument of the British state blocking growth, but it is certainly the keystone. Many reports show how better forecasting (including at the Bank of England) could have prevented post-Covid high inflation. Better forecasting would also caution against ineffective and costly regulations (by more accurately estimating the costs they impose), and drive policy creation with a closer eye on how macro patterns can emerge non-linearly from dynamic interactions of heterogeneous agents. In other words, small changes can have big effects due to dynamic effects on individual decision-making. Reforming the Treasury, especially those elements which allow it to produce poor-quality reports based on highly political internal groupthink, is the first step. With a better Treasury at her command, even this Chancellor would likely have made fewer mistakes.

*　　*　　*

For many years, the proposition that immigration is a driver of economic growth enjoyed widespread acceptance. On a global scale, the movement of people from less productive regions to more productive ones appears self-evidently beneficial. Even at the national level, economic models suggested that a greater supply of labour – a key input to production – would naturally increase output and thus raise GDP.

Yet this consensus rested on assumptions that have, over time, proven mistaken. The fiscal contribution of unskilled migrants, for instance, has often been negative. Estimates show that the average non-EEA low-skilled worker is likely to cost the state more than they contribute over their lifetime, particularly when dependants are taken into account. These calculations typically exclude wider economic and social externalities, such as the upward pressure on housing costs, increased demand on overstretched public services and the added burden on physical infrastructure.

At the start of the twenty-first century, many migrants arriving in the UK, whether from the EU or further afield, shared similar levels of education and social background with the resident population. Non-EU migrants, subject to stricter entry criteria, were often drawn from the middle classes of Commonwealth countries. However, the composition of immigration has shifted significantly in the post-Brexit period. According to the OBR, recent inflows have skewed more heavily towards categories such as international students and dependants, groups with historically lower rates of workforce participation.

Policymakers had assumed that the economy would respond elastically to these changes. Housing supply would rise with demand; utilities and public services would scale to match population growth; the labour market would absorb new entrants without consequence for native employment or wages; cheap labour would not alter business investment decisions; and social cohesion would remain intact. In short, immigration would follow the neat logic of economic models. In reality, none of these assumptions held. Migrant workers differ from natives not only in productivity, but in the price at which they are willing to supply their labour, the sectors in which they are concentrated, their levels of social capital and their preferences as consumers, particularly in housing, where immigrant and native populations often prefer to live in different neighbourhoods. The UK's housing supply, constrained by planning regulations and a financial system heavily reliant on high property values, failed to expand in step with population growth. The result has been a surge in rents, decreased housing affordability and a notable reduction in living space per person. The phenomenon of 'shrinkflation' now extends beyond food packaging to residential property, with homes being subdivided or downsized in ways that do not register in headline economic statistics, but which materially diminish quality of life.

The government's official housing plans, based on annual net migration of 170,000, anticipated the need for approximately 72,000 new homes per year. In 2022, net migration stood at over 900,000. Even with strong house-building figures, supply is nowhere near sufficient. In London, nearly 70 per cent of private rentals are headed by individuals born outside the UK, and immigration in 2022 alone was responsible for a 10 per cent rise in rents. Public services have also failed to keep pace. Over the past decade, the population has grown by 6.6 per cent, yet the number of general practitioners has increased by just 4 per cent. The country's electricity-generation capacity fell by over 14 per cent in the same period. Across housing, transport, energy and healthcare, the UK's capacity is demonstrably insufficient to accommodate immigration on anything like its current scale.

The ONS projects that the UK population will rise from 67 million in 2021 to 73.7 million by 2036, with 91 per cent of that increase attributable directly to immigration. Much of the remainder will be due to the children of recent migrants. Without stronger economic growth, such rapid demographic expansion will render per capita public spending and infrastructure investment increasingly difficult to sustain.

In addition to the economic miscalculations, policymakers also underestimated the political and social consequences. They assumed immigration would not lead to political polarisation, that the UK would not become a magnet for illegal immigration (which by 2022 was estimated to cost £14 billion annually, with a further £4.7 billion spent on asylum support) and that a shadow labour market, in which undocumented migrants work in substandard or exploitative conditions, would not emerge. Each of these assumptions has proven either misguided or incorrect. The failure to distinguish clearly between different types of migration – in terms of skill level, fiscal impact or intention – has led to a system overwhelmed in both numbers and complexity. And yet the tools for addressing these problems remain largely untouched.

* * *

One of the most damaging ideas to British long-term economic growth has been the influence of environmental activism, particularly when it comes to energy policy. Britain's failure to invest adequately in North Sea gas production, at a time when we needed to reduce reliance on Russian gas, reflects a deeper strategic failure. Political decisions in Westminster (including green levies and windfall taxes) and long-standing obstructionism from devolved administrations in Scotland have discouraged investment in domestic energy. The underlying belief, driven by environmental ideology rather than economic logic, was that by making domestic fossil fuel production uneconomic, the country would be forced to transition to renewables. In practice, as local supply dwindles, Britain has simply turned to foreign imports to meet demand – at significant cost. Without the infrastructure, storage capacity or grid investment to support a large-scale switch to renewables, the country is left paying foreign suppliers while failing to meet energy security goals. Indeed, the Energy and Climate Intelligence Unit warns that gas import dependence could rise by 60 per cent by 2035.

This approach is akin to trying to lose weight by throwing away your cooker – the result is not lower consumption, but higher spending on convenience food. The UK now spends £100 billion annually importing gas, primarily from Norway, which continues to exploit the same North Sea reserves the UK has chosen to abandon. There is no real environmental benefit – only a transfer of costs and control. And Norway is no guaranteed long-term supplier. Analysts warn that as Norway's production slows and its politics shift, the vacuum may be filled by Russian exports. The implications are not just economic but geopolitical. Meanwhile, nuclear power – long opposed by the same environmental factions – has suffered decades of neglect, despite being one of the few proven paths to both energy security and decarbonisation. The UK government's exclusion of nuclear energy from its own Green Financing Framework in 2021, citing activist investor preferences, reveals how deeply these anti-growth ideas have permeated decision-making.

These mistakes have left Britain with some of the highest electricity prices in the developed world – four times higher than in the US. This has led to deindustrialisation, not because British industry is uncompetitive, but because it has been priced out by domestic policy. A case in point is Tata Steel's Port Talbot site, deemed inefficient and unprofitable by its owners, yet given £500 million in government funding to build an electric arc furnace powered by prohibitively expensive energy. At the same time, new energy grid connections are being blocked by a regulatory body established to help meet aggressive decarbonisation targets, because the grid itself lacks the capacity to handle the surge in new projects driven by state subsidies. The entire strategy depends on continued high public spending and subsidies to paper over structural weaknesses created by policy.

Instead of pursuing an anti-growth, anti-industrial agenda dressed in environmental language, Britain could have led on green diplomacy, using its market and capital to secure global supply chains for critical inputs like uranium, lithium and gallium, while maintaining stable domestic energy prices. Strategic investments in proven technologies such as nuclear, along with focused support for areas of British expertise like nuclear fusion, could have preserved the UK's industrial base and positioned it as a leader in the global energy transition. Yet successive governments failed to grasp the importance of affordable inputs to economic growth, allowing ideology to drive decisions that made Britain less competitive at the exact moment when we need to build, invest and lead.

*　*　*

Britain must now design a growth strategy not as an economic vanity project, but as a geopolitical necessity. In an era where liberal democracy is embattled by the rise of 'managed democracies' and increasingly confident authoritarian powers, economic dynamism and strategic capability are prerequisites for diplomatic influence. A stagnant Britain cannot shape the standards of AI, the rules of green finance or the institutional norms governing cyberspace and trade. It cannot lead multilateral reform, nor counter disinformation and proxy authoritarian warfare without economic and technological weight to back its principles. Every major decision, from tax reform to planning, energy, immigration and investment, must be filtered through a singular strategic lens: does this policy make Britain stronger, more agile and more relevant in an era of systemic competition?

The UK's 2025 Strategic Defence Review acknowledges that hostile state actors are challenging the international order not just with arms but through economic coercion and infrastructure control. Only with growth can Britain project an effective response and avoid dependence on foreign regimes. Through competitive energy prices, advanced manufacturing and specialisation in frontier technologies where we have a latent advantage, Britain could become a supplier of strategic goods – from nuclear technology to cybersecurity services – to other democracies in need of alternatives to authoritarian capital.

A credible plan to 'go for growth', particularly while clear-eyed that our economy must also serve our soft and hard power influence to bring about specific desirable outcomes, must give treatment to one of the most expensive but most important sources of both – our nuclear deterrent. The recommendations of *A Greater Britain* support the Strategic Defence Review 2025 in its conclusion that developing tactical nuclear capacity would bolster Britain's defence offering and provide the ultimate insurance in the event that the guarantee of US tactical nuclear capability being used to protect us comes under question. It would, unlike our strategic deterrent, be usable outside the explicit consent and knowledge of the US, and would therefore guard against the possibility that the US could judge that using tactical nukes on our behalf was too risky for them, against the possibility that they have a vacuum of leadership or have competing priorities. It would form the most expensive yet most important component of our platform of global influence.

Any decision to establish a British tactical nuclear capability must be judged first and foremost as an economic programme as much as a military one. These are significant resources, raised at a time when the tax burden is already too high, and they have many productive alternative uses. The UK already has large, ongoing nuclear commitments: the replacement and sustainment of the strategic deterrent represents a multi-decade, multi-billion-pound effort, and the government already needs a major near-term commitment to strategic warhead modernisation and to replace Trident. Extending that posture to include an additional, sub-strategic capability would therefore add a distinct and measurable set of costs.

There are two realistic acquisition pathways, and each carries very different price tags. The lower-cost option is a NATO-style approach in which the United States provides warheads that are forward-based, or which are made available to Royal Air Force delivery platforms under agreed arrangements. This route requires procurement of compatible dual-capable aircraft or integration kits, hardened storage and security facilities, extensive certification and training, and long-term hosting and operational costs. Upfront bills under this model are modest by comparison with building an indigenous warhead – on the order of hundreds of millions to a few billion pounds in initial capital spending – but they carry a persistent political and operational dependence on the US and require recurring costs for basing, security and life-cycle support.

The higher-cost, fully sovereign pathway is to design, test, produce and integrate a UK warhead and the associated delivery architecture under British control. That option is expensive and slow. Reconstituting a sovereign warhead design and production base; regenerating specialist scientific and manufacturing skills; creating bespoke safety and certification regimes; and integrating the warhead with a domestic or purchased delivery system (an air-launched cruise missile, for example) would most plausibly run to a programme of tens of billions of pounds from concept to initial operational capability. In round terms, an indigenous tactical programme could reasonably be expected to require an initial investment in the single-figure to low-double-digit billions (for example, roughly £5–£20 billion) and then further sustainment and replacement costs across subsequent decades that together would make the life-cycle bill materially larger. The Strategic Defence Review also quotes a cost exceeding £15 billion. The benefits are a tactical option, independent of the United States, than can be used, or threatened, with a lower (but non-zero) risk of mutually assured destruction.

How would those figures sit inside the political defence envelope under discussion? Defence spending trajectories under recent allied agreements envisage a substantial rise in defence expenditure over the coming decade. Using a conservative baseline for the UK economy, a 1 per cent-of-GDP change is worth roughly £29 billion a year. If the UK moves from a near-term defence burden of roughly 2.4 per cent of GDP to an eventual target of 5 per cent of GDP, the annual uplift in defence spending would be on the order of £70–80 billion a year. Amortising a £10–20 billion indigenous tactical programme over ten years implies an annualised charge of about £1.0–£2.0 billion a year – equivalent to only a single-digit percentage of the total annual uplift required to reach a 5 per cent target. Even a larger, more conservative life-cycle figure amortised over a longer period would remain a modest share of the total new annual defence resources envisaged under a 5 per cent outcome.

None of this should be read as an argument that cost is trivial. For our current purposes, it should be read instead as arguing that Britain *can* afford such an expense even without expanding beyond the 5 per cent NATO target. It should also underscore the central thesis of this chapter: that Britain must cut tax and spending else-where and must focus on real sources of power and influence, and in aligning our many sources of power, hard and soft, into a coherent strategy.

This chapter calls for nothing short of dramatic economic reform. Planning reform must unlock housing, transport and green energy infrastructure. The tax system must reward capital formation and skilled work, not punish ambition. Immigration policy must benefit the British people or else immigration itself must be curtailed. And critically, the UK must take energy security seriously. A reliance on imported gas, while decommissioning domestic sources and under-investing in nuclear, has left Britain exposed.

The good news is that our national fortunes have turned around before, and very quicky. Our economic goal for this century is to make Britain globally indispensable: a hub of innovation, specialist regulation and capital that advances liberty by its example.

CHAPTER 10

SOFT POWER

The idea of soft power is something that has caused Britain, and our leaders, significant problems. As we have argued, there has been a tendency for leaders and diplomats to hide behind claims of 'credibility' when doing things that reduce the long-term strategic capability of the UK. In many places in this book, I have argued that how the UK acts domestically and internationally will affect its ability to influence global actions. In a few instances, such as security and finance and – with careful management – future industry in cybersecurity and nuclear fusion, the UK is apt to be powerful enough to have a very distinct and influential voice, even in an age of superpowers and transnational blocs. In each case we have answered with deference to an implicit principle of soft power: how will this soft power pay for itself in terms of hard power?

In this chapter, I lay out the justification and strategy of Britain's soft power gambit – the Knowledge Power Doctrine (KPD). KPD is a doctrine through which Britain can align its many sources of soft power into powerful and strategically useful sources of influence. If we can overcome the domestic challenges outlined in this book, and restore balance over the bureaucracy and judiciary, this chapter lays out the blueprint to build Westminster's global influence. By leveraging our disproportionate soft power, institutional credibility and global networks, Britain can position itself not merely as a participant in world politics, but as the go-to source for solving the most pressing international challenges. This model – part diplomacy, part thought leadership, part strategic entrepreneurship – might also be called *ideas-first diplomacy*.

Soft power is and must be thought of as a substitute for hard power; as such, the costs of obtaining soft power are justified in so far as it is able to do the job of hard power. Joseph S. Nye, who coined the term, defined soft power as 'the ability to get what you want through attraction rather than coercion or payment. It arises from the attractiveness of a country's culture, political ideals and policies'. Conceptually, soft power can therefore never be a goal in itself. It is desired as a result of its ability to replace hard power. Soft power is often the product of things that are themselves goals of good statecraft: a strong economy, thriving social and political institutions and an educated and open-minded citizenry. Soft power can be ephemeral and, contrary to the beliefs of naive appeasers, it is not distributed by merit or morality. It can come from activity, strength and recognisability much more straightforwardly than from good deeds.

Britain has been described as a 'soft power superpower', largely due to its global cultural footprint, historic diplomatic reach, recognisable institutions like the BBC, leading universities and its role in shaping liberal norms through bodies such as the Commonwealth. The English language, the legacy of empire and the global aspiration to British arts, education and legal traditions have all contributed to this perception. Some of those also point to Britain's ability to convene international coalitions, influence global debates and export governance expertise as evidence of its enduring soft power. This reputation is often asserted uncritically. Calling Britain a soft power superpower can be misleading if it ignores the crucial test: does this influence translate into real outcomes? Influence without effect is branding, not power. Britain's cultural recognisability does not automatically yield diplomatic results, nor does it shield the country from strategic irrelevance in a world increasingly shaped by hard economic and military realities. Without a clear strategy linking soft power assets to foreign policy goals – and the institutional capacity to act on them – Britain risks mistaking visibility for effectiveness, and naive moral esteem for leverage. There is a real risk that moralising leaders flatter themselves into thinking the world is more impressed than it really is.

Nothing underscores this better than Chagos and Israel–Palestine. Britain's leaders broadcast that they were 'completing the process of decolonisation of Mauritius'. As we saw in Chapter 2, Philippe Sands KC, Starmer's close friend from his days as a barrister, announced to the Lords International Relations and Defence Committee that the Chagos deal was 'enhancing Britain's position in the world'. While recognising, of course, that Sands has a client in the Mauritians, the idea, ubiquitous throughout the current government, is that this handover earns us soft power. That idea, quite frankly, is for the birds.

At that Committee meeting, Sands (evidently believing he was strengthening his case) argued that 'Mauritius has many other islands it could give to China'.[1] Far from showing that Britain was a serious dealmaking power, the deal broadcast that Britain is willing to compromise fundamental interests and throw away hard power. It bears repeating: doing things that sound 'moral' does not boost our soft power if we come out looking foolish and naive. Soft power is not a prize for the most agreeable, moralising country. It is a prize for countries which lead, influence and project reliability and capability. In short, Chagos is a priceless military base, costing £30 billion in exchange for a reduction in our respectability as a nation. We can see this when China praises the deal. We can see this when Caribbean states now start pestering the UK for their own reparation demands. Apology and handouts do not increase our influence. Confidence and steadfastness do.

Israel–Palestine, by contrast to Chagos, is of enormous significance for the soft power of Britain and her allies. It's clear that Hamas has been positioning its military and terroristic assets under schools, mosques and churches such as to generate the maximum possible international outrage when Israel determined whether or not to eliminate the stronghold. Those involved in security will have to reflect on the strategy employed by Hamas to take hostages and hide behind the innocent, particularly since it seems to be working spectacularly well for them: Hamas terrorists enjoy more support worldwide than ever before, while Israel is increasingly viewed as a pariah state. Regardless of the very complex dynamics, the facts are that, rightly or wrongly, Britain's support for Israel is a profound source of reputational damage. To believe that self-immolation on Chagos matters, while we are judged harshly on Israel–Palestine, shows how out of touch the Home Office, and the Prime Minister, really are.

Britain needs to move on from its simplistic, moralising conception of soft power, and return to the more pragmatic world that is international relations. The strategy of appeasement and apology is not a good one. Soft power must justify itself in terms of hard power and influence. We use soft power to protect our interests, not sacrifice our interests to earn soft power. On this understanding, we can recognise that the English language, our global news reach, our foundational role in the Atlantic Charter and as the more reputable, thinking right hand of US global power is the real source of our respectability.

*   *   *

Practically speaking, it is no longer feasible to imagine that the UK has the military capacity to act independently or to rely principally on traditional hard power to shape the wider world, except under the wing of the US. This is why, ultimately, Britain must deploy alongside our US allies. Britain is a strategic nuclear power, but our nuclear deterrent is the NATO deterrent – it cannot be used autonomously from the United States. To compensate for our declining traditional hard power, we should develop tactical nuclear weapons that are autonomous from the United States as the ultimate insurance policy.

The nuclear deterrent rests upon credible hard power foundations. Influence cannot endure if it is dependent on another nation's permission to act. Britain's nuclear deterrent, though an essential pillar of Western security, remains tied in important respects to American technology and decision-making. Should Washington's political priorities ever diverge from our own, London could find its freedom of action constrained at the very moment independence matters most. Firstly, as we have seen, the UK does not have a tactical nuclear capability. Currently, threats to the UK would have to reach the point that they warrant using a strategic nuclear weapon, at which stage we might expect retaliation from any nuclear power. Secondly, our current strategic nuclear weapons can only practically be used with the knowledge and consent of the United States.

Developing limited, sovereign tactical nuclear capabilities, even if costly, would therefore enhance the credibility of Britain's diplomacy. A tactical nuclear option, under British control and built on British platforms, would not be a repudiation of NATO but a reinforcement of it: an insurance policy against uncertainty in Washington. It would also signal to allies and adversaries alike that Britain is prepared to carry its share of the strategic burden. Even while courting some criticism and even challenge from nuclear non-proliferation agreements, self-reliance would amplify our soft power. Nations take seriously those partners who can defend themselves. The combination of moral authority abroad and credible deterrence at home is the surest way to restore Britain's standing in a fractured world.

The UK also retains other considerable sources of soft power and could do much to enhance this. Some of this power is a matter of luck: the enduring value of English as an international language is not a reflection of the UK's importance but that of the US. But it still matters that, even after the UK has left the EU, English remains the core language simply because it is so widely learned. It is important to consider, however, that each source of soft power does not build upon the others in a linear fashion. There is not an automatic causal link which converts cultural influence or the dominance of many areas of English law into positive outcomes in negotiations. These many sources of soft power must be organised so as to support and reinforce one another, and there must be a doctrine for leveraging them to bring about a concrete outcome. The core concept of soft power in international relations is that it makes other powers (or their citizens) more willing to cooperate and to accept specific goals. In effect, the relative value depends both on the social and cultural output (current and historical) of Britain as well as wider global perceptions of the nation. Any successful doctrine to leverage these sources of influence must produce soft power that can genuinely bring about specific goals and therefore replace hard power. In the context of international challenges, perhaps the single most influential cultural output a nation can have is its output of ideas on good governance and innovation. Our doctrine therefore takes knowledge and expertise as its two central pillars.

*　*　*

The KPD articulates a strategic vision grounded in Britain's most enduring comparative advantage: its exceptional capacity to generate, curate and apply knowledge at the highest level. It recognises that intellectual capital is not merely a by-product of national life but a deliberate instrument of statecraft. There is, in other words, work to do to make sure the institutions that produce, apply and disseminate our ideas, innovations and norms are working in the same direction and building around a shared centre of gravity. Britain's universities, research institutes and policy think tanks rank among the world's finest, consistently producing ideas and evidence that shape global debates. From pioneering achievements in science and medicine to leadership in law, governance and regulatory design, Britain has long excelled at defining the intellectual parameters of international discourse.

A defining feature of this form of power lies in Britain's ability to convene – to bring together nations, institutions and individuals to find common ground on complex global issues. From the San Francisco Conference of 1945 that laid the foundations of the modern multilateral system, to leadership within the G7, COP summits and the Northern Ireland peace process, the UK has repeatedly demonstrated its aptitude for turning dialogue into consensus and consensus into coordinated action. This convening skill transforms the reach of British ideas, converting them into shared frameworks and operational commitments that shape international norms.

In practical terms, the KPD would align the UK's academic, policy and diplomatic communities into a coordinated engine of influence. We might call this the *think-tank nation model*. Evidence-based policymaking would be deliberately linked with public diplomacy, ensuring that British ideas and convening initiatives reach key decision-making centres in foreign capitals, international organisations and global corporations. This integration would position the UK as the world's most credible and trusted source of policy design, governance expertise and institutional standard-setting, giving it a level of influence disproportionate to its economic or military weight.

Traditional concepts of power help to clarify why the KPD represents a distinct and timely evolution. Hard power, or the ability to compel through military or economic means, is constrained by Britain's limited relative resources compared to superpowers such as the US or China. Soft power, the capacity to attract and persuade through culture, values and diplomacy, remains a national strength, underpinned by the English language, global media such as the BBC and the influence of British education and diaspora networks. Yet soft power alone, as we have discussed at length, often lacks precision and does not always translate into tangible policy outcomes. Politicians adopt confused versions of ideas about 'credibility' that fail to align with concrete British interests.

Knowledge power, by contrast, is the ability to define the agenda itself: to produce the intellectual frameworks, technical standards and institutional blueprints that others adopt, and to convene the right actors to make them operational. It is the quiet but decisive force that determines how problems are understood, how solutions are designed and what becomes 'normal' in global governance. Knowledge power works from the top down and the inside out, by embedding British thinking within the operating systems of international institutions.

By consciously integrating this intellectual capital and convening capacity into a coherent grand strategy, Britain could secure a form of enduring influence suited to the twenty-first century. In an age where credibility and expertise often shape the global order more decisively than force, knowledge power offers a sustainable foundation for Britain's international leadership.

KPD is by no means the only doctrine through which Britain can bring its soft power to bear, yet it is perhaps the most coherent approach to turn many smaller, disparate sources of soft power influence and direct them so as to be a genuine substitute for hard power. For instance, Britain aspires to be a successful multi-ethnic democracy. The UK has diaspora communities from many countries (especially parts of the Commonwealth) while it also has a diaspora of its own (although they're normally called expats, bound to return one day) particularly in the US, Australia and Spain. Equally, English and its international relevance drives students to attend British universities. These students' experience and positive perceptions and memories drive rapprochement between Britain and many nations around the world. Considering only the University of Oxford, world leaders from Bill Clinton, Imran Khan and Aung San Suu Kyi to King Abdullah II of Jordan and Viktor Orbán have been educated in its hallowed halls. Its alumni include business leaders such as Mukund Rajan (of Tata Sona Ltd in India), as well as financiers like Antony Jenkins, John Templeton and Michael von

Clemm. Each have returned to Oxford, with Templeton endowing his own college there.

This educational and cultural diaspora of the UK includes some of the more influential people on earth. Britain has also spent billions on foreign aid. It comes second to the US on global scales of soft power, with this recognised in the 2021 Integrated Review of Security, Defence, Development and Foreign Policy.[2] Yet concrete examples of the dividends paid by this soft power are harder to pin down. If nobody pays attention, the billions we have spent in Sudan and Yemen on aid mean, quite frankly, nothing in terms of soft power. The KPD, in this limited example, would favour the alignment of foreign aid spending with the involvement of our cultural and educational diaspora. Our diaspora must be used to amplify the impact of our spending, and our spending must be used to raise the profile and impact of our diaspora.

When British policymaking expertise, media influence and diplomatic experience are added in, it becomes clear how sources of soft power build upon each other and can be directed to valuable strategic outcomes. Current British statecraft, however, leaves all these elements of potential global influence largely unused. Our media broadcasts our failures and projects colonial embarrassment rather than national confidence. Our diasporas are underutilised. Our diplomatic and global problem-solving experience is directionless without a coherent grand strategy, or even a cultural conception of our own national interest. Building that coherent grand strategy starts with bolstering our sources of soft power and reputation and ends with aligning them to concentrate intellectual and policymaking activity in London.

To deliver the first half, it is vital to improve our perception and our soft power resources. It is a prerequisite that cultural and economic problems constraining growth and dynamism in the UK are resolved, from taxes and the bureaucracy to immigration and the judiciary, a programme of reforms we explored from Chapters 1–9. The UK's response to Russia's invasion of Ukraine is also an example of how a perception can shift for the better. The UK government pandered to Putin's elite for almost thirty years but, following its clear support for Ukraine, Britain is now seen as a reliable state, perhaps the *most* reliable state, willing to directly challenge aggression.

*   *   *

The network Russia Today is set up to project soft power for the Putin regime but these days few, if any, see it as anything but an instrument of the Russian state. By contrast, the BBC, especially the World Service, manages to retain an independence of voice, despite numerous attempts by both Labour and Conservative governments to ensure it is more reliably the voice of their own immediate interests, and ongoing scandals over its failure on reporting bias.[3] It is important to resist this manner of short-term politicised thinking. The corporation is still a trusted source of news, including in its various non-English forms, and related bodies such as BBC Media Action help sustain journalism and democracy while challenging misinformation internationally. The challenge for Britain's leaders is how we can ensure the BBC shows the good that Britain does and doesn't just air our dirty laundry. Leadership and cultural change, both in the BBC and throughout society, characterised by confidence, honesty and humility, is the key.

Many states are aware of the importance of their media. Some, such as Russia Today (and other Russian-sponsored sites), are not really designed to be watched or listened to in a coherent manner. Instead, key segments are broken out and used as part of social media campaigns. Allied nations such as France and Germany are also putting considerable emphasis on their media as a route to soft power, with the former growing its English-language offering substantially.

*   *   *

Major sporting events are often used by states for political and promotional purposes. Sometimes this is blatant, such as the 1936 Olympics in Nazi Germany or the 2022 Olympics in China. Both were designed to showcase the regime, despite some misgivings and partial boycotts.[4] So far, the UK government has made little use of sport as a component of soft power, nor has it really gone past platitudes that structures such as English football's Premier League are a great national strength.[5] This is beyond doubt: a British Council report suggested that 10 per cent of the world claim to support Manchester United and almost five billion people watch Premier League games.[6] This may be overstated, but it is indicative of the fact that some aspects of the UK's sporting portfolio trigger a wider association with the UK. What is missing is any step between this and practical action. In fact, Parliament seems set to pass a Football Governance Bill which threatens the independence of the Premier League – independence which has been the precise cause of its global domination. This instinct to regulate something that does so much to boost the visibility of Britain is justified by lawmakers in terms of inequality and fan involvement; it will involve the creation of a new quango, the Independent Football Regulator. Why the government is considering regulating something that is working so remarkably well speaks to wider governmental failure, not just a failure to recognise its importance for soft power.

There has been awareness of the importance of showcase events such as the 2012 London Olympics. The Foreign Office set out its basic goal as, 'To contribute to UK foreign policy goals by using the profile of the Olympics to promote British culture and values at home and abroad. To cement Britain's reputation as a valuable bilateral partner and a vibrant, open and modern society, a global hub in a networked world.'[7] The question, again, is one of follow-up. Any soft power that will derive from these kinds of public relations exercises will fade. High-cost items like these ought to be justified in terms of the hard power that they can replace. In reality, however, Britain did not cash in on the global attention to advance any particular cause.

Part of the UK's reputation as a cultural superpower stems from the ways in which members of a multicultural society create global links. As with sport, however, there is a tension in that what *really* produces cultural power is civil society and the actions of individuals, and any benefits can be lost if this cultural power is seen as the product of overt state sponsorship. (As with sporting events, hosting major cultural events is a well-trodden path for many authoritarian regimes.)

In effect, cultural soft power stems most effectively from its natural development rather than as a state-mandated project. It also comes from wider investment in cultural, academic and research issues going beyond existing major assets; in effect it needs ongoing support for this advantage to be sustained. However, while it may be produced naturally by free individuals, soft power is most effectively *used* within a doctrine such as the KDP.

There is also the influence of our entertainment media. Though

Boris Johnson was once ridiculed for mentioning it, it is true that Harry Potter, Peppa Pig, Paddington Bear and Doctor Who drive sympathy with the UK and with British on-screen characters. British output, from *The Lord of the Rings* and *The Chronicles of Narnia* to *Downton Abbey*, drive interest in the UK and tell our stories even in homes where politics is not discussed.

*   *   *

Overall, the UK has more universities in the global top 100 than any country apart from the US.[8] This is also a reflection of English as the language of research. Papers published in English have the most citations and therefore help boost the country's universities in the rankings. Research in fields such as wind, tidal and wave energy is world leading and the UK overall is second only to the US for investment in life sciences – an advantage that became clear during the worst of the Covid pandemic. The silicon fen in Cambridge is arguably more productive for technology research than the US – but often the technologies they help innovate are ultimately commercialised in the US and will become US companies. Imperial College, Oxbridge and St Andrews are world leaders in spy recruitment, leading to British and British-educated spooks informing government on the most intimate strategic insights.

Equally, the sector is international. Almost half of academic research staff at Universities UK member institutions were non-UK nationals. Non-UK students at both undergraduate and postgraduate levels are a critical part of institutional funding. As we have seen, the diaspora of British-educated leaders continues to grow around the world. Not every trend is positive. Brexit has broken many UK–EU links for students and researchers: many possible postgraduate students already have families who will now need their own visas if they are to come to the UK when they study. The breakdown in the accessibility of the UK to researchers is a casualty of the governmental failure to prevent mass low-skilled migration. The smaller number of rule-following, highly educated and high potential immigrants is easier to target, and then nothing is done about the unskilled immigration which British society continues to object to at every opportunity at the ballot box.

The last government decided to make the bulk of funding dependent on student fees. However, this has created two major problems. First, the fees have been frozen for the last ten years while the costs of universities have gone up. Clearly raising fees would be politically unpopular. The second problem, as ministers were warned at the time, is the fees are often not paid. Students do not have to repay the costs till they graduate and earn a certain amount. Many do not succeed, or take courses which are unrewarded in the jobs market, meaning they never make significant repayments. This doesn't directly affect the institutions, but it does increase the overall cost to the Treasury and Student Finance England, leading to less money to invest and higher interest rates on those that do repay. The upshot for soft power is clear: Britain needs to ensure that its universities are solvent if they are to do their job educating Britain's finest and the cream of the global student body. It is unsustainable that fees continue to be frozen. Delivering a high quality of education and research is simply more important than delivering a breadth of lower-quality degrees.

Two unfortunate developments have emerged. One is that British private education is now being taxed. This makes it a global outlier: Britain is one of the only nations on earth that taxes private provision of a public good. As a policy it amounts to fiscal, social and moral vandalism. The world's rich and influential have long sent their children to British, particularly English, public schools, but now many of these will not survive without the benefits of their charity status. Narrowing the numbers receiving top-quality education and skewing their demographic more heavily in favour of global elites is not helpful. The second unfortunate development is the proliferation of low-quality courses for the express purpose of obtaining UK visas. Large numbers of generic courses at UK institutions are increasingly catering to students from China and India who have very poor levels of English. City University, Middlesex University and Edinburgh Napier University have become notorious for this practice. They are effectively abusing their position as a guaranteed visa sponsor to cash in on low-quality courses.

Research funding is mostly at a UK level but consists of two main strands. The bulk is derived from grants gained by (groups of) academics, which can fund anything from individual small grants to major multi-year research projects. For the university, the problem is that the various sponsors want as much to go to their particular project, making it harder to fund the wider support for research. This is supplemented by institutional funding, on the basis of previous research record, that is meant to cover the extra costs to the university separately – and in addition to this, the Department for Culture Media and Sport (DCMS), Education (DfE) and the UKRI give spurious grant funding worth £8 billion a year, increasingly to woke research projects (including, for example, 'decolonising 120,000 dried plants').[9] These kinds of projects are expensive and embarrassing – what little effect they do have on soft power is profoundly negative.

It would be beneficial to recalibrate our funding systems to disempower public quangos such as UKRI and to restore more modest grant funding to the universities themselves, which benefit from credible and important research and lose reputation for publishing drivel. We also need to change the way that student funding works to allow interest rates to vary by course. This will incentivise students to choose courses that increase their productivity and employability if, after all, it will be the public purse paying to indulge them. It would have the additional advantage of lower interest rates for students heading into science, technology, engineering and mathematics, including computer science, which are the skills upon which Britain's enduring international soft power and influence are fundamentally based. We cannot afford to have an unserious, wasteful and untargeted funding system for higher education in a world which is now competing so intently for the industries that Britain must seek to lead in.

* * *

Britain harbours ambitions to lead in artificial intelligence but lacks one thing: energy. It has a proud history, beginning with Charles Babbage and Ada Lovelace, of leading the development of computers. It has a large white-collar workforce, many of whom are educated well in natural sciences, computer sciences and mathematics. It has some of the most in-demand university courses training computer scientists, for example the 'comp sci' courses at Imperial College London and Cambridge. And Britain has one of the most well-developed and capitalised tech industries, supported by venture and private capital.

AI is not a new concept in computing but started as a tool designed around rules and applied mostly to relatively well-defined problems. In medicine, an early application was to check the results of cancer scans and over time it proved to be more accurate than professionals in its decision-making. The key to this process was that the improvement was directed: in effect false positive and false negative decisions were reviewed for systemic reasons and then the underlying algorithm was corrected.[10] The related approach was not to seek to replace human judgement but to improve the quality of that judgement. So, in terms of cancer screening, the norm now is to have an AI system review the raw data, indicate positives and those that are marginal and these will then be reviewed by a human.

For a long time, raw computing power was a limit. Computing was initially reliant on vacuum tubes and fixed connections, and by the end of the Second World War was dependent on huge rooms even as electronic and digital approaches were adopted. The first programmable personal computer, ENIAC, needed 1,000 square feet of space and 18,000 vacuum tubes, with each panel wired individually. Microprocessors were introduced in the 1970s leading to steady growth in power and reductions in size. This is on the threshold of being changed substantively with the adoption of quantum computing, which may remove almost all the current constraints on computing power. At its most far-reaching, this could render any attempts at data protection meaningless (as any password protection can be broken), and also any problem that has a mathematical basis becomes solvable. In terms of AI, this means that the current restriction (of processing power) will not apply.

The approach now is towards generic AI that can address any issue. ChatGPT, as the most common language model used by the general public, is not designed to address a particular problem; in theory at least, it can be used in almost any circumstance. Equally, it does not rely on written code for its approach, as it can draw context from images, speech as well as text and works from that data probabilistically. The new generation of agentic AIs are a shift from AI responding to inputs to an approach where the AI seeks to understand its environment and then considers how to respond to meet goals.

The EU has taken a regulatory approach that limits the scope of AI, places specific requirements where the application is deemed to be high-risk and requires companies to be clear where they are using generative AI. Linked to existing privacy rules, this sets a standard and, for the moment, sees the UK well in advance of the US, which is still developing an overall approach. China, too, has developed a comprehensive approach.[11] There is a focus on the underlying information, specific controls applied to how AI is used to make recommendations and a demand that the data used to train the AI is 'true and accurate'. Unless Britain can carve out a significant lead in quantum computing, or else quickly reverse course on its plan for costly electrical power, Britain will squander its position of advantage in AI. The regulatory approach best for Britain, and best to make up for our costly energy, is to adopt the widest possible regulatory permissibility, recognising as sufficient both the EU and the US approach to regulation.

China is another matter, however. By progressing well beyond the US in this regard, it is building up substantive technical ability in AI regulation. The Chinese seem to be prioritising caution over speed in AI development. This approach is based on information control and the CCP's internal agendas; they may become a trendsetter and regulatory influence for those many elites who aspire to even greater control over the economic and social lives of their subjects. As such, their regulatory model does not credibly compete with the US's for the development of AI in the market and in the free world. But their regulatory approach is focused on how AI is affecting society – so if models are to be used to set salaries, say, the rules, data and criteria must be clear to all. As of now, China is seeking a regulatory framework that fits its internal concerns rather than aiming to become a global setter of AI regulations. If the EU has placed data privacy at the core of its approach (or rather, debating about privacy), this is, predictably, missing from China's concerns.

This internal focus of China has left the US and EU effectively setting the rules and indeed the focus of AI. The critical difference is that while the EU is only regulating, the US is both innovating and regulating. The US is more responsive to the demands of the sort of IT companies that seek limited control over their actions and prefer a risk-based approach rather than a hazard-based one. The EU, predictably Luddite in its regulatory response, has progressed the debate in AI ethics but has thus far failed to flesh out an alternative regulatory model since it has no true AI giants of its own. They are on the cusp of making a potentially calamitous geopolitical failure: shutting down AI with overbearing regulations would be the single most expensive regulatory error in the history of the EU institutions. Clearly, the UK would do well to align firmly with the US, but has nothing to gain by not additionally recognising EU rules as equivalent in the UK. By nurturing the AI industry with appropriate educational and economic policy, our businesses can expect to hold their share of the industry's influence over US regulation. By having access to the EU and US market from one place, Britian can enjoy economic rents caused by the inefficiencies between EU and US data flows and regulatory barriers.

While early signs are pushing us into regulatory alignment with the EU, particularly through Keir Starmer's 'EU reset', Starmer's UK–US Tech Prosperity Deal has established a firm regulatory link between the UK and US AI sectors. Alignment with the EU would likely have seen US AI products altered or unavailable in our market. Our businesses would be faced with similar challenges on the production side, finding themselves unable to compete in the US market. This is not to mention that the fundamental value of AI is in its ability to revolutionise productivity in its industrial applications, including in our all-important service sector. To throw away both a market and a productivity gain (as well as some limited US regulatory influence if we can build successful AI businesses in Britain) would be the height of madness. A repeating theme in Britain's next century will be whether we 'pick' the EU. In trade and production standards we really need not pick; we can accept both as equivalent to our own.

This could, in theory, lead the EU to increase inspections or impose additional checks on UK exports entering the single market. However, there is no automatic legal obligation for the EU to do so. More importantly, Brussels may be reluctant to take a hardline enforcement approach if it perceives the UK moving closer to US regulatory frameworks. Doing so could risk pushing Britain further out of the EU's economic orbit – a strategic outcome the EU is likely keen to avoid. In this context, a balanced and independent UK position that treats both EU and US standards as equivalent could deter excessive trade friction while preserving flexibility and competitiveness.

It should not be surprising that many of the recent AI Nobel Prize winners have had a British connection: either being born here, educated here, or having moved here to work. It is hard to exaggerate just how important this opportunity is for us: we can truly build the future through our people, our institutions and by the force of our example.

CONCLUSION

It now falls to us to draw the British strategy to as fine a point as possible. At this stage, with the broad trends and opportunities explored, it should be obvious that the UK's approach must be as a hybrid economy, pitched between the EU and US by recognising, mutually or unilaterally, the regulatory standards of each. When we are forced to make a choice, such as potentially in data and military deployments, we should operate as an extension of the United States except in those key areas where we can specialise and secure soft and hard power of our own.

Our key goals for the next century include the preservation of the international legal order as the most prized and valuable achievement Britain can hope for. While the US can afford to watch the world turn inward on itself, Britain cannot. We have been a net importer of food for the last 300 years. We have looked to trade for our wealth since the first ports at Dordrecht and Calais in the early fourteenth century. A continuous strain of British foreign policy has been about securing the international environment for trade and prosperity for Britain at home, and from 1833 onwards, to stamp out slavery and despotism abroad. The Imperial Preference system, which allowed the UK privileged trading access to its many colonies and protectorates, secured this goal until it became unviable after the Second World War. The EEC was positioned as the natural pivot, giving up our 'walled garden' of Commonwealth nations in exchange for guaranteed trade within Europe, something particularly appealing following half a century of fascism, communism and war.

The underlying goal is to bring prosperity to Britain. From this, springs the preservation of the legal order and the chance for specialisation in those key industries of the future where we have a considerable advantage. This means prosperity in economic terms, in terms of a peaceful global environment and also in the sense of a good life shared in common. We should, therefore, be aiming for a rich and prosperous Britain for the good of the British people. In service of that goal, we seek global influence where we can achieve it, we build hard power and exercise it alongside our allies and we make ourselves a destination for the capital – financial and human – that can develop the high-value industries of the future. These industries will enrich us and ensure that we have expertise and services to trade well into the next century.

There are key domestic failures that are holding the UK back. In our domestic policy, economic growth has dried up, as Britain attempts to be all things to all people. Finance, pharmaceuticals, law, education and consulting propelled us through the 1980s and 1990s to rank once again among the richest nations on earth. But rather than reinvesting that into a foothold in higher technology productive capacity, we taxed our high-performing industries to fund day-to-day government spending and welfare. The City, in particular, which was the engine of talent and productivity and facilitator of growth, was over-regulated after the financial crash, causing consistently lower rates of return in London than New York, without any difference in risk. There is only so long that a government can bleed its most productive industries before they start to lose their edge globally. We must not throw good money after bad.

A key problem with the current government is that their pivot back towards the EU is stronger than it needs to be. The EU offers too much protectionism, too much precaution and hazard-based regulation and is too internally divided to allow us to pull our weight in this new authoritarian century. If we want to help preserve the legal order, an independent seat at the table is the only viable way to do that. Yet, as we have explored in this book, this requires a reassessment of our priorities. On some issues, such as AI regulation, it may be necessary to recognise that our botched attempt at reaching net zero has priced us out of that industry for the next thirty years. This approach boils down to picking our battles. Britain is not attempting to be a great power: we are aiming to lead and specialise in those areas to ensure we continue to be indispensable to the world. We need something to offer. A little bit of everything, while we fall into relative economic decline, will *not* do.

Britain's priority must be to become truly competitive again. This means an end to the practice of holding back our most productive sectors in order to keep the unproductive parts on life support. This means massively reducing the number of civil servants and releasing those young and educated workers into the private productive workforce. It means securing cheaper energy by drilling in the North Sea. It means committing to being a high-skilled economy and rejecting arguments that low-skilled workers must be brought in to keep low-skilled industries alive. A reform of state pensions is necessary, which will ultimately reduce the generosity of the scheme as pensioners live longer. We'll also need to recognise that the tax rates and unavailability of housing is driving high-skilled young workers overseas. A reform of welfare is necessary to tackle the incentive structure for the long-term unemployed and long-term sick. Tax reform is required to simplify the system, reduce its most distortionary effects, increase capital investment and encourage the relocation of multinational corporations and high-net-worth individuals to the UK. Immigration must take on a high-skill character immediately or else be curtailed to the low tens of thousands. It is only through economic growth that Britain can once again afford to invest in its own global influence.

It is through this opportunity for high-tech growth that Britain, within certain sectors, may have a chance to lead globally. Nuclear fusion power and legal, educational and banking services are areas where the UK need not fall behind the US regulators or any other global partner. We can do better with standards tailored to our interests as an independent power and as a crossroads between superpowers. Our leaders must have the capability to align our various sources of soft power to make a more coherent bid for leadership in these areas. In a sense, the US and the EU are competitors within these industries. This category includes our joint role in CANZUK, which together would control the vast majority of proven reserves of almost all rare earth metals and fuels needed to power the energy transition and hence the next century of human development, as well as being a large Western bloc committed to the principles of free trade. In the Commonwealth, particularly those nations being targeted by China for aggressive investment and alignment, the UK is the only nation aside from the US with the influence and corporate power to offer an alternative. It should be clear that we are not seeking to upend the order of things or bend them to our particular preference, but to be a vehicle to keep the world free, open and in business.

Having defined our leaning between the US and EU, economic growth comes second only to security as the defining goal of our global engagement. Our trade policy should be as maximally permissive as possible, including trade with China in non-strategic industries such as buying their electric vehicles. Our role as an intermediate power, both in the sense of our size and our positioning, will allow us to collect dividends from our more flexible relationship, and trade with considerable advantage with smaller economies in Africa, South America and the Indian subcontinent which lack opportunities for deep trade agreements with the US or EU. Our specialisation, achieved via domestic economic reform – particularly in financial and legal services and high-tech production – make trade with those developing economies that have raw materials, solid agricultural production and primary manufacturing highly beneficial and capable of sustaining the foreign dollar reserves necessary to trade.

The challenge for the government is to ensure that the benefits of this scramble for productivity reach those who are less able to take part. Government funding must be available to direct investment to regions. The government has a clear role to play in developing transportation infrastructure and in reforming the social safety net to improve incentives. Workers must be allowed to try out jobs without immediately losing their benefits. The most important role for government, society and its leadership is to inspire change in the political culture. An awareness of how network effects drive firms and government departments to institutionalise high-status, postmodern 'woke' beliefs must give way to a motivated, confident and humble political culture that is not too embarrassed to police crime, enforce the law equally or control immigration to the benefit of the country.

Social and political change is also a prerequisite for the confident foreign policy stance with respect to third nations. A conviction to defend Britain's interests even if we draw criticism has been missing from British statecraft for more than two decades. We must be willing to listen to what other countries really think of us, particularly on Israel–Palestine and Ukraine, rather than project about the trendy issues of decolonisation and reparations. We must be seen as a restrained, diligent negotiator but also a stalwart defender of our own interests that is willing to state them loud and clear. That is how we earn the respect of other nations, become predictable partners and grow our soft power. It is not by placation and issuing platitudes – the modern world is not the Model UN.

From a coherent and solid base, Britain will seek to uphold the rules-based international order that we helped build with the US. We must be willing to invest in our soft power, provided it pays for itself in terms of the hard power it can replace. Our hard power should come from our status as a specialised and rapidly deployable arm of the US Armed Forces, focusing on technologies developed in the UK by BAE, Lockheed Martin UK (with US partners) and focusing on key operational capacities in logistics and reconnaissance in line with the Strategic Defence Review. Any conventional deployments we make will be with the US, or not at all. Our nuclear deterrent is, in reality, a NATO deterrent – it cannot be used independently. We have made the economic, legal, diplomatic and military case for developing tactical nuclear weapons that are autonomous from the US to compensate for a declining conventional military power. We must also learn to reconceptualise our deployment, given that it will be alongside the United States, according to the logic of US grand strategy.

Importantly, all of these steps will mean internalising the realist competition that is underway between the United States and China and the logic of offshore balancing: that the US need not police regions, except for its home region, where a stable balance of power has been achieved. Rather, it must maintain the capacity to intervene to stop any other power, or combination of powers, from seizing hegemony. No potential hegemon exists in Europe or the Middle East; the theatre of great power competition is Asia. The same geostrategic logic applies to Canada, Australia and New Zealand.

Approaching British policy from this angle yields important insights. First, that China doesn't need to spend the same resources as the United States maintaining legacy systems or in checking the balance of power across the globe. Beijing can apply its full weight to its home region. Second, that the West's three-decade-long focus on fighting counter-insurgency missions and against weaker militaries such as Iraq distracted development, research and hardware away from competition with a near-peer rival. Britain must help the United States ensure that the European Union is prepared for its own defence, which will permit a focused deployment in east Asia. Britain must also focus its rearmament efforts on preparing for operations against a technological equal. Of course, this eastward pivot places yet more importance on the network of military bases in the region, including Diego Garcia.

Nowhere is a pivot towards the US more important than in

recognising their standards in high-tech industry. Recognition of the US regulatory model is a condition of ever entering the global market for AI, data and cybersecurity, given the overwhelming dominance and technical superiority of their firms. The recent Tech Prosperity Deal proves that there is appetite in the US to leverage Britain's considerable research and development firepower. That agreement should be a model that guides a wider facilitation of trade and development in the most high-tech and high-value industries. In lower tech industries, and in those where geography favours the European Union (such as food products), we should agree to follow EU standards – though without paying for the privilege of being told what to do.

Our influence and involvement at international institutions must come from our being an agent of the post-war economic order which, although we did not create it alone, sustains us. As well as language, law and our nuclear deterrent, we must make use of perhaps the richest diplomatic inheritance of any nation on earth: the Commonwealth. Through focusing on the Commonwealth, CPTPP and CANZUK, Britain can still play an outsized role in reinforcing the WTO and the US-led legal order. By getting this right, the UK could become by far the most well-connected major economy in the world. Together with CPTPP partners in Asia, plus Canada, Australia and New Zealand, we can hold open the door until such a time as the US might be willing to re-engage. With Brexit, the UK remains the most energised actor in international trade, even under a Labour government, which has signed landmark deals with India and the US. In this area, we must remain aligned with the trading models the US has produced and remain firmly *out* of the regulatory and customs orbit of the EU, and hence trading with nations and economies that are independent and growing.

Britain needs to accept our diminished but specialised role in this new bipolar world without repeating the mistakes of the late 1960s and early 1970s. We must adapt early to our new reality; it will pay dividends in achieving our national priorities. We can expect to take a share in the high-value industries of the future. We can build an independent tactical nuclear deterrent. We can work to shut down the expropriation of nations by corrupt governments, cooperating against terrorism by developing and sharing our clout in counter-terrorism, joining the US in proscribing organisations including the IRGC and uprooting their smuggling and laundering operations. With Brexit, we have given up our role as a referee shaping Europe's regulatory future. But at that price we've bought ourselves the opportunity to play for ourselves and throw our weight behind our own people and our own values.

With this plan, Britain has a blueprint. Although the country is heading down the wrong path, we still have so much going for us. What we can all do – a prerequisite of a confident yet humble democracy – is make noise about the good that Britain does. We must be bullish about the contribution we've made: from the beaches in Normandy to the great arsenal of British inventions, no country has done more than Britain to spread prosperity and democracy around the earth. If we back ourselves, dare to compete and assert our right to choose our own future based on our British values, we can make a very British comeback, snatching victory from the jaws of defeat.

Britain deserves to be a strong power in the new century. It has many advantages, as well as a significant history upon which new leaders, statesmen and founders can build. It need only play to its many strengths. If this is done, there is no reason why the twenty-first century can't be the finest and most significant in Britain's bittersweet and beautiful history. Let us talk ourselves up, with confidence and a plan: 'All for our vantage. Then, in God's name, march. True hope is swift, and flies with swallow's wings; Kings it makes gods, and meaner creatures kings.'

NOTES

INTRODUCTION
1   Ahmadi, A. A. (2025).
2   Wessner, C., and Sharma, S. (2025).
3   Balla, R. (2023).

CHAPTER 1
1   Schmitt, C. (2007).
2   Dworkin, R. (1977).
3   Oakeshott, M. J. (1962).
4   Ibrahim, A. (2022).
5   Stiglitz, J. E. (2002).
6   Lee, D. (2018).
7   Vogel, E. F. (2011).
8   Brown, K. (2022).
9   Kachmar, O. (2021).
10 Maçães, B. (2018).
11 Bokhari, K. (2023).
12 MOD (2025).
13 Morton, B. (2024b).
14 Jones, S. G. (2024).

CHAPTER 2
1   Media – Lockheed Martin (2025).
2   Diver, T. (2025).
3   Lord West of Spithead (2025).
4   Caplan, B. (2011).
5   Sumption, J. (2020).
6   Dworkin, R. (1986).
7   Simor, J. (2025).
8   Thompsons Solicitors (2024).
9   Chapman, R. (2021).
10 Clark, R. (2025).
11 Foss, N., and Klein, P. (2022).
12 Parkin, F. (1968).
13 Wagner, W. (2024).
14 Sands, P. (2023).
15 Münchau, W. (2017).
16 Merrick, R. (2018).

17 Drazen, A., and Masson, P. R. (1994).
18 Frontier Economics (2024).
19 Al Jazeera (2024).
20 Kimball, R. (2020).
21 Rawls, J. (1971).

CHAPTER 3

1   World Meteorological Foundation (2024).
2   United Nations (2015).
3   Fendt, L. (2021).
4   Gladwell, M. (2000).
5   United Nations (2023).
6   Ince, M. (2024).
7   Lakhani, N. (2024).
8   Tingley, D., and Tomz, M. (2021).
9   Barnes, P. W., Bornman, J. F., Pandey, K. K., Bernhard, G. H., Bais, A. F., Neale, R. E., Robson, T. M., Neale, P. J., Williamson, C. E., Zepp, R. G., Madronich, S., Wilson, S. R., Andrady, A. L., Heikkilä, A. M., and Robinson, S. A. (2021).
10 Ince, M. (2024).
11 Spyro, S. (2025).
12 Dahl, M. H. (2024).
13 World Bank (2021).
14 Eir Nolsøe (2025).
15 Puzder, A. (2024).
16 Climate and Freedom Accord (2024).
17 It should be pointed out that a hypothetical capital tax of 20 per cent decreases investment profitability by *more* than 20 per cent, since tax is levied on gross profit before the costs of employing that capital (including taxes, fees and interest) have been paid. For example, if platform, exchange, transaction and intermediary costs are 30 per cent, a 20 per cent capital tax reduces profitability by some ~28 per cent. A 40 per cent tax would reduce profitability by ~57 per cent. Hence this should be considered a large increase to green project viability.
18 Taylor, R. (2022).
19 The Commonwealth (n.d.).
20 Alayza, N., Laxton, V., and Neunuebel, C. (2023).
21 Oliver, M. (2024).

CHAPTER 4

1   UNHCR (2024).
2   Sturge, G. (2024).
3   Tudor, S. (2022).
4   Vargas-Silva, C., Sumption, M., and Walsh, P. W. (2024).
5   BBC (2015).
6   Sökefeld, M. (2016).
7   Starmer, K. (2025).
8   Anon (2016).
9   Gov.uk (2025).
10 UNHCR (2023).
11 Dunford, D. (2025).
12 United Nations High Commissioner for Refugees (2023).
13 International Organization for Migration (2024).
14 Vera Delzo, P. (2023).
15 Center, E.-M. (2021).
16 Earth Day (2020).
17 International Rescue Committee (2023).
18 Middle East Eye (2024).
19 Ibrahim, A. (2025).
20 Nyberg-Sorensen, N., Hear, N. V., and Engberg-Pedersen, P. (2002).
21 Ibrahim, A. (2022).

22 Christensen, J. (2011).
23 International Consortium of Investigative Journalists (2016).
24 *The Economist* (2018).
25 Fitzgibbon, W. (2021).
26 Starkman, D. (2021).
27 Augusto, D. (2023).
28 Leask, D. (2017).
29 Department for Business, Energy and Industrial Strategy (2018).
30 Interpol (2024).
31 Salt, J. (2000).

CHAPTER 5
1   Cicero (2025).
2   O'Driscoll, C. (2023).
3   Ibrahim, A. (2017).
4   Raustiala, K., and Slaughter, A.-M. (2002).
5   Mearsheimer, J. J. (1994).
6   Kydd, A. H. (2005).
7   Amin, R. (2010).
8   Kotkin, S. (2008).
9   Gat, A. (2007).
10 O'Brien, R.C. (2020).
11 West, E. (2024).
12 Truss, L. (2024).
13 University of Law (2024).
14 Ibrahim, A. (2022).
15 Ward, A. (2019).
16 Wang, J. (2021).
17 Nixey, J. (2019).
18 Kirchick, J. (2017).
19 Wesslau, F. (2016).
20 Riley-Smith, B. (2025).
21 COP26 (2021).
22 Schreurs, M. A. (2016).
23 Mills, C., Shalchi, A., Gower, M., Johnston, N., and Woodhouse, J. (2022).
24 Hamilton, C. (2018).
25 Leigh, S. (2024).
26 CAMERA (2019).
27 Atlantic Council (2020).

CHAPTER 6
1   Badenoch, K. (2024).
2   Davey, W. J. (2022).
3   Ibid.
4   OBR (2022).
5   Thomas, D. (2023).
6   Babington, T. (2015).
7   McBride, J., and Siripurapu, A. (2022).
8   Posen, A.S., Petri, P., and Banga, M. (2021).
9   USTR (2001).
10 Schneider-Petsinger, M. (2023).
11 Europarl (2023).
12 Sen, A. (2024).
13 Huld, A. (2023).
14 Bloomberg (2023).
15 Bloomberg (2024).
16 Williams, S. (2013).
17 Xlinks (2024).

18 Bartholemew, C., and Cleveland, R. (2021).
19 BBC (2015a).
20 Schneider-Petsinger, M. (2023).
21 Wood, J. (2024).
22 Morita-Jaeger, M. (2024).

CHAPTER 7
1 Ibrahim, A. (2022).
2 Belton, C. (2020).
3 Abrahms, M. (2008).
4 Ibrahim, A. (2017).
5 Kirk-Wade, E., and Allen, G. (2020).
6 Jay, A. (2014).
7 Montgomery, S. (2024).
8 Johnston, N. (2024).
9 Gold, J. (2022).
10 College of Policing (2021).
11 Ibid.
12 US Treasury (2024).
13 Nicolle, E. (2024).
14 Reuters (2023).
15 FCA (2023).
16 Mulhall, J. (2022).
17 Ibrahim, A. (2022)
18 Hymas, C. (2024).
19 Ibrahim, A. (2017).
20 Searle, N. (2017).
21 Maizland, L., and Fong, C. (2024).
22 Tarabay, J. (2021).
23 Ibrahim, A. (2022).
24 Belton, C. (2020).
25 Borshchevskaya, A. (2020).
26 Foy, H. (2021).
27 Thompson, S. A. (2022).
28 Panjwani, A., Mills, C., Dawson, J., Woodhouse, J., Gower, M., and Johnston, N. (2025).
29 He, L. (2023).
30 Gracie, C. (2015).
31 Denmark, A. (2018).
32 Jie, C. (2024).
33 Muelle, R. (2019).

CHAPTER 8
1 Adams, S., and Canvin, A. (2023).
2 National Crime Agency (2025).
3 Transparency International (2025).
4 National Crime Agency (2019).
5 Belton, C. (2020).
6 *The Economist* (2022).
7 Starkman, D. (2021).
8 Morgan, K., and Kinossian, N. (2023).
9 Tax Justice Network (2022).
10 Department for Business, Energy and Industrial Strategy (2018).
11 Belton, C. (2020).
12 Burgis, T. (2024).
13 Ibid.
14 Head, C. (2022).
15 Transparency International (2019).
16 The Regional Law Revision Centre, Turks and Caicos Islands (2025).

17 Fitzgibbon, W. (2020).
18 Lawrence, D. (2022).
19 Apergis, N., and Katsaiti, M.-S. (2018).
20 Gorny, T. (2021).
21 Cherry, K. (2017).
22 *Geographical* (2023).
23 Pianese, B. (2024).
24 Shalchi, A. (2021).
25 City of London (2022).

CHAPTER 9

1   Keep, M., and Brien, P. (2023).
2   MacQueen, R., Mortimer-Lee, P., and Bhattacharjee, A. (2022).
3   Denham, A. (2022).
4   Şerban, A. C., Aceleanu, M. I., Dospinescu, A.S., Ţîrcă, D.-M., and Novo-Corti, I. (2020).
5   Vargas-Silva, C., Sumption, M., and Walsh, P. W. (2024).
6   US Treasury (2025).
7   Dibb, G. (2023).
8   Mitra, P. (2024).
9   Titcomb, J., and Penna, D. (2024).
10 Business Plus Ireland (2024).
11 Mustoe, H. (2024).
12 Dorrell, C. (2024).
13 Warrington, J., and Holl-Allen, G. (2024).
14 Markson, T. (2024).
15 Reeves, R. (2024).
16 OBR (2024).
17 Bradshaw, T., Gross, A., and Millard, R. (2025).
18 Law Society (2022).
19 McWilliams, D., and Singham, S. (2024).
20 Singham, S. (2019).
21 Singham, S. (2023).
22 Hussain, A., and Davies, M. (2024).
23 Reenen, J. V. (2023).
24 Chadha, J., and Venables, T. (2024).
25 Cecil, N. (2024).
26 Herring, D. (2024).
27 Cornforth, E. (2024).
28 Feld, L. P., and Heckemeyer, J. H. (2011).
29 Gutteridge, N. (2025).
30 Mengden, A. (2024).
31 Tax Foundation (2023).
32 Murphy, L. (2022).
33 Wallace, T. (2024).
34 Burton, L. (2024).
35 Vaisanen, I. (2024).
36 Wilkes, G., Bartrum, O., and Clyne, R. (2024).
37 Truss, L. (2023).
38 Nelson, E. (2025).
39 Halligan, L. (2024).
40 Ibid.
41 OBR (2023).
42 Wilkes, G., Bartrum, O., and Clyne, R. (2024). *Treasury 'orthodoxy'*. [online] Institute for Government. Available at: https://www.instituteforgovernment.org.uk/publication/treasury-orthodoxy.

CHAPTER 10

1   International Relations and Defence Committee (2025).
2   West, L. (2024b).

3   Foreign Affairs Committee (2024).
4   Brancati, D., and Wohlforth, W. C. (2021).
5   Jarvie, G., and Macdonald, S. (2024).
6   Dubber, J., and Worne, J. (2015).
7   Foreign Affairs Committee (2011).
8   Ibid.
9   Turner, C. (2022).
10   Dembrower, K., Crippa, A., Colón, E., Eklund, M., and Strand, F. (2023).
11   Sheehan, M. (2023).

BIBLIOGRAPHY

Abrahms, M. (2008). What Terrorists Really Want: Terrorist Motives and Counterterrorism Strategy. *International Security*, 32(4), pp.78–105.

Adams, S., and Canvin, A. (2023). UK Finance: Promoting global trade in financial services is central to UK economic recovery. [online] UK Finance. Available at: https://www.ukfinance.org.uk/press/press-releases/uk-finance-promoting-global-trade-in-financial-services-is-central-to-uk-economic-recovery.

Al Jazeera (2024). UN committee slams UK over racism, incitement affecting minorities. [online]. Available at: https://www.aljazeera.com/news/2024/8/23/un-committee-slams-uk-over-racism-incitement-affecting-minorities.

Alayza, N., Laxton, V., and Neunuebel, C. (2023). Developing Countries Won't Beat the Climate Crisis Without Tackling Rising Debt. World Resources Institute. [online] Available at: https://www.wri.org/insights/debt-climate-action-developing-countries.

Allen, C. (2009). *God's Terrorists*. Da Capo Press.

Allison, G. (2010). Nuclear Disorder: Surveying Atomic Threats. *Foreign Affairs*, [online] 89(1), pp.74–85. doi: https://doi.org/10.2307/20699784.

Amin, R. (2010). Controlling Behavior – Not Arms: Moving Forward On An International Convention For Cyberspace. [online] The Belfer Center for Science and International Affairs. Available at: https://www.belfercenter.org/publication/controlling-behavior-not-arms-moving-forward-international-convention-cyberspace [Accessed 12 Jul 2025].

Anon (2016). 'Mrs May, we are all citizens of the world,' says philosopher. BBC News. [online] 29 Oct. Available at: https://www.bbc.co.uk/news/uk-politics-37788717.

Apergis, N., and Katsaiti, M. S. (2018). Poverty and the resource curse: Evidence from a global panel of countries. *Research in Economics*, 72(2), pp.211–223. doi: https://doi.org/10.1016/j.rie.2018.04.001.

Arrighi, G. (2009). *Adam Smith in Beijing: Lineages of the Twenty-First Century*. W. W. Norton & Co Inc.

Ashley, P. R. (n.d.). Foresight Future Flooding. [online] Available at: https://assets.publishing.service.gov.uk/media/5a74c78de5274a3f93b48beb/04-947-flooding-summary.pdf.

Atlantic Council (2020). Iranian Digital Influence Efforts: Guerrilla Broadcasting for the Twenty-First Century. [online]. Available at: https://www.atlanticcouncil.org/in-depth-research-reports/report/iranian-digital-influence-efforts-guerrilla-broadcasting-for-the-twenty-first-century/.

Augusto, D. (2023). Only 3 of 631 Scottish limited partnerships formed by Scots residents. [online] *The Ferret*. Available at: https://theferret.scot/only-3-631-scottish-limited-partnerships-formed-residents-scotland/.

Babington, T. (2015). *Critical and Miscellaneous Essays, Volume 3*. New York: Appleton, p.367.

Badenoch, K. (2024). The role of the UK in the global trade landscape. [online] Chatham House – International Affairs Think Tank. Available at: https://www.chathamhouse.org/2024/03/role-uk-global-trade-landscape.

Barnes, P. W., Bornman, J. F., Pandey, K. K., Bernhard, G. H., Bais, A. F., Neale, R. E., Robson, T. M., Neale, P. J., Williamson, C. E., Zepp, R. G., Madronich, S., Wilson, S. R., Andrady, A. L., Heikkilä, A. M., and Robinson, S. A. (2021). The success of the Montreal Protocol in mitigating interactive effects of stratospheric ozone depletion and climate change on the environment. *Global Change Biology*. doi: https://doi.org/10.1111/gcb.15841.

Bartholemew, C., and Cleveland, R. (2021). Annual Report to Congress. [online] www.uscc.gov. Available at: https://www.uscc.gov/annual-report/2021-annual-report-congress.

BBC (2015a). China and 'the Osborne Doctrine'. BBC News. [online] 18 Oct. Available at: https://www.bbc.co.uk/news/world-asia-china-34539507.

BBC (2015b). Paris attacks: Who were the attackers? BBC News. [online] 16 Nov. Available at: http://www.bbc.co.uk/news/world-europe-34832512.

BBC (2025). BBC statement on claims made about Gaza reporting. [online] Available at: https://www.bbc.co.uk/mediacentre/statements/bbc-statement-on-claims-made-about-gaza-reporting.

Belton, C. (2020). *Putin's People*. Farrar, Straus and Giroux.

Bloomberg (2023). How China is incentivising production of electric vehicles. [online] *The National*. Available at: https://www.thenationalnews.com/business/technology/2023/09/16/how-china-is-incentivising-production-of-electric-vehicles/.

Bloomberg (2024). China's EV Makers Got $231 Billion Aid over 15 Years, Study Says.

Bloomberg.com. [online] 21 Jun. Available at: https://www.bloomberg.com/news/articles/2024-06-21/china-s-ev-makers-got-231-billion-in-aid-over-last-15-years.

Bokhari, K. (2023). Iran's Protests – A Close Examination. [online] Media Hub. Available at: https://mediahub.newlinesinstitute.org/state-resilience-fragility/irans-protests-a-close-examination/ [Accessed 11 Jul. 2025].

Boland, H. (2024). M&S and Sainsbury's chiefs urge Reeves to slash tax on retailers. [online] *The Telegraph*. Available at: https://www.telegraph.co.uk/business/2024/10/07/marks-spencer-sainsburys-lead-reeves-slash-tax-bills/?msockid=01f5ba8bd2c0655939cdaee8d3e764c2 [Accessed 13 Jul. 2025].

Borshchevskaya, A. (2020). Russia's Growing Interests in Libya. [online] The Washington Institute. Available at: https://www.washingtoninstitute.org/policy-analysis/view/russias-growing-interests-in-libya [Accessed 13 Jul. 2025].

Bradshaw, T., Gross, A., and Millard, R. (2025). What is Keir Starmer's plan to turn Britain into an AI superpower? [online] @FinancialTimes. Available at: https://www.ft.com/content/b02ba1bd-1075-4703-9b7d-800e2efa4513.

Brancati, D., and Wohlforth, W. C. (2021). Why Authoritarians Love the Olympics *Foreign Affairs*. [online] www.foreignaffairs.com. Available at: https://www.foreignaffairs.com/articles/china/2021-03-25/why-authoritarians-love-olympics.

Brown, K. (2022). *Xi*. Icon Books.

Burgis, T. (2024). How oligarchs took on the UK fraud squad – and won. [online] *The Guardian*. Available at: https://www.theguardian.com/news/2024/sep/12/enrc-oligarchs-took-on-serious-fraud-office-and-won.

Burton, L. (2024). Public sector pay officials backed inflation-busting rises to counter austerity. [online] *The Telegraph*. Available at: https://www.telegraph.co.uk/business/2024/12/18/public-sector-pay-officials-backed-inflation-busting-rises/?msockid=01f5ba8bd2c0655939cdaee8d3e764c2 [Accessed 13 Jul. 2025].

Business Plus Ireland (2024). Half of UK bosses 'to cut jobs and raise prices' after Reeves budget. [online]. Available at: https://businessplus.ie/news/prices-jobs-uk-budget/.

Camera (2019). Latest Report on BBC Coverage of Israel-Hamas War Highlights Old Problems, Raises New Concerns. [online]. Available at: https://www.camera.org/article/latest-report-on-bbc-coverage-of-israel-hamas-war-highlights-old-problems-raises-new-concerns/ [Accessed 12 Jul. 2025].

Caplan, B. (2011). *The Myth of the Rational Voter Why Democracies Choose Bad Policies New Edition*. Princeton University Press.

Casciani, D. (2019). Tommy Robinson: The rancour, rhetoric and riches of brand Tommy. BBC News. [online] 11 Jul. Available at: https://www.bbc.co.uk/news/uk-48942411.

Cecil, N. (2024). Keir Starmer vows to 'fire up' training of skilled workers in UK and end 'over-reliance' on immigration. [online] *The Standard*. Available at: https://www.standard.co.uk/news/politics/keir-starmer-skilled-workers-immigration-labour-training-business-b1172057.html.

Center, E.-M. (2021). Middle East and North Africa: Heatwaves of up to 56 degrees Celsius without climate action. [online] Phys.org. Available at: https://phys.org/news/2021-04-middle-east-north-africa-heatwaves.html.

Chadha, J., and Venables, T. (2024). Boosting productivity: why doesn't the UK invest enough? [online] Economics Observatory. Available at: https://www.economicsobservatory.com/boosting-productivity-why-doesnt-the-uk-invest-enough.

Cherry, K. (2017). What Is the Scarcity Principle? [online] *Explore Psychology*. Available at: https://www.explorepsychology.com/scarcity-principle/.

Christensen, J. (2011). The looting continues: tax havens and corruption. *Critical perspectives on international business*, 7(2), pp.177–196. doi: https://doi.org/10.1108/17422041111128249.

Cicero (2025). *Cicero: On Duties*. [online] Google Books. Available at: https://books.google.co.uk/books?id=PuONLmVUW4QC.

City of London (2022). London leads the world as the top destination for foreign investment in financial and professional services. [online] Available at: https://news.cityoflondon.gov.uk/london-leads-the-world-as-the-top-destination-for-foreign-investment-in-financial-and-professional-services.

Clark, R. (2025). The radical barristers who really lay down the law in Britain. [online] *The Spectator*. Available at: https://www.spectator.co.uk/article/the-radical-barristers-who-really-lay-down-the-law-in-britain/.

Climate and Freedom Accord (2024). A Straw Proposal for an International Free Market Climate Agreement. [online] Available at: https://clean capitalistleadership council.org/wp-content/uploads/climatefreedomaccord-straw-230202.pdf.

College of Policing (2021). Solving problems. [online]. Available at: https://www.college.police.uk/guidance/neighbourhood-policing/solving-problems.

Cooke, M. (2024). Trump to target EU over UK in trade war as he wants to see 'successful Brexit', former staffer claims. [online] *The Independent*. Available at: https://www.independent.co.uk/news/uk/politics/donald-trump-reeves-free-trade-tariffs-b2644505.html?os=wtmbzegmu5hw&ref=app.

COP26 (2021). COP26 Goals. [online] UN Climate Change Conference (COP26) at the SEC – Glasgow 2021. Available at: https://ukcop26.org/cop26-goals/.

Cornforth, E. (2024). Which taxes are best and worst for growth? [online] *Economics Observatory*. Available at: https://www.economicsobservatory.com/which-taxes-are-best-and-worst-for-growth.

Dahl, M. H. (2024). The Panama Canal Is Running Dry. [online] *Foreign Policy*. Available at: https://foreignpolicy.com/2024/01/15/panama-suez-canal-global-shipping-crisis-climate-change-drought/.

Davey, W. J. (2022). WTO Dispute Settlement: Crown Jewel or Costume Jewelry? *World Trade Review*, 21(3), pp.1–10. doi: https://doi.org/10.1017/s1474745622000106.

Dembrower, K., Crippa, A., Colón, E., Eklund, M., and Strand, F. (2023). Artificial Intelligence for Breast Cancer Detection in Screening Mammography in Sweden: a prospective, population-based, paired-reader, non-inferiority Study. *The Lancet Digital Health*, [online] 5(10). doi: https://doi.org/10.1016/s2589-7500(23)00153-x.

Denham, A. (2022). How much did the Covid crisis cost? [online] *The Spectator*. Available at: https://www.spectator.co.uk/article/how-much-did-the-covid-crisis-cost-/.

Denmark, A. (2018). 40 years ago, Deng Xiaoping changed China – and the world. [online] *The Washington Post*. Available at: https://www.washingtonpost.com/news/monkey-cage/wp/2018/12/19/40-years-ago-deng-xiaoping-changed-china-and-the-world .

Department for Business, Energy and Industrial Strategy (2018). Limited partnerships: reform of limited partnership law. [online] Available at: https://www.gov.uk/government/consultations/limited-partnerships-reform-of-limited-partnership-law.

Dibb, G. (2023). UK has under-invested to the tune of half a trillion pounds, or 30 Elizabeth lines, says IPPR. [online] IPPR. Available at: https://www.ippr.org/media-office/uk-has-underinvested-to-the-tune-of-half-a-trillion-pounds-or-30-elizabeth-lines-says-ippr.

Dimaranan, B., and Mevel, S. (2008). The COMESA Customs Union: A Quantitative Assessment. *AgEcon Search*. [online] Available at: https://ageconsearch.umn.edu/record/331712/?v=pdf [Accessed 13 Jul. 2025].

Diver, T. (2025). Chagos case judge Xue Hanqin is ex-China official who backed Russian invasion of Ukraine. [online] *The Telegraph*. Available at: https://www.telegraph.co.uk/politics/2025/02/11/chagos-case-judge-china-official-backed-russian-in-ukraine/?msockid=201ea57b4ed3670d2fe9b0b04fac6657 [Accessed 11 Jul. 2025].

Dorrell, C. (2024). Budget tax hike could destroy 100,000 jobs, Deutsche Bank estimates. *City AM*. [online] Available at: https://www.cityam.com/budget-tax-hike-could-destroy-100000-jobs-deutsche-bank-estimates/.

Draper, R. (2020). *To Start a War*. Penguin.

Drazen, A., and Masson, P. R. (1994). Credibility of Policies Versus Credibility of Policymakers. *The Quarterly Journal of Economics*, 109(3), pp.735–754. doi:https://doi.org/10.2307/2118420.

Dubber, J., and Worne, J. (2015). Playing the game: the soft power of sport | British Council. [online] Britishcouncil.org. Available at: https://www.britishcouncil.org/research-insight/soft-power-sport.

Dunford, D. (2025). Government draws link between good weather and small boat crossings – but they are rising during bad conditions too. [online] Sky News. Available at: https://news.sky.com/story/government-draws-link-between-good-weather-and-small-boat-crossings-but-theres-been-a-rise-in-bad-conditions-too-13378394.

Dworkin, R. (1977). *Taking Rights Seriously*. London: Bloomsbury.

Dworkin, R. (1986). *Law's Empire*. Oxford: Hart.

Earth Day (2020). Climate change, water woes, and conflict concerns in the Middle East: A toxic mix. [online] Available at: https://www.earthday.org/climate-change-water-woes-and-conflict-concerns-in-the-middle-east-a-toxic-mix/.

Europarl (2023). EU's response to the US Inflation Reduction Act (IRA) | Think Tank | European Parliament. [online] Available at: https://www.europarl.europa.eu/thinktank/en/document/IPOL_IDA(2023)740087.

Europol (2022). Migrant smuggling in the EU. [online] Available at: https://www.europol.europa.eu/publications-events/publications/migrant-smuggling-in-eu.

FCA (2022). FCA fines Santander UK £107.7 million for repeated anti-money laundering failures. [online] Available at: https://www.fca.org.uk/news/press-releases/fca-fines-santander-uk-repeated-anti-money-laundering-failures.

Feld, L. P., and Heckemeyer, J. H. (2011). FDI and Taxation: A Meta-study. *Journal of Economic Surveys*, 25(2), pp.233–272. doi: https://doi.org/10.1111/j.1467-6419.2010.00674.x.

Fendt, L. (2021). Why did the IPCC choose 2°C as the goal for limiting global warming? [online] Massachusetts Institute of Technology Climate Portal. Available at: https://climate.mit.edu/ask-mit/why-did-ipcc-choose-2deg-c-goal-limiting-global-warming.

Financial Conduct Authority (2023). Crypto: The basics. [online] Available at: https://www.fca.org.uk/investsmart/crypto-basics.

Fitzgibbon, W. (2020). Notorious tax haven British Virgin Islands to introduce public register of company owners – ICIJ. [online] International Consortium of Investigative Journalists. Available at: https://www.icij.org/investigations/fincen-files/notorious-tax-haven-british-virgin-islands-to-introduce-public-register-of-company-owners/.

Fitzgibbon, W. (2021). While foreign aid poured in, Jordan's King Abdullah funnelled $100m through secret companies to buy luxury homes – ICIJ. [online] International Consortium of Investigative Journalists. Available at: https://www.icij.org/investigations/pandora-papers/jordan-king-abdullah-luxury-property.

Foreign Affairs Committee (2024). Evidence Session: BBC World Service and soft power – Committees – UK Parliament. [online] Parliament.uk. Available at: https://committees.parliament.uk/committee/78/foreign-affairs-committee/news/203805/evidence-session-bbc-world-service-and-soft-power/.

Foreign Affairs Committee (2011). The FCO's strategy for the 2012 Olympics: The Olympic and Paralympic Games 2012. [online] publications.parliament.uk. Available at: https://publications.parliament.uk/pa/cm201011/cmselect/cmfaff/581/58107.htm.

Foss, N., and Klein, P. (2022). Why Do Companies Go Woke? *Academy of Management Perspectives*, 37(4). doi: https://doi.org/10.5465/amp.2021.0201.

Foy, H. (2021). Vladislav Surkov: 'An overdose of freedom is lethal to a state'. *Financial Times*. [online] 18 Jun. Available at: https://www.ft.com/content/1324acbb-f475-47ab-a914-4a96a9d14bac.

Frank-Keyes, J. (2024). 'Hammer blow': Family firms call for inheritance tax consultation. [online] *City AM*. Available at: https://www.cityam.com/hammer-blow-family-firms-call-for-inheritance-tax-consultation/ [Accessed 13 Jul. 2025].

Frontier Economics (2024). *Report: Quantifying the opportunities for economic growth*. [online] Best for Britain. Available at: https://www.bestforbritain.org/growth_report.

Garfinkel, I. (2025). BBC apologises after 'ambushing' rabbi on air with hostile questions about Israel. [online] *The Jewish Chronicle*. Available at: https://www.thejc.com/news/bbc-apologises-after-ambushing-rabbi-on-air-with-hostile-questions-about-israel-x2ncxm4t.

Gat, A. (2007). The Return of Authoritarian Great Powers. [online] *Foreign Affairs*. Available at: https://www.foreignaffairs.com/articles/china/2007-07-01/return-authoritarian-great-powers.

Geographical (2023). The hidden costs of Bitcoin go beyond its carbon footprint. [online] Available at: https://geographical.co.uk/science-environment/the-hidden-costs-of-bitcoin.

Gladwell, M. (2000). *The Tipping Point*. London: Abacus.

Gold, J. (2022). Improving community relations in the police through procedural justice – an action learning initiative. *Action Learning: Research and Practice*, [online] 19(3), pp.1–18. doi: https://doi.org/10.1080/14767333.2022.2129586.

Gorny, T. (2021). Virtual Currencies: FATF's New Sanctions Guidance. sanctions.io. [online] Sanctions.io. Available at: https://www.sanctions.io/blog/the-fatfs-new-sanctions-compliance-guidance-for-the-virtual-currency-industry.

Gov.uk (2025). Hong Kong UK welcome programme – guidance for local authorities. [online] Available at: https://www.gov.uk/guidance/hong-kong-uk-welcome-programme-guidance-for-local-authorities.

Gracie, C. (2015). China and 'the Osborne Doctrine'. BBC News. [online] 18 Oct. Available at: https://www.bbc.co.uk/news/world-asia-china-34539507.

Gutteridge, N. (2025). Starmer endorses UN's high-tax manifesto. [online] *The Telegraph*. Available at: https://www.telegraph.co.uk/politics/2025/07/05/starmer-commits-uk-un-high-tax-manifesto/.

Halligan, L. (2024). Britain has developed a dangerous credibility gap in the markets. [online] *The Telegraph*. Available at: https://www.telegraph.co.uk/business/2024/12/22/britain-has-developed-dangerous-credibility-gap-in-markets/?msockid=01f5ba8bd2c0655939cdaee8d3e764c2.

Hamilton, C. (2018). Australia's Fight Against Chinese Political Interference. [online] *Foreign Affairs*. Available at: https://www.foreignaffairs.com/articles/australia/2018-07-26/australias-fight-against-chinese-political-interference.

He, L. (2023). China relaxes capital controls to entice badly needed foreign investment. | *CNN Business*. [online] CNN. Available at: https://edition.cnn.com/2023/09/22/economy/china-loosens-capital-controls-intl-hnk/index.html.

Head, C. (2022). *The City of London: A Pandora's Box?* [online] Disruption Banking. Available at: https://www.disruptionbanking.com/2022/09/28/the-city-of-london-a-pandoras-box.

Heathershaw, J., Cooley, A., and Mayne, T. (2021). The UK's kleptocracy problem. [online] Chatham House – International Affairs Think Tank. Available at: https://www.chathamhouse.org/2021/12/uks-kleptocracy-problem.

Herring, D. (2024). The UK's International Tax Competitiveness: 2024 Update – The Centre for Policy Studies. [online] The Centre for Policy Studies. Available at: https://cps.org.uk/research/the-uks-international-tax-competitiveness-2024-update/.

Hill, C., and Beadle, S. (2014). The Art of Attraction: Soft Power and the UK's Role in the World. [online] Available at: https://www.thebritishacademy.ac.uk/documents/322/the-art-attraction-soft-power-and-uks-role-world.pdf.

House of Commons (2015). HM Government support for UK victims of IRA attacks that used Gaddafi-supplied Semtex and weapons inquiry – Committees – UK Parliament. [online] Available at: https://committees.parliament.uk/work/3751/hm-government-support-for-uk-victims-of-ira-attacks-that-used-gaddafisupplied-semtex-and-weapons-inquiry/news/ [Accessed 13 Jul. 2025].

Huld, A. (2023). EU–China Relations: Trade, Investment, and Recent Developments. [online] China Briefing News. Available at: https://www.china-briefing.com/news/eu-china-relations-trade-investment-and-recent-developments/.

Hussain, A., and Davies, M. (2024). The perils of earning £100,000 and why it's about to get worse. [online] Thetimes.com. Available at: https://www.thetimes.com/business-money/money/article/why-its-tough-earning-100000-and-soon-it-can-become-even-worse-5jhrvchbo?msockid=01f5ba8bd2c0655939cdaee8d3e764c2 [Accessed 13 Jul. 2025].

Hymas, C. (2024). Police accused of 'appalling' attack on free speech with probe into *Telegraph*'s Allison Pearson. [online] *The Telegraph*. Available at: https://www.telegraph.co.uk/news/2024/11/13/police-appalling-attack-on-free-speech-allison-pearson/.

Ibrahim, A. (2017). *Radical Origins: Why We Are Losing the Battle Against Islamic Extremism? And How to Turn the Tide.* Simon & Schuster.

Ibrahim, A. (2019). The Prospective Foreign Policy of a Corbyn Government and its U.S. National Security Implications. [online] Hudson Institute. Available at: https://www.hudson.org/national-security-defense/the-prospective-foreign-policy-of-a-corbyn-government-and-its-u-s-national-security-implications.

Ibrahim, A. (2022). *Authoritarian Century*. Hurst Publishers.

Ibrahim, A. (2025). The Prospective Foreign Policy of a Corbyn Government and its U.S. National Security Implications. [online] Hudson Institute. Available at: https://www.hudson.org/research/15311-the-prospective-foreign-policy-of-a-corbyn-government-and-its-u-s-national-security-implications.

Ince, M. (2024). *Delivering Climate Security Requires an Intelligence-Led Response*. [online] Rusi.org. Available at: https://rusi.org/explore-our-research/publications/commentary/delivering-climate-security-requires-intelligence-led-response.

International Consortium of Investigative Journalists (2016). *The Panama Papers: Exposing the Rogue Offshore Finance Industry*. [online] ICIJ. Available at: https://www.icij.org/investigations/panama-papers/.

International Organization for Migration (2024). *World Migration Report 2024*. [online] IOM UN Migration. Available at: https://worldmigrationreport.iom.int/msite/wmr-2024-interactive/.

International Relations and Defence Committee (2025). 11 June 2025 – Implications of the transfer of sovereignty of the Chagos Archipelago – Oral evidence – Committees – UK Parliament. [online] Available at: https://committees.parliament.uk/event/24477.

International Rescue Committee (2023). The Central Sahel: How conflict and climate change drive crisis. | International Rescue Committee (IRC). [online] Available at: https://www.rescue.org/article/central-sahel- how-conflict-and-climate-change-drive-crisis.

Interpol (2024). The issues. [online] Available at: https://www.interpol.int/en/Crimes/Human-trafficking-and-migrant-smuggling/The-issues.

Isle of Man Financial Services Authority (2019). Background. [online] Iomfsa.im. Available at: https://www.iomfsa.im/amlcft/background/.

Jarvie, G., and Macdonald, S. (2024). Sport and Britain's UK Soft Power Council. [online] Available at: https://education-sport.ed.ac.uk/sites/default/files/2024-12/Response%20to%20UK%20Government%20Soft%20Power%20Council%20Strategy%20Group.pdf.

Jay, A. (2014). Inquiry into Child Sexual Exploitation in Rotherham. [online] Rotherham Metropolitan Borough Council. Available at: https://www.rotherham.gov.uk/downloads/file/279/independent-inquiry-into-child-sexual-exploitation-in-rotherham.

Jie, C. (2024). The UK's next government must redefine its confused relationship with China. [online] Chatham House – International Affairs Think Tank. Available at: https://www.chathamhouse.org/2024/06/uks-next-government-must-redefine-its-confused-relationship-china.

Johnston, N. (2024). Police review after liaison officer tells group of Muslims to 'discard' any weapons in mosque. [online] *The Telegraph*. Available at: https://www.telegraph.co.uk/news/2024/08/05/police-review-liaison-officer-muslims-weapons-mosque/.

Jones, S. G. (2024). The U.S. Industrial Base Is Not Prepared for a Possible Conflict with China. [online] features.csis.org. Available at: https://features.csis.org/preparing-the-US-industrial-base-to-deter-conflict-with-China/.

Jozepa, I., and Browning, S. (2019). *Trade in services: Parting with the EU?* [online] House of Commons Library. Available at: https://commonslibrary.parliament.uk/trade-in-services-parting-with-the-eu/.

Kachmar, O. (2021). The Uyghur Genocide: An Examination of China's Breaches of the 1948 Genocide Convention. [online] New Lines Institute. Available at: https://newlinesinstitute.org/rules-based-international-order/genocide/the-uyghur-genocide-an-examination-of-chinas-breaches-of-the-1948-genocide-convention/.

Kaku, M. (2024). *Quantum Supremacy*. Vintage.

Keep, M., and Brien, P. (2023). Public spending during the Covid-19 pandemic. House of Commons Library. [online] Available at: https://commonslibrary.parliament.uk/research-briefings/cbp-9309/.

Kimball, R. (2020). *Who Rules?* Encounter Books.

Kirchick, J. (2017). *Russia's plot against the West.* [online]POLITICO. Available at: https://www.politico.eu/article/russia-plot-against-the-west-vladimir-putin-donald-trump-europe/.

Kirk-Wade, E., and Allen, G. (2020). Terrorism in Great Britain: the statistics. commonslibrary.parliament.uk. [online] Available at: https://commonslibrary.parliament.uk/research-briefings/cbp-7613/.

Kotkin, S. (2008). *Armageddon Averted*. Oxford University Press.

Kydd, A. H. (2005). Trust and mistrust in international relations. Editorial: Princeton, N. J.; Woodstock: Princeton University Press.

Lakhani, N. (2024). Corporations invested in carbon offsets that were 'likely junk', analysis says. *The Guardian*. [online] 30 May. Available at: https://www.theguardian.com/environment/article/2024/may/30/corporate-carbon-offsets-credits.

Lang, A. F., O'Driscoll, C., and Williams, J. (2013). *Just war: authority, tradition, and practice.* Washington DC: Georgetown University Press.

Law Society (2022). *The Law Society*. [online] @thelawsociety. Available at: https://www.lawsociety.org.uk/contact-or-visit-us/press-office/press-releases/england-and-wales-hailed-as-legal-centre-of-the-world.

Lawrence, D. (2022). Redefine the Commonwealth now to safeguard its future. [online] Chatham House – International Affairs Think Tank. Available at: https://www.chathamhouse.org/2022/10/redefine-commonwealth-now-safeguard-its-future.

Leask, D. (2017). Full extent of multi-billion dollar bank heist's links to Scottish firms revealed. [online] *The Herald*. Available at: https://www.heraldscotland.com/news/15792485.True_scale_of_Scotland_s_shell_firms_links_to_multi_billion_dollar_global_heist_revealed/.

Lee, D. (2018). The tactics of a Russian troll farm. BBC News. [online] 16 Feb. Available at: https://www.bbc.co.uk/news/technology-43093390.

Leigh, S. (2024). Pouria Zeraati: TV station Iran International faced 'heavy threats' before stabbing. BBC News. [online] 30 Mar. Available at: https://www.bbc.co.uk/news/uk-68698366.

Lord West of Spithead (2025). Averting a Strategic Misstep. [online] Policy Exchange. Available at: https://policyexchange.org.uk/publication/averting-a-strategic-misstep/.

Lynch, D. (2025). Trump meets with military leaders over Iran, after PM insists he wants peace. [online] The Standard. Available at: https://www.standard.co.uk/news/politics/donald-trump-iran-president-john-healey-national-security-council-b1233498.html.

Maçães, B. (2018). Belt and road: a Chinese world order. London: Hurst & Company.

Macmillan, M. (2003). Paris 1919: Six Months That Changed the World. New York: Random House Trade Paperbacks.

MacQueen, R., Mortimer-Lee, P., and Bhattacharjee, A. (2022). Powering Down, Not Levelling Up – NIESR. [online] NIESR. Available at: https://niesr.ac.uk/publications/powering-down-not-levelling-up?type=uk-economic-outlook.

Maizland, L., and Fong, C. (2024). China and Russia: Exploring Ties Between Two Authoritarian Powers. [online] Council on Foreign Relations. Available at: https://www.cfr.org/backgrounder/china-russia-relationship-xi-putin-taiwan-ukraine.

Markson, T. (2024). Civil service headcount rises again – now same size as 2006. [online] Civil Service World. Available at: https://www.civilserviceworld.com/professions/article/civil-service-headcount-rises-again-now-same-size-as-2006.

McBride, J., and Siripurapu, A. (2022). What's Next for the WTO? [online] Council on Foreign Relations. Available at: https://www.cfr.org/backgrounder/whats-next-wto.

McCulloch, S. (2015). Report: 50 per cent cut in Air Passenger Duty could add £1bn to Scotland's economy. [online] businessInsider. Available at: https://www.insider.co.uk/news/report-50-cut-air-passenger-9892286.

McWilliams, D., and Singham, S. (2024). The Autumn 2024 Growth Budget. [online] Available at: https://www.growth-commission.com/wp-content/uploads/2024/10/FINAL-TEXT-GC_Autumn-Growth-Budget-2024.pdf.

Mearsheimer, J. J. (1994). The False Promise of International Institutions. Cambridge, Ma: MiT Press, pp.5–49.

Media – Lockheed Martin. (2025). Norway Becomes First F-35 Partner Nation to Fulfil its Program of Record. [online] Available at: https://news.lockheedmartin.com/2025-04-01-Norway-Becomes-First-F-35-Partner-Nation-to-Fulfill-its-Program-of-Record.

Mengden, A. (2024). International Tax Competitiveness Index 2024. [online]

Tax Foundation. Available at: https://taxfoundation.org/research/all/global/2024-international-tax-competitiveness-index.

Merrick, R. (2018). Brexit: Theresa May warned hard Irish border can only be avoided if UK stays aligned with EU rules for time being. *The Independent*. [online] Available at: https://www.independent.co.uk/news/uk/politics/brexit-ireland-hard-border-theresa-may-avoid-north-eu-rules-mp-report-latest-news-a8258081.html.

Middle East Eye (2024). UK accused of trying to suppress criticism of UAE role in Sudan war. [online] Middle East Eye. Available at: https://www.middleeasteye.net/news/uk-accused-suppress-criticism-uae-role-sudan-war.

Mills, C., Shalchi, A., Gower, M., Johnston, N., and Woodhouse, J. (2022). Countering Russian influence in the UK. [online] Available at: https://researchbriefings.files.parliament.uk/documents/CBP-9472/CBP-9472.pdf.

Mitra, P. (2024). Tax hike triggers record equity fund outflows. [online] Funds Europe. Available at: https://funds-europe.com/tax-hike-triggers-record-equity-fund-outflows/.

MOD (2025). Strategic Defence Review. [online] Available at: https://assets.publishing.service.gov.uk/media/683d89f181deb72cce268025/The_Strategic_Defence_Review_2025_-_Making_Britain_Safer_-_secure_at_home__strong_abroad.pdf.

Momani, B., Karns, M. P., Mingst, K. A., Kirton, J. J., and Stefanova, R. N. (2006). International Organizations: The Politics and Processes of Global Governance. *International Journal*, [online] 61(3), p.773. doi: https://doi.org/10.2307/40204209.

Montgomery, S. (2024). Watch: Hammer-wielding man seeks revenge during riots. [online] *The Telegraph*. Available at: https://www.telegraph.co.uk/news/2024/11/07/hammer-wielding-man-middlesbrough-riots-jailed/.

Morgan, K., and Kinossian, N. (2023). Dismantling Londongrad: the dark geography of dirty money. *European Planning Studies*, 32(1), pp.1–17. doi: https://doi.org/10.1080/09654313.2023.2221283.

Morita-Jaeger, M. (2024). Can the UK lead on Data Flow Governance? Insights from the EU–Japan protocol on free data flows and personal data protection. UK Trade Policy Observatory. [online] Sussex.ac.uk. Available at: https://blogs.sussex.ac.uk/uktpo/2024/07/23/can-the-uk-lead-on-data-flow-governance-insights-from-the-eu-japan-protocol/.

Morton, B. (2024b). Keir Starmer to meet Chinese President Xi Jinping at G20 summit. BBC News. [online] 17 Nov. Available at: https://www.bbc.co.uk/news/articles/c1dp6wgk72ro.

Muelle, R. (2019). Report On The Investigation Into Russian Interference In The 2016 Presidential Election. https://www.justice.gov/storage/report_volume2.pdf.

Mulhall, J. (2022). Tommy Robinson: Putin's Useful Idiot? [online] HOPE not hate. Available at: https://hopenothate.org.uk/2022/03/17/tommy-robinson-putins-useful-idiot/.

Murphy, L. (2022). Not working. [online] Resolution Foundation. Available at: https://www.resolutionfoundation.org/publications/not-working/.

Mustoe, H. (2024). Business confidence tumbles to two-year low following Reeves's raid on employers. [online] *The Independent.* Available at: https://www.independent.co.uk/news/business/employment-budget-rachel-reeves-b2661326.html.

National Crime Agency (2019). National Economic Crime Centre leads push to identify money laundering activity. [online] Available at: https://www.nationalcrimeagency.gov.uk/news/national-economic-crime-centre-leads-push-to-identify-money-laundering-activity.

National Crime Agency (2025). Bribery, corruption and sanctions evasion [online] Available at: https://www.nationalcrimeagency.gov.uk/what-we-do/crime-threats/bribery-corruption-and-sanctions-evasion.

Nelson, E. (2025). Soaring Bond Yields Put U.K. Government's Economic Plan at Risk. *The New York Times.* [online] 14 Jan. Available at: https://www.nytimes.com/2025/01/14/business/bonds-gilt-yield-britain-economy.html.

Neufeld, D. (2023). Mapped: The Top Global Financial Centers in 2023. [online] Visual Capitalist. Available at: https://www.visualcapitalist.com/top-global-financial-centers-in-2023/.

Nicolle, E. (2024). Binance Attempts to Restart UK Business Hampered by New Marketing Rules. [online] Bloomberg.com. Available at: https://www.bloomberg.com/news/articles/2024-02-01/binance-attempts-to-restart-uk-business-hampered-by-new-marketing-rules.

Nixey, J. (2019). Address Russian Rule-breaking. [online] Chatham House International Affairs Think Tank. Available at: https://www.chathamhouse.org/2019/06/address-russian-rule-breaking.

Nolsøe, E. (2022). How an incorrect recession forecast helped spark the mini-Budget market chaos. [online] *The Telegraph.* Available at: https://www.telegraph.co.uk/business/2022/09/30/how-mistaken-recession-forecast-helped-spark-mini-budget-market/.

Nolsøe, E. (2025). Net zero to cost Britain £800bn. [online] *The Telegraph.* Available at: https://www.telegraph.co.uk/business/2025/07/10/net-zero-cost-britain-800bn/ [Accessed 11 Jul. 2025].

Nyberg-Sorensen, N., Hear, N. V., and Engberg-Pedersen, P. (2002). The Migration-Development Nexus: Evidence and Policy Options. *International Migration*, 40(5), pp.49–73. doi: https://doi.org/10.1111/1468-2435.00211.

Oakeshott, M. J. (1962). *Rationalism in Politics and Other Essays.* Indianapolis: Liberty Fund.

O'Brien, R. C. (2020). How China Threatens American Democracy. [online] www.

foreignaffairs.com. Available at: https://www.foreignaffairs.com/articles/china/2020-10-21/how-china-threatens-american-democracy.

O'Driscoll, C. (2023). Just War Theory: Past, Present, and Future. *International political theory*, pp.339–354. doi: https://doi.org/10.1007/978-3-031-36111-1_18.

OBR (2022). The latest evidence on the impact of Brexit on UK trade. [online] Available at: https://obr.uk/box/the-latest-evidence-on-the-impact-of-brexit-on-uk-trade.

OBR (2023). An international comparison of the cost of energy support packages. [online] Available at: https://obr.uk/box/an-internationalcomparison-of-the-cost-of-energy-support-packages/.

OBR (2024). Economic and fiscal outlook – October 2024. [online] Available at: https://obr.uk/efo/economic-and-fiscal-outlook-october-2024/#chapter-2.

Oliver, M. (2024). Britain paying highest electricity prices in the world. [online] *The Telegraph*. Available at: https://www.telegraph.co.uk/business/2024/09/26/britain-burdened-most-expensive-electricity-prices-in-world/?utmsource=email&msockid=01f5ba8bd2c0655939cdaee8d3e764c2.

Panjwani, A., Mills, C., Dawson, J., Woodhouse, J., Gower, M., and Johnston, N. (2025). Countering Russian influence in the UK. [online] House of Commons Library. Available at: https://commonslibrary.parliament.uk/research-briefings/cbp-9472/.

Parkin, F. (1968). *Middle Class Radicalism: The social bases of the British campaign for nuclear disarmament*. Manchester: Manchester University Press.

Peace, T. (2016). Who becomes a terrorist, and why? *Washington Post*. [online] Available at: https://www.washingtonpost.com/news/monkey-cage/wp/2016/05/10/who-becomes-a-terrorist-and-why/.

Perliger, A. (2012). *Challengers from the sidelines: understanding America's violent far-right*. West Point, NY: The Combating Terrorism Center At West Point.

Pianese, B. (2024). Labour's big plans to stir up the City on illicit finance [online] Thebanker.com. Available at: https://www.thebanker.com/Labour-s-big-plans-to-stir-up-the-City-on-illicit-finance-1718107596.

Posen, A. S., Petri, P., and Banga, M. (2021). *The Interconnected Economy*. PIIE. Available at: https://www.piie.com/commentary/testimonies/interconnected-economy-effects-globalization-us-economic-disparity.

Press Association (2016). Osborne rejected safeguards over Chinese role in Hinkley Point, says ex-minister. [online] *The Guardian*. Available at: https://www.theguardian.com/uk-news/2016/aug/01/osborne-rejected-safeguards-over-chinese-role-in-hinkley-point-says-ex-energy-minister.

Puzder, A. (2024). Britain's Disastrous Path to Net Zero Is a Warning to the U.S. [online] *National Review*. Available at: https://www.nationalreview.com/2024/02/britains-disastrous-path-to-net-zero-is-a-warning-to-the-u-s/ [Accessed 11 Jul. 2025].

Qiang, X. (2019). The Road to Digital Unfreedom: President Xi's Surveillance State, Journal of Democracy. [online] *Journal of Democracy*. Available at: https://www.journalofdemocracy.org/articles/the-road-to-digital-unfreedom-president-xis-surveillance-state/.

Rawls, J. (1971). *A Theory of Justice*. Cambridge: Harvard University Press.

Redwood, J. (2024). The New Great Inflation: How Western Central Banks Got It Wrong... and What They Should Do About It. [online] Institute of Economic Affairs. Available at: https://iea.org.uk/publications/the-new-great-inflation-how-western-central-banks-got-it-wrong-and-what-they-should-do-about-it/#Conclusions.

Reenen, J. V. (2023). Chronic under-investment has led to productivity slowdown in the UK. [online] London School of Economics and Political Science. Available at: https://www.lse.ac.uk/News/Latest-news-from-LSE/2023/k-November-2023/Chronic-under-investment-has-led-to-productivity-slowdown-in-the-UK.

Reeves, R. (2024). National Minimum Wage increase is proof Labour improves living standards. [online] *The Mirror*. Available at: https://www.mirror.co.uk/news/politics/national-minimum-wage-increase-proof-34325501 [Accessed 13 Jul. 2025].

Reuters (2007). Blair defends dropping Saudi fraud probe. *Reuters*. [online] 9 Aug. Available at: https://www.reuters.com/article/world/uk/blair-defends-dropping-saudi-fraud-probe-idUSL1660210S/.

Reuters (2023). Crypto's role in terrorist financing.. [online] 23 Oct. Available at: https://www.reuters.com/technology/cryptos-role-terrorist-financing-2023-10-23/.

Riley-Smith, B. (2025). My 48 hours watching Trump make a mockery of the G7. [online] *The Telegraph*. Available at: https://www.telegraph.co.uk/politics/2025/06/18/my-48-hours-watching-trump-make-a-mockery-of-the-g7/.

Salt, J. (2000). Trafficking and Human Smuggling: A European Perspective. *International Migration*, 38(3), pp.31–56. doi: https://doi.org/10.1111/1468-2435.00114.

Sampson, E., Chutel, L., and Schuetze, C. F. (2024). What to Know About the Attacks on Israeli Soccer Fans in Amsterdam. *The New York Times*. [online] 8 Nov. Available at: https://www.nytimes.com/2024/11/08/world/europe/amsterdam-israel-soccer-fans-attacks.html.

Sands, P. (2023). *The Last Colony*. Knopf.

Schmitt, C. (2007). *The Concept of the Political*. Chicago, Ill.: Univ. of Chicago Press.

Schneider-Petsinger, M. (2023). Global trade in 2023 – What's driving reglobalization? [online] Smart Thinking. Available at: https://smartthinking.org.uk/report/global-trade-in-2023/.

Schreurs, M. A. (2016). The Paris Climate Agreement and the Three Largest Emitters: China, the United States, and the European Union. *Politics and Governance*, 4(3), p.219. doi: https://doi.org/10.17645/pag.v4i3.666.

Searle, N. (2017). To defeat terrorists we have to get inside their minds. [online] *The Guardian*. Available at: https://www.theguardian.com/commentisfree/2017/mar/17/defeat-terrorists-terrorism.

Sen, A. (2024). The EU's tariff hike on electric vehicles from China: The data behind the decision – UK Trade Policy Observatory. [online] Sussex.ac.uk. Available at: https://blogs.sussex.ac.uk/uktpo/2024/06/28/the-eu-tariff-hike-on-electric-vehicles-from-china-the-data-behind-the-decision/.

Șerban, A. C., Aceleanu, M. I., Dospinescu, A. S., Țîrcă, D.-M., and Novo-Corti, I. (2020). The Impact Of EU Immigration On Economic Growth Through The Skill Composition Channel. *Technological and Economic Development of Economy*, 26(2), pp.479–503.

Shalchi, A. (2021). Unexplained Wealth Orders. Available at: https://commonslibrary.parliament.uk/research-briefings/cbp-9098/.

Shaxson, N. (2021). The City of London Is Hiding the World's Stolen Money. *The New York Times*. [online] 11 Oct. Available at: https://www.nytimes.com/2021/10/11/opinion/pandora-papers-britain-london.html.

Sheehan, M. (2023). China's AI Regulations and How They Get Made. [online] Carnegie Endowment for International Peace. Available at: https://carnegieendowment.org/research/2023/07/chinas-ai-regulations-and-how-they-get-made?lang=en.

Simor, J. (2025). Why Lord Sumption is dangerously wrong about our human rights law. [online] *Prospect*. Available at: https://www.prospectmagazine.co.uk/ideas/law/63339/lord-sumption-ehcr-human-rights-law.

Singham, S. (2019). *The Case for Growth*. [online] Available at: https://www.growth-commission.com/about-us/.

Singham, S. (2023). The Growth Challenge: The decline in GDP per capita growth in advanced economies. [online] Available at: https://www.growth-commission.com/wp-content/uploads/2023/07/64ae4fd40046a0f0dbd8f7f8_The-Growth-Challenge-1.pdf.

Sökefeld, M. (2016). The Kashmiri Diaspora in Britain and the Limits of Political Mobilisation. In A. Wonneberger, M. Gandelsman-Trier and H. Dorsch (Ed.), *Migration – Networks – Skills: Anthropological Perspectives on Mobility and Transformation* (pp. 23-46). Bielefeld: transcript Verlag. https://doi.org/10.1515/9783839433645-002

Spyro, S. (2025). Ed Miliband U-turns on drilling of North Sea – despite branding idea 'climate vandalism'. [online] *Express*. Available at: https://www.express.co.uk/news/politics/2071063/ed-miliband-u-turns-drilling-north [Accessed 11 Jul. 2025].

Starkman, D. (2021). Frequently asked questions about the Pandora Papers and ICIJ [online] International Consortium of Investigative Journalists. Available at: https://www.icij.org/investigations/pandora-papers/frequently-asked-questions-about-the-pandora-papers-and-icij/.

Starmer, K. (2025). PM remarks at Immigration White Paper press conference: 12 May 2025. [online] GOV.UK. Available at: https://www.gov.uk/government/speeches/pm-remarks-at-immigration-white-paper-press-conference-12-may-2025.

Stiglitz, J. E. (2002). *Globalization and its discontents*. New York: W. W. Norton & Co.

Sturge, G. (2024). Asylum Statistics. commonslibrary.parliament.uk. [online] Available at: https://commonslibrary.parliament.uk/research-briefings/sn01403/.

Sumption, J. (2020). *Trials of the State*. London: Profile Books.

Tarabay, J. (2021). How Hackers Hammered Australia After China Ties Turned Sour. [online] Bloomberg. Available at: https://www.bloomberg.com/news/features/2021-08-30/covid-origin-probe-calls-australian-government-businesses-universities-hacked.

Tax Foundation (2023). United Kingdom Archives. [online] Available at: https://taxfoundation.org/location/united-kingdom/.

Tax Justice Network (2022). Financial Secrecy Index [online]. Available at: https://fsi.taxjustice.net/.

Taylor, R. (2022). UK aid spending: Statistics and recent developments. [online] House of Lords Library. Available at: https://lordslibrary.parliament.uk/uk-aid-spending-statistics-and-recent-developments/.

The Commonwealth (n.d.). *Commonwealth Climate Change Programme*. [online] Available at: https://thecommonwealth.org/our-work/Commonwealth-Climate-Change-Programme.

The Economist (2018). London's financial flows are polluted by laundered money. [online] The Economist. Available at: https://www.economist.com/leaders/2018/10/11/londons-financial-flows-are-polluted-by-laundered-money.

The Economist (2022). Why does so much dodgy Russian money end up in Britain? [online] The Economist. Available at: https://www.economist.com/the-economist-explains/2022/02/04/why-does-so-much-dodgy-russian-money-end-up-in-britain.

The Ferret (2023). Only 3 of 631 Scottish limited partnerships formed by Scots residents. [online] The Ferret. Available at: https://theferret.scot/only-3-631-scottish-limited-partnerships-formed-residents-scotland/.

The Regional Law Revision Centre, Turks and Caicos Islands (2025). 16.14 Confidential Relationships Ordinance. [online] Fliphtml5.com. Available at: http://online.fliphtml5.com/fizd/bnyp/#p=3.

Thomas, D. (2023). More risk, fewer rules: the plan to revive the City of London. *Financial Times*. [online] 15 Feb. Available at: https://www.ft.com/content/477318a9-5b05-4305-9e0d-f605431692db.

Thompson, S. A. (2022). How Russian Media Uses Fox News to Make Its Case. *The New York Times*. [online] 15 Apr. Available at: https://www.nytimes.com/2022/04/15/technology/russia-media-fox-news.html.

Thompsons Solicitors (2024). Store Workers Win Landmark Equal Pay Case Against Next. [online] Thompsons Solicitors. Available at: https://www.thompsonstradeunion.law/news/employment-law-review/weekly-issue-868/next-workers-win-equal-pay-claims-what-this-means-for-employees.

Tingley, D., and Tomz, M. (2021). The Effects of Naming and Shaming on Public Support for Compliance with International Agreements: An Experimental Analysis of the Paris Agreement. *International Organization*, 76(2), pp.1–24. doi: https://doi.org/10.1017/s0020818321000394.

Titcomb, J., and Penna, D. (2024). Rachel Reeves's inheritance tax raid 'to cost more than it makes'. [online] *The Telegraph*. Available at: https://www.telegraph.co.uk/business/2024/12/16/reeves-inheritance-tax-raid-cost-more-than-it-makes/.

Transparency International (2019). Toward transparency in Britain's offshore financial centres. [online] Transparency International UK. Available at: https://www.transparency.org.uk/toward-transparency-britains-offshore-financial-centres.

Transparency International (2025). Stop the flow of dirty money. [online] Transparency International UK. Available at: https://www.transparency.org.uk/what-we-do/corruption-and-uk/stop-flow-dirty-money.

Truss, L. (2023). Liz Truss exclusive: 'I assumed upon entering Downing Street my mandate would be respected. How wrong I was'. *The Telegraph*. [online] 4 Feb. Available at: https://www.telegraph.co.uk/politics/2023/02/04/liz-truss-downing-street-reflection-mini-budget-boris-johnson/.

Truss, L. (2024). *Ten Years to Save the West*. Biteback.

Tudor, S. (2022). Refugees and asylum-seekers: UK policy. [online] House of Lords Library. Available at: https://lordslibrary.parliament.uk/refugees-and-asylum-seekers-uk-policy/.

Turner, C. (2022). £27m of taxpayer money 'wasted' on woke projects such as 'decolonising 120,000 dried plants'. [online] *The Telegraph*. Available at: https://www.telegraph.co.uk/news/2022/11/04/27m-taxpayer-money-wasted-woke-projects-decolonising-120000/.

US Treasury (2024). Fact Sheet: Countering ISIS Financing. [online] Available at: https://home.treasury.gov/system/files/136/Fact-Sheet-Countering-ISIS-Financing-2-27-24.pdf.

US Treasury (2025). Debt to the Penny. Fiscal Data. U.S. Treasury. [online] fiscaldata.treasury.gov. Available at: https://fiscaldata.treasury.gov/datasets/debt-to-the-penny/debt-to-the-penny.

UNFCCC (2015). Paris Agreement. [online] unfccc.int. United Nations. Available at: https://unfccc.int/sites/default/files/english_paris_agreement.pdf.

UNHCR (1951). The 1951 Refugee Convention and 1967 Protocol Relating to the Status of Refugees. [online] Available at: https://www.unhcr.org/media/1951-refugee-convention-and-1967-protocol-relating-status-refugees.

UNHCR (2023a). Asylum in the UK. [online]. Available at: https://www.unhcr.org/uk/asylum-uk.

UNHCR (2023b). Global Trends. [online]. Available at: https://www.unhcr.org/global-trends.

UNHCR (2024). UNHCR – Refugee Statistics. [online]. Available at: https://www.unhcr.org/refugee-statistics.

University of Law (2024). Ex-Supreme Court justice backs a British Bill of Rights to replace the 'ideological' European Court of Human Rights. [online] Law.ac.uk. Available at: https://www.law.ac.uk/about/press-releases/the-judges-podcast-lord-sumption/.

USTR (2001). Background Information on China's Accession to the World Trade Organization. [online] Ustr.gov. Available at: https://ustr.gov/archive/Document_Library/Fact_Sheets/2001/Background_Information_on_China%27s_Accession_to_the_World_Trade_Organization.html.

Vaisanen, I. (2024). Autumn Budget 2024: A summary. [online] Inspired PLC. Available at: https://inspiredplc.co.uk/insights/industry-news/policy-regulation/autumn-budget-2024-a-summary/.

Vargas-Silva, C., Sumption, M., and Walsh, P. W. (2024). The Fiscal Impact of Immigration in the UK. [online] Migration Observatory. Available at: https://migrationobservatory.ox.ac.uk/resources/briefings/the-fiscal-impact-of-immigration-in-the-uk/.

Vera Delzo, P. (2023). Venezuelan Migration in Peru: Perceptions and Realities [online] Center for Strategic Studies of the Army of Peru (CEEEP). Available at: https://ceeep.mil.pe/2023/03/23/venezuelan-migration-in-peru-perceptions-and-realities/?lang=en.

Vogel, E. F. (2011). *Deng Xiaoping and the Transformation of China.* Cambridge, Massachusetts: The Belknap Press of Harvard University Press.

Wagner, W. (2024). Contesting Western support for Ukraine. The radical left in the European Parliament. *Journal of European Integration*, pp.1–23. doi: https://doi.org/10.1080/07036337.2024.2424186.

Wallace, T. (2024). As public sector pay soars, Britain braces for it to rocket even higher. [online] *The Telegraph.* Available at: https://www.telegraph.co.uk/business/2024/12/20/public-sector-pay-surges-its-heading-even-higher/?msockid=01f5ba8bd2c0655939cdaee8d3e764c2.

Wang, J. (2021). China's approach to global economic governance | Summary. [online] Chatham House – International Affairs Think Tank. Available at: https://www.chathamhouse.org/2021/12/chinas-approach-global-economic-governance/summary.

Ward, A. (2019). Ideas for modernizing the rules-based international order [online]

Available at: https://www.chathamhouse.org/sites/default/files/publications/research/2019-06-10-Expert-Perspectives.pdf.

Warrington, J., and Holl-Allen, G. (2024). Pubs and restaurants tell Reeves they face closures and 'drastic' job cuts after tax raid. [online] *The Telegraph*. Available at: https://www.telegraph.co.uk/business/2024/11/10/pubs-restaurants-tell-reeves-closures-job-cuts-tax-raid/.

Wesslau, F. (2016). Putin's friends in Europe [online] ECFR. Available at: https://ecfr.eu/article/commentary_putins_friends_in_europe7153/.

Wessner, C., and Sharma, S. (2025). Competing with China's Public R&D Model: Lessons and Risks for U.S. Innovation Strategy. [online] Available at: https://www.csis.org/analysis/competing-chinas-public-rd-model-lessons-and-risks-us-innovation-strategy.

West, E. (2024a). How bad will a Labour government be? [online] *The Spectator*. Available at: https://www.spectator.co.uk article/how-bad-will-a-labour-government-be/.

West, L. (2024b). UK ranked second most powerful country in 'soft power'. [online] *UK Defence Journal*. Available at: https://ukdefencejournal.org.uk/uk-ranked-secondmost-powerful-country-in-soft-power.

Whipple, T. (2025). Why are UK energy bills so high? The costs explained. [online] archive.ph. Available at: https://archive.ph/gLJfl.

Wilkes, G., Bartrum, O. and Clyne, R. (2024). *Treasury 'orthodoxy'*. [online] Institute for Government. Available at: https://www.instituteforgovernment.org.uk/publication/treasury-orthodoxy.

Williams, S. (2013). NZ lambs 'better for the environment'. [online] Wales Online. Available at: https://www.walesonline.co.uk/news/wales-news/nz-lambs-better-environment-2240702.

Wolfgang Münchau (2017). Europe's four freedoms are its very essence. [online] @FinancialTimes. Available at: https://www.ft.com/content/49dc02dc-c637-11e7-a1d2-6786f39ef675.

Wood, J. (2024). The what and why of the EU–US Trade and Technology Council. [online] World Economic Forum. Available at: https://www.weforum.org/agenda/2024/04/eu-us-trade-technology-council-agreement.

World Bank (2021). Climate Change Could Force 216 Million People to Migrate Within Their Own Countries by 2050. [online] World Bank. Available at: https://www.worldbank.org/en/news/press-release/2021/09/13/climate-change-could-force-216-million-people-to-migrate-within-their-own-countries-by-2050.

World Data (2024). The 50 largest economies in the world. [online] Worlddata.info. Available at: https://www.worlddata.info/largest-economies.php.

World Meteorological Foundation (2024). State of the Global Climate 2023.

[online] Available at: https://library.wmo.int/viewer/68835/download?file=1347_Global-statement-2023_en.pdf&type=pdf&navigator=1.

Xlinks (2024). Frequently Asked Questions. [online] Xlinks. Available at: https://xlinks.co/faq/.

Youngs, I. (2025). BBC pulls Gaza film as it carries out checks over Hamas links. BBC News. [online] 21 Feb. Available at: https://www.bbc.co.uk/news/articles/clydv5yngq40.

INDEX